Craig Murray is Rector of the University of Dundee and an Honorary Research Fellow at the University of Lancaster School of Law.

He was born in West Runton in 1958 and gained the degree of MA (Hons) in Modern History with first class honours from the University of Dundee. He joined the British diplomatic service in 1984 and served in Nigeria, Poland and Ghana before becoming British ambassador to Uzbekistan. Craig Murray was sacked from that position in 2004 after protesting about the use by US and UK secret services of intelligence gained by torture there, as part of the "war on terror". He resigned from the diplomatic service in 2005 and published his first book, *Murder in Samarkand*, an immediate non-fiction bestseller.

Craig lives in Shepherds Bush with his partner, Nadira, and his two children from a previous marriage.

The Catholic Orangemen of Togo
And Other Conflicts I Have Known

CRAIG MURRAY

Atholl

An Atholl Hardback

First Edition 2009
Published by Atholl Publishing
31 Sinclair Gardens
West Kensington
London
W14 0AU

Typeset in Palatino Linotype
by Atholl Publishing

ISBN 978-0-9561299-0-1

In accordance with the policy of Atholl Publishing
carbon offset has been purchased
to reduce the environmental impact of this book

For Robert Cameron Brunton Murray 1930-1999

Watch what you say!
They'll be calling you a radical, a liberal,
A fanatical criminal.
Won't you sign up your name?
We want to feel you're acceptable, presentable,
Respectable, a vegetable.

The Logical Song
By Roger Hodgson and Richard Davies (Supertramp)

Contents

Author's Preface

I spent the eve of the Millennium in my garden, on the spacious lawns of Devonshire House in Accra, hosting a seven course meal for 120 people, with dancing, fireworks and unlimited champagne. Despite the hysterical rubbish with which the Foreign and Commonwealth Office had been bombarding me for weeks, the World's computers didn't crash, and the future looked bright.

Osama Bin Laden doesn't use the Christian calendar so wasn't celebrating that night. He had already accepted the idea – not originally his – of suicide attacks involving hijacked aircraft. His al-Qaida network had about 180 members. Al Gore looked pretty safe to win the democratic nomination and the Presidency.[1] George Bush was a blip on the horizon whose record as a Vietnam draft-dodger would surely scupper his chances.

The World was on the brink of unhappier times. But we didn't know it, and I was happily immersed in what remains my first and abiding concern: the freedom and development of Africa

Six years later, when I first published *Murder in Samarkand,* I faced a credibility problem. Many people simply did not believe that the US and UK governments had been willing to resort to the most stark and brutal forms of torture of helpless prisoners as part of the War on Terror. An accumulation of indisputable evidence from hundreds of sources has since forced acceptance upon the media and thus awareness upon the public. *Murder in Samarkand* in essence is a simple tale. The British government was actively complicit in torture; I opposed this internally, and so I got sacked.

That book's interest comes from its detailed documentation of the terrible oppression of the Uzbek people, of Western collusion with that oppression, and of the heroic work of some Uzbek individuals against that oppression. I also found that people reacted well to my frank account of

---

[1] Which, of course, in truth he was to do

1

myself. Autobiography is a form in which individuals recount highly edited versions of their own lives, in which they observe sharply the failings of others, but are themselves near-perfect. *Murder in Samarkand* showed a man warts and all. In doing so, I hope it illustrated that it is not always the man society finds most respectable who is likely to try to do what is right.

Emboldened by the strong response I received, I now write this further memoir, *The Catholic Orangemen of Togo and Other Conflicts I have Known*, which I hope may shed some light on some well known foreign policy questions in which I was involved. I hope it will also give some food for thought on the future of Africa, and perhaps show that freedom and progress there are not impossible.

This book should also explain further why I acted as I did in Uzbekistan. Hundreds, if not thousands, of senior British diplomats, civil servants and members of the military knew of our policy of acceptance of torture. A great many were much more actively involved, particularly in extraordinary rendition, than I.

Why they did nothing to stop it is, in fact, not the difficult question. Thousands of good, nice Germans were caught up at least tangentially in the administration of the concentration camps. They did nothing. Doing nothing is the norm, when it safeguards your life, your family and your livelihood. The difficult question is why was Craig Murray, by no means a conventionally good man, one of the tiny handful of those involved not to go along with the torture policy of the Bush and Blair years? This delve deeper into my past is an opportunity for us both to look for answers.

Doubtless some reviewers will again seize on the fact that I made mistakes, particularly in my private life. Well, I have news for you – I know that already. I had no illusion that I am perfect. The conflicts of the title are intended to embrace those internal ones with which we all struggle, and the conflicts in my personal life, as well as the obvious external ones. But, as one perceptive blog commenter said of US reviews of *Murder in Samarkand* (or *Dirty Diplomacy*, to give its US title), you don't have to be a saint to call torture when you see it.

The thing that I did differently from other diplomats was that I cared. Diplomats rather pride themselves on not caring. The culture of the Foreign and Commonwealth Office has been perceptively described by Carne Ross as "A cult of Machiavellianism". Carne and I quit in the Bush/ Blair years because we both cared passionately about those values which are meant to be fundamental to British policy, whichever party happens to be in power. I care for human rights, democracy and international development. I care for freedom. I care passionately for Africa.

The strange thing is that this is exactly the same list of things that Tony Blair declared, at every possible opportunity, that he was passionate about too. I was one of the very few in the FCO who was delighted by the announcement of an "Ethical foreign policy" by Robin Cook when New Labour took office. I had spent the first thirteen years of my career working for Conservative governments which I viewed with varying degrees of distaste.

How extraordinary to find that those Conservative governments were much more honourable in their pragmatism than the reckless neo-conservative contempt for international law that Blair was about to introduce as this story begins. Blair believed he alone was the judge of right, and didn't care how many had to die to prove it. I hope that this book illustrates that, in his very first year of office, Blair's role in the "Arms to Africa affair" displayed the cavalier disregard for the United Nations and for international law that was to do such huge damage to the United Kingdom's international reputation when applied to Iraq and the "War on Terror".

Blair's policy of "Projection of Hard Power" was simply the return of formal Imperialism. His motives had not changed from Kipling's "White man's burden." We should establish protectorates over dusky peoples who don't know much at all. It's for their own good. However many we kill now, in time they will come to thank us.

I apologise to my many friends in Ghana, including very good people with whom I worked in the High Commission, who are not mentioned in the book. That does not in any way mean that I did not value your company, or your contribution. A few names have been changed where people requested it or to protect the guilty.

3

Grateful thanks are due to Ailsa Bathgate of Mainstream Publishing for her help with editing and to Margaret Binns for the index.

The book has been subject to approval and minor censorship by the Foreign and Commonwealth Office.

Shepherds Bush, November 2008

1
Ethical Foreign Policy

It was possibly the worst thing I had ever done, and my conscience was bothering me. As my wife Fiona was nudging our overloaded Saab 9.3 around a Polish lake, through fog so dense it looked like solid mass, I felt uneasy. Mariola had been perhaps the nicest, kindest, gentlest mistress I ever had. Her red curls framed a face of pre-Raphaelite perfection, her lithe but well curved body was the incarnation of allure, and more precious still, her soul was deep, gentle and romantic. She was also discreet, reliable, faithful and inexpensive. Yet I was running away, leaving the country without even saying goodbye. Worse, without even telling her I was going. I hadn't been able to face it. I just left. What a bastard I was. I reached up to the steering wheel and squeezed my wife's hand for comfort.

What I was doing to Mariola was really, really bad. Even worse than sleeping with both her sisters. I wondered if they would tell her.

I had hugely enjoyed my time in Poland as First Secretary at the British Embassy. I had been in charge of the Embassy's Political, Economic and Information sections at an exciting time, as Poland transformed from communism to capitalism at astonishing speed. Most of my work concentrated on preparing Poland for eventual EU membership. It had been a happy and successful period and my career was going well.

It was mid December 1997 and we were driving back to London through the fog on minor roads, because the main trunk road through Poznan was a nightmare of speeding, overloaded trucks and traffic jams caused by the frequent accidents. The infrastructure hadn't kept up with the burgeoning of East/West trade. Smaller roads some fifty miles north of the main one were in fact faster. Unless you were enveloped in fog, as we now were. That night we slept in a beautiful old castle, still government owned. Under communism it had been one of many rest facilities for branches of the Party. One of the great pleasures of our time in Poland had been the numerous castles and aristocratic lodges throughout the country where you could hire the entire building for £50 per night and live, among the original furnishings, in vast decaying splendour. Oak panelling, oil paintings of armoured aristocrats, pianos everywhere and acres of mildewing gold and scarlet velvet curtain. Four poster beds with two foot high pillows stuffed with sharp quills. Hot water brought to you in the morning in great steaming porcelain jugs. I loved it. My enthusiasm was not entirely shared - the family preferred plumbing.

The next night we slept in the Berlin Hilton, returning to modern efficiency and comfort. Another night later we were at home in Gravesend.

I had bought the house in Gravesend, on a massive mortgage, in my second year with the FCO, just before going out to Lagos on our first posting. I didn't really know London or the South East. I had settled on Gravesend by starting from my workplace in Whitehall and going out on the commuter lines until I came upon the first decent sized house I could afford. That was in Gravesend.

The town has fallen on hard times, and appears to have forgotten its former glories. It was right at the heart of darkness, one of the greatest ports of Britain's Empire. Several of Nelson's ships at Trafalgar were built in Gravesend. But even more remarkable is how many of the journeys that made the Empire started from there. Gordon left for Khartoum, Burton left for Mecca, Clive for India and Livingstone set off for Africa, all from Gravesend. It was the portal of Empire for four hundred years. Famously Captain John Smith returned there with Pocahontas, and her remains still lie under St George's church in the town.

One of Nelson's ships of the line at the battle of Cape St Vincent, the 74 gun *Colossus*, was built in Gravesend for the Admiralty at the yard of a private contractor called Cleveley. Badly knocked about after its heroic role in that battle, it accompanied Nelson back to Naples. There it was the scene of one of the worst blots on the history of the Royal Navy, as liberal opponents of the despotic Neapolitan regime were "tried" and shot or hung (depending on social status) on the ship, it being feared the people might rise to free them if they were tried in Naples itself. That the Napo-

6

leonic Wars were fought largely to uphold highly reactionary regimes, is a part of our history that still escapes popular culture.

In Naples Nelson was shacked up in his ménage a trois with Sir William Hamilton and his wife, Emma. Sir William was tremendously wealthy and had married far beneath him. His wife was thirty years younger than he, and by the standards of the time she was a tremendous beauty. She was also, even by the standards of the time, a right slapper.

Sir William was a highly influential connoisseur of art and played a pivotal role in starting the fashion for collecting Grecian urns, about which Keats was to wax so lyrical. (What's a Grecian urn? About 20,000 euros a year plus another 30,000 in EU subsidy scams.) Hamilton had amassed the greatest collection of ancient urns the world had seen, or will ever see again. The collection was absolutely priceless and irreplaceable. He had a beautiful catalogue made by artists in Naples, who reproduced on paper every detail of the designs.

This turned out to be fortunate.

The *Colossus* was sent back to the UK for repair due to her battle damage. Nelson agreed that the Hamilton urn collection, packed with enormous care into two hundred and twenty crates, could be sent to London on the ship. The captain of the *Colossus,* a brilliant and daring Scot named (what else?) Murray, was not best pleased at this. The unusual sexual arrangement between the Hamiltons and Nelson had been the source of much ribaldry in the fleet. Conveying the Admiral's tart's pots was not what Murray felt he had joined the Royal Navy for.

He had other worries. The *Colossus* was cannibalised by Nelson for other ships which were remaining on active service in the Mediterranean. Among the items taken were the anchor cable and the main anchor, which went to the *Vanguard*. On the return voyage the *Colossus* had to anchor in the Scillies to ride out a fierce storm. The makeshift anchor cable parted, and the ship was driven onto the rocks. The Hamilton urn collection was dashed into tiny fragments. Its value can be judged by the fact that when some tiny shards were picked up by divers recently, the British Museum still considered them important enough to join its permanent display.

Murray's outstanding leadership and cool seamanship saved all of the crew, except the carpenter, but Murray still faced an ignominious court martial.

Gravesend is now shabby and dispirited with almost no sign of its fantastic maritime heritage. One thing that does still remain is the Port of London Authority. Ships have to stop at Gravesend and take on a qualified local pilot before proceeding up the Thames. In the 1860s when this long-standing practice was formalised, the Port of London Authority built a long line of identical semi-detached houses for the pilots. One of these was now ours. Pilots were retired sea captains, and the house, though a modest five bedrooms in size, gave an idea of their status, with marble fireplaces and mahogany fittings. We had put many hundreds of hours of our own toil into its restoration.

My son Jamie was nine, my daughter Emily three. Jamie was at Wellesley House, a tremendously posh preparatory (boarding) school in Broadstairs. We had been obliged to send Jamie there when it became plain that he was not happy or learning at the British School in Warsaw. I had been heartbroken when he left, which I tried to hide under a façade of humour. The US Ambassador in Warsaw, a lady, had asked me about my son going away to school, and asked how old he was.

"He's six," I replied.

"He went away to school at six! Why that's terrible!" said the Ambassador.

"Yes I know," I rejoined, "But they won't take them any younger."

I could not have been happier about my new job in the Foreign and Commonwealth Office. I was to be Deputy Head of Africa Department (Equatorial). The FCO had three African departments. There was Near East and North African Department (NENAD), dealing with the Mediterranean countries. Then there were African Department (Equatorial) and African Department (Southern). My new berth, African Department (Equatorial), or AD(E), dealt with over forty states. It had two deputy heads, one for West Africa and one for East Africa. I was to be the one in charge of West Africa. That may have made me a small cog in a very large machine – but I was a very happy cog.

For one thing, I governed my own bit of the machine. I used to define what I did by saying that there was nobody senior to me who did nothing but West Africa. And as West Africa was not exactly fashionable, I had the subject much to myself.

And I love West Africa. When I first joined the FCO in 1984, I had no doubt that I wanted to work on Africa. I believed that the empowerment of the people of Africa, and the removal of poverty, disease, despotism and economic subordination from the continent, was the greatest challenge in World politics. I still feel that today.

I had joined the FCO through the fast stream entry competition, and my Civil Service Selection Board score had been stellar – in the top three for all 80,000 applicants from the whole country. I was marked down as a high flyer, and high flyers want to get involved in real power. That means they spend their careers in Washington, New York, Brussels, Moscow, Berlin, Beijing and Paris. My desire to work on Africa confused the FCO, but they went along with it. My first job was a political desk in London dealing with South Africa, at a time when Mrs Thatcher was proclaiming Nelson Mandela a terrorist. I then wanted to go to Africa – and not even Pretoria, to black Africa – on my first posting. Personnel department suggested that Lagos would "Get Africa out of my system". But it didn't. I had the great job of dealing with agriculture and water resources, so despite the chaos and violence of Lagos, my travels all around Nigeria rubbed the red soil of Africa right into my blood. And once it is in there, you can't get it out.

My new boss was now to be Ann Grant, Head of AD(E). I was delighted about that, too. Ann was as passionate about Africa as I was, and we shared a similar political outlook. In particular, with New Labour having been in power less than a year, we were both enthusiasts for Robin Cook's ethical foreign policy. The idea that human rights, democracy, fair trade and development should take precedence over narrow self interest, was exactly the prescription that both Ann and I had been advocating for our Africa policy ever since we started our diplomatic careers.

We were perhaps unusual in this; the large majority of senior British diplomats viewed Cook's ideas with amused cynicism.

Within a month of becoming Prime Minister, Blair had bounced Cook at a Cabinet meeting over the sale of British Aerospace Hawk jets to Indonesia. The Indonesian regime had a record of ruthless use of air power on civilian populations to crush dissent. Cook had wanted to prevent the sale of further jets. Blair, with Jack Straw[2] and Gordon Brown, had ensured that not only was Cook overruled at Cabinet, but he was crushed in a humiliating fashion. This strengthened the hand of the FCO mandarins even further; they knew that if in conflict with Cook over ethical foreign policy, Blair would always overrule his Foreign Secretary, especially if the interest of the British arms industry could be invoked,. So there was a sense in which Cook was a lame duck almost from the start of his tenure.

It was the Arms to Africa affair which brought Robin Cook's ethical foreign policy to widespread public ridicule. It is a matter of great irony that at the heart of the affair were Ann Grant and I, two of the very few senior figures in the FCO who actually supported Cook.

I started my new job on 5 January 1998. My area of responsibility covered the 21 states of West Africa. These included the coastal states, from Gabon in the East to Equatorial Guinea in the West, and the huge French speaking Sahelian territories of Mali, Burkina Faso and Upper Volta.

I had reached the level of seniority in the FCO where I finally got my own room. The FCO is run on very traditional lines, where the majority of the work is done in a "Third room". How this name came about I do not know – possibly the Head and the Deputy Head of Department had their individual rooms, so everyone else was in the "Third Room." Here, typically a First Secretary will sit supervising a gaggle of Second and Third Secretaries plus some clerical staff. It is actually a very good system, as important items like briefings or submissions to ministers or answers to parliamentary questions will be submitted up the chain through the First Secretary anyway, and it allows for hands-on mentoring. In fact Departments nowadays will have a series of third rooms, housing the Department's Sections. A big country like Nigeria or Russia might be

---

2Straw had strong constituency connections with British Aerospace and a BAE board member, Lord Taylor of Bradford, had contributed 50% of Straw's 1997 election expenses according to the Commons Register of Members' interests.

covered by its own Section in its own room with several staff dedicated to it, while smaller countries will be grouped together to make up a Section. As far as room layout allows in the rambling palatial buildings, there is generally one Section per room, but there are variations.

So you can be quite a senior First Secretary and still sit in a common room with the staff you supervise – I had done so as head of Maritime and of Cyprus Sections. But now finally I was to have my own room, and a very nice one it was. If you stand at the Cenotaph and look at Gilbert Scott's splendid Italianate building, mine was the ground floor second window to the right of the great doors. The window is some twelve feet high and the ceiling looms above that, with deep cornices and pilasters, and a great marble mantelpiece carved in clean lines with a contrasting puritan severity. Everything had been painted over white some years before, and dirt was notably gathering in corners and crevices. The panelled door, also painted white, was ten feet tall and commensurately wide. The room appeared to have been designed for a larger race. Great billows of dirty grey net curtain loomed over the windows. These are bomb blast curtains, made of a special plastic. Much longer than the window and with a heavy chain tied to the bottom, the chain and yards of spare material are packed into an open topped wooden box on the window sill. In the event of a bomb blast the curtains billow out, absorbing the energy of the glass shards and catching them in their capacious folds. I know that they work well in the event of at least a reasonably distant blast, as I had lost my office windows some years earlier to an IRA explosion. You can of course get windows that are highly blast proof and do not fragment into sharp shards; that would be more effective. It would however also be more expensive; it would cost about .02% of the cost of the first day of our bombardment of Iraq. The Foreign and Commonwealth Office had decided that the yards of curtaining sufficiently mitigated the chances of its employees being shredded, at a reasonable cost.

I was glad that I had an old mahogany desk, topped with green leather that had darkened with age so you could scarcely make out the ink blots. I hated the new, flimsy beech desks they were putting in everywhere. On my grand old desk there was a huge leather framed blotter of similar vintage, a green shaded desk lamp and various bits of dark bronze metal-

11

work of uncertain purpose. I put in a requisition for a leather settee, and was surprised to be called by the Property Services Agency the next day.

"Hello there, sir, this is Estates. I see you've put in for a sofa. May I ask why you want it?"

"Certainly: I like to take a small nap in the afternoons."

"Oh. Right you are then, sir. We'll have it with you in a jiffy."

And they did.

The Department was divided into a number of sections, each with its own head. Frances Macleod was head of Nigeria section. She was a fiercely bright, red-haired Scot in her mid thirties, who had bumped into the FCO's notorious glass ceiling. As with so many women in the FCO, she was condemned to working for a series of chinless wonders who were not nearly as bright as she was. Including me, except for the chinless bit. Frustration tended to turn such women into ferocious turf-battlers, and Frances was plainly not pleased to have a boss who had actually served in Nigeria and knew even more about the country than she did. But fortunately Frances was so good that I was happy to leave Nigerian affairs almost entirely to her.[3]

Sierra Leone was the most pressing problem in West Africa. A failed state, most of the country was under the control of the Revolutionary United Front (RUF), a ragtag guerilla group of disaffected peasants. They were in an alliance of convenience with the Armed Forces Ruling Council, a military junta who in May 1997 had ousted the democratically elected President Tejan Kabbah in a coup. Many of the RUF's fighters were child soldiers, or former child soldiers who had been abducted as children, often with their parents butchered in front of their eyes.

I didn't know it then, but I was to get to know some of them quite well.

The RUF had become internationally notorious for their practice of lopping off the arms of civilians with machetes (or matchets, as they are called in English speaking West Africa). They would do this if they suspected villagers of hoarding grain, of being informers or just being government supporters. They did it to adults, to babies and to small children. It became a kind of cult. The scale of it was horrendous. At that

---

3Frances has since very sensibly left the FCO and gone to put her considerable talents at the service of the Scottish Executive.

time nobody could know exactly how many had been amputated, but around twelve thousand amputees ultimately survived the conflict. Probably a larger number died.

The conflicts in Sierra Leone and neighbouring Liberia were intertwined, and the RUF were sponsored by, and effectively part of the forces of, then Liberian President Charles Taylor. They also received arms and money from Colonel Gadaffi's Libya, and had the tacit and sometimes material support of the governments of Ivory Coast, Togo and other Francophone West African states. The RUF controlled most of Sierra Leone's diamond fields, the most productive in the world. Control of these diamonds was the first goal of every group in the conflict.

Nobody knew how long the alliance would last between the RUF and the military junta. Meanwhile the Economic Community of West African States (ECOWAS) was attempting to negotiate a peaceful return to power for President Kabbah. This was complex because, as always in West Africa, there were political, family and diamond smuggling connections between all the key players. The Francophone states and Libya broadly supported the RUF. Nigeria and Ghana backed Kabbah. Nigeria was by far the dominant force in ECOWAS, with well over half its people and over 75% of its economy.

The conflict in Sierra Leone was inextricably linked with the equally terrible and bloody one in neighbouring Liberia, with fighting groups ranging freely over the borders. Liberia, as a state created by the US for the return of freed slaves, had powerful support among Black American politicians of all parties. US political pressure had resulted in ECOWAS sending a powerful military force, ECOMOG, to end the conflict there. (The MOG stands euphemistically for monitoring group.) ECOMOG consisted largely of Nigerian and Ghanaian forces, plus other contributions, with the Ghanaians being the key fighting troops. Money, equipment and logistics came principally from the US government. ECOMOG had fought hard battles, taking serious casualties, to subdue the Liberian factions. The end result was to secure the most powerful Liberian warlord, Charles Taylor, in the Presidential palace. Taylor had always been a Nigerian client. ECOMOG now stood poised to enter Sierra Leone if negotiation failed

The military junta (AFRC) in Sierra Leone was in a weak position as it had the backing of no regional government, and had no roots or popular support in the country. It was purely military. It needed the alliance with the RUF, and increasingly the AFRC looked the prisoner of the RUF. While the RUF continued to exercise terror in the areas they felt opposed them, at least there was no hot war at present, and the rate of deaths and maimings was at its lowest for some years.

The cult of amputation was not the only weird thing about the RUF. They were given to wearing amulets and mirrors which they believed rendered them bullet proof. Some RUF fighters ate pieces of flesh from their victims in a ritual to absorb their strength, though this practice was not widespread.

So far, so horrible. But our policy in Sierra Leone was bedevilled by the great fallacy of the Blair years – that foreign conflicts can be seen in black and white, as goodies versus baddies; therefore all we have to do is side with the goodies and join in. Even the most complex conflicts were sim-plified in this way. Thus the RUF was treated as though it were an alien phenomenon, a thing of pure evil that had been visited on us for no cause whatsoever. I was to find that to suggest otherwise was unacceptable within the FCO. But in fact while the RUF was undeniably horrible, it had its roots in real grievance. The RUF was caused.

And in truth, on the other side of the equation, there are seldom any real "goodies" among those vying for power and resources. The Kabbah government were certainly not all goodies, as was to become obvious after the British army eventually restored them. Blair's fevered adoption of "goodies" where there are none, particularly in ethnic conflicts in the Balkans and Africa, was to lead to recurring foreign policy blunders.

As with most current African conflicts, much of the cause of the Sierra Leone war can be traced back to colonial occupation. The colonial motiv-ation in Sierra Leone was initially muddled but noble. On 22 June 1772 Lord Mansfield, the Chief Justice of England, had ruled that nobody could own another person in England[4], and by 1797 there was something

---

4Lord Mansfield was of course a good Scot, born in Perth, and another Murray – William Murray. His ruling didn't apply in Scotland, but slavery was already illegal there, the Scots being ahead of the English as always. Although generations of schoolchildren had to learn it, William Murray in fact never said "the air of England is too pure for a slave to

of an accumulation of free Africans in London, many of whom did not want to be there.

The capital of Sierra Leone, Freetown, was established by the British in 1797 as a colony to which they could return freed slaves, just as its better known twin, Liberia, was to be established by the Americans. As Simon Schama has pointed out[5], popular history has written out the undoubted fact that British anti-slavery laws were a primary cause of the American rebellion. George Washington was fighting for the right to keep black people in chains. Unsurprisingly, quite a lot of black people fought against him. These black "Empire loyalists" formed the majority of the first returnees to Freetown. Such is the confusion of history that the next wave was made up primarily of rebellious slaves from British Jamaican plantations deported as troublemakers.[6]

The native tribes, notably the Mende and the Temne, showing a laudable lack of colour prejudice, viewed all the colonists, black or white, as invaders, and started attacking Freetown pretty well from the day of its foundation. The colony was overrun several times in its first fifty years.

The tension between the natives and the colonists, white and black, never stopped and there is no doubt that the RUF and the conflict of the 1990s had direct links to this root, whatever the complicating factors. A situation developed where a coastal elite, consisting of the colonist families increasingly in alliance with the Mende, came to dominate the rich coastal trade and to squeeze those in the hinterland who were dependent on the coast for access to markets for their produce. In essence that situation is little changed today. The inland tribes considered the coastal elite to be wealthy parasites; the coasters considered the inlanders to be rude and idle peasants. Those attitudes still persist.

British rule was not imposed on the interior of Sierra Leone until 1896, and the subsequent taxation led in 1898 to one of Britain's most vicious,

---

breathe." Given the smell of late eighteenth century London, it would have risked derision if he had!

5 Schama, *Rough Crossings*, passim

6 A number of unfortunate white prostitutes were also deported to Sierra Leone. Of the white settlers, both official and convict, over 100 out of 140 died of disease in the first year.

and most forgotten, colonial wars. Again the local tribes attacked both whites and non-native blacks. The official enquiry concluded that

"the rioters, identifying all English-speaking people with the English government, and believing that in one way or other they had taken part with and aided the government in bringing the hut tax, with its con-comitant grievances, upon them, were wrought up to the desire of taking vengeance upon them."[7]

Many brave people fought on all sides, and thousands died, in that war, but their history is almost entirely unwritten. It took two British relief expeditions to subdue the country, and many hundreds of British soldiers were killed, but they were mostly black West Indians, so they didn't trouble the history books too much. The Sierra Leone War of 1898 to 1900 rates not a mention even in Thomas Pakenham's magisterial survey *The Scramble for Africa*. Niall Ferguson's *Empire* mentions Sierra Leone just twice. He notes its founding in 1797, and then next gives us the year 2000 and the views of Tony Blair and his acolyte Robert Cooper on how Sierra Leone justifies "a new kind of imperialism".[8] In missing out the intervening years of actual Empire, Ferguson shows the same lack of historical perspective as undermined Blair and Cooper's analysis. Of course the latter two aren't pretending to be historians.[9]

The 1898 "rebellion" of the newly annexed tribes was finally put down with great ferocity, and when the fighting was over, a hundred and twenty indigenous "rebels" were formally tried and executed – hung slowly from trees by the country that had invaded them. The large majority of the colonial black settlers supported the hangings and applauded them vigorously.

Freetown and Sierra Leone remained formally separate, respectively as colony and protectorate, until they were merged on independence in

---

7 Quoted in Richard Gott *Sierra Leone and New Labour Miiltarism, http://www.zmag.org/CrisesCurEvts/sierra_leone.htm*
8 Ferguson, *Imperialism, pp373-6.*
9 CLR James covers the Sierra Leone War more comprehensively in his *History of Pan-African Revolts (1969).* Unfortunately, though a great man and a great writer, covering ground unjustifiably neglected, James is a poor historian, and many of his claims, particularly on the annihilation of white battalions, give too much credence to oral history. Nonetheless it is a very valuable exercise in recovering the ordeal of the colonised.

1961. The colony of Freetown fostered an educated elite of black settlers who monopolised the rich maritime trade of Freetown, exploiting the native inland people who actually worked to produce the trade goods – including diamonds. There was little intermarriage between settler and indigenous families, and the settler-dominated and usually military governments of Freetown post 1961 were a byword for massive corruption, even by African standards.

In its forty years of independence Sierra Leone had been a nation in continual turmoil, where physical control of the diamond mines, usually by employing foreign mercenary guards, was the key political factor. The latest of these foreign mercenary forces controlling the diamonds was from a company called Sandline International. They had the same ownership and management as Executive Outcomes. This was the euphemistic name for as enthusiastic a band of white killers as has been unleashed on Africa since King Leopold ran the Congo.

The backbone of Executive Outcomes were South African apartheid era special forces members who were hired to get back to killing black people. Their modus operandi was to seize by physical force key natural resources – oil fields, diamond and gold mines – in countries torn apart by conflict. They worked for private corporations who would bribe their way to huge natural resource concessions from corrupt governments, given on condition that Executive Outcomes took physical possession of the assets from rebel forces. As EO were able to deploy modern weaponry and highly trained forces and only sought to seize specific natural resource targets, they were able to operate with some success. Their largest operation had been in Angola, where the prizes were oil and diamonds, and where Executive Outcome's hired white killers had gained a reputation for random attacks with heavy machine guns on "rebel" villages, often from the air.

The management of Executive Outcomes and subsequently of Sandline included Simon Mann, the old Etonian mercenary currently in jail in Equatorial Guinea for his attempt to organise a coup in that oil-rich state. There has been a great deal of public sympathy in the UK for the British Officer sweltering in an African jail. I believe that is because the public do not realise the true facts of mercenary involvement in Africa. While I would welcome an alleviation of his living conditions, I do not feel it would be unjust if he were to be kept in prison until he is too old to organise the death of another African.[10]

DFID had made a high-minded attempt to break the cycle of bad governance by organising and securing the more or less democratic election of President Tejan Kabbah in 1996. Kabbah was however overthrown after one year by a military junta, the Armed Forces Ruling Council, who claimed to be acting against government corruption. Naturally, the AFRC then proceeded itself to loot the country.

British policy was to restore the democratically elected government of President Kabbah. It could hardly have been otherwise. But unfortunately it failed to take cognisance of the fact that the Kabbah government had indeed been hideously corrupt, and as pre-occupied as all previous Sierra Leonean governments with venal deals in the diamond fields. Kabbah himself was a former UN official, which I regret to tell you too often means corrupt and untrustworthy[11]. After the Sandline affair became public, Kabbah was to be repeatedly disingenuous about his role in it.

10Interestingly Simon Mann has claimed from jail in an interview with Channel 4 News that the British Government knew and approved of his coup plot. That was exactly the same defence his then partner, Tim Spicer, was to deploy in "The Sandline Affair".
11I am a huge supporter of the UN, but I am afraid to say that the money-changers are running the temple.

2

Arms to Africa

I have a high regard for the British military. I come from a family with centuries of tradition of military service. Members of the diplomatic service often work very closely with the military, and I had done so in my career. We share Embassies with military attaches and their staff, and I had almost always got on extremely well with them, forging friendships which still endure today – I had often found their company more congenial than that of many of my FCO colleagues. On home postings, as head of Cyprus section I had worked very closely with the UK sovereign military bases on the island and with the British contingent of the UN peacekeeping force there, and with my military counterparts in the MOD.

The UK contingent of the UN peacekeeping force in Cyprus was at that time funded from the FCO budget. In consequence the living conditions of our peacekeeping troops, particularly those in married quarters, had deteriorated until we were asking our soldiers and their families to live in quite appalling conditions. Together with Brigadier Dick Lamb I had devoted a lot of energy to freeing up resources to improve things. This had made me popular with the Army, but not in some parts of the FCO (almost none of my diplomatic colleagues could imagine why I was bothered about military living conditions).

Then as Head of Maritime Section I had worked very closely indeed with the Navy on a whole variety of issues. As Head of the FCO section in the Embargo Surveillance Centre following the Iraqi invasion of Kuwait, I had lived in a (literally) underground establishment for months working with largely military personnel.

So I was very comfortable with the military. When on my second day in my new office I received a friendly phone call from Lt.-Col Tim Spicer saying he wished to come and see me, it rang no alarm bells with me. The defence industry is full of newly retired military personnel, and we provide military training to governments all around the world. I should confess that I didn't yet on 6 January 1998 mentally attach the word "mercenary" to Sandline, and I did not connect Sandline with Executive Outcomes during that initial telephone conversation with Spicer.

As Spicer briefly explained it, Sandline were involved in providing security to expatriate companies in Sierra Leone and training to forces loyal to the legitimate government of Sierra Leone. Spicer asked if he could come to see me and brief me on what his company was doing, and I readily agreed. I felt I could do with all the briefing I could get.

The next day I mentioned Spicer's call to John Everard, my predecessor as Deputy Head, who was engaged in a week's handover with me. John asked if I was sure I wanted to meet Spicer. He said that as our policy was to avoid further military conflict in Sierra Leone, he had thought it best to avoid direct contact with Spicer, and to have only telephone contact with him.

It had not occurred to me that there could be a problem, and I was a bit taken aback by what John had said. But it would be difficult now for me to cancel the appointment I had agreed.

I thought it through, and decided that I really couldn't see the moral difference between having a conversation on the telephone, as John Everard did, and having it face to face. Indeed you could sum someone up much better if you could see their body language rather than just hear their voice. I spoke to Tim Andrews, head of the section which included Sierra Leone, who told me that it was indeed very sensitive, but that Spicer had been chasing a contract to train forces loyal to President Kabbah. Tim agreed with my suggestion that we should see Spicer, as we needed to know what was happening. But Tim did mention he believed Sandline were connected to Executive Outcomes. That put me on my guard.

Perhaps I should have researched further. But I was in just my second day in a big new job. I had 21 new countries to update myself on, involving thousands of pages of material to read through. I worked over a hundred hours that first week. I decided Spicer could wait until I met him. I didn't particularly see him as a danger to me.

I underestimated Spicer. That was a bad error of judgement.

19 January, the day that Tim Spicer arrived, was extremely busy. We had ministerial briefings and parliamentary questions on Sierra Leone and a consular crisis in Nigeria. So when I was informed that Colonel Spicer was here to see me, it took me a few seconds to recall who he was.

As he was shown up, I asked Tim Andrews to come and sit in with me and take a note of the conversation. You would normally only do this for important visitors – otherwise you would just make a brief note yourself after the meeting – but given John Everard's words of caution, I thought it was probably wise to have Tim Andrews present. Besides, he knew the subject much better than I yet did.

Tim Spicer was short for a soldier, but well built and exceedingly well manicured and coiffured. His conventional good looks were marred by a slight hooding of the eyes or squint. He wore the thin, inch apart pin-stripes that seem to be universally favoured by the British military out of uniform. He smelt of expensive after-shave.

Spicer told us that Sandline now had a contract to provide training to the Kamajors, a militia force loyal to Sam Hinga Norman and currently prepared to fight for President Kabbah. He said that the aim was to pre-pare the Kamajors for a quick campaign, in support of the Nigerian-led ECOMOG forces, to retake Sierra Leone from the RUF and military junta. The contract covered training and "non-lethal" equipment. Spicer used the phrase "non-lethal" several times, and I took it as his intention to stress that he was not providing weapons and was therefore acting leg-ally.

I told him that we did not favour a military solution and that any armed intervention by ECOMOG would require prior agreement from the UN Security Council; it was essential that any such military action be as quick and limited as possible. The laws of armed conflict and the human rights of civilians must be respected.

I asked Spicer, who was funding the Sandline contract, and why? He replied that he was not free to tell me who was funding it, but that it related to the securing of some mineral assets within the country. I asked him who Sandline were? I had heard that they were related to Executive Outcomes, whose reputation in Africa was not good. Were Sandline related to Executive Outcomes, and was Mr Tony Buckingham involved in Sandline?

Spicer replied that he did not have authority to discuss Sandline's corporate structure or confidential business matters. He was here to brief me on the wider situation with regard to their strategy on Sierra Leone.

Spicer then said that he had intelligence that the junta may be attempting to acquire Eastern European weapons, shipped via Nigeria. I said that we could ask the Nigerian government to intercept any such weapons shipments under UN Security Council Resolution 1132. I asked Tim Andrews to show him the relevant passage.

Tim Andrews did not have a copy of the resolution on him, so he went back to his own office to get one. He took it down from where it was pinned, on the cork board behind the desk officer Linda St Cook's desk. He returned to my room and read aloud the appropriate clause:

Decides that all States shall prevent the sale or supply to Sierra Leone, by their nationals or from their territories, or using their flag vessels or aircraft, of petroleum and petroleum products and arms and related matériel of all types, including weapons and ammunition, military vehicles and equipment, paramilitary equipment and spare parts for the aforementioned, whether or not originating in their territory;

Spicer responded to this by saying that he had understood that the UN-SCR applied only to the RUF, and not to the government. I said that this was wrong, and that it was a geographic prohibition covering the whole country.

Spicer then asked whether the prohibition applied to "dual-use" items, which could have either a military or a civilian application. He gave the example of night vision equipment, which he said could be used by the military or in mining. I said that such "dual-use" items would be subject to export control licensing by the Department of Trade and Industry, who would consult other departments including the FCO and MOD.

Spicer then asked if military items could be exported to a neighbouring country such as Guinea, and then on to Sierra Leone. I said no, they couldn't.

While it was now obvious to me that Spicer was really considering the potential for himself to export arms to the government of Sierra Leone, I felt that Tim Andrews and I had made it plain that this was not allowed. The language of the Resolution which Tim Andrews read out to Spicer is admirably plain. I was surprised that a former British Army Lieutenant Colonel, who must by training have been familiar with UN Security Council Resolutions in conflict situations and how to interpret them, appeared to be quite so ignorant of the basic rules governing his operations in a theatre in which he was already involved. But I took it that this was because his existing contract covered only training and non-lethal equipment, as he had stated, and he was just making preliminary enquiries about the possibility of expanding this to include arms.

I am quite certain that, when Tim Andrews read Spicer the Security Council Resolution, he did not say anything like "Well, that's awkward, because the contract we expect to sign does include the sale of weapons".

It was not only to Tim Andrews and I that Spicer went out of his way to stress that his contract was for "non-lethal" equipment. My first day in the Department had been 5 January, but as is FCO practice I had a few days "handover" from my predecessor who was still doing the job for the first few days. On 5 January John Everard had sent a minute to Ann Grant to say that Spicer had told Everard that his contract would include medical and communications equipment "and nothing higher profile".[12]

It has been put to me, not least at the House of Commons Foreign Affairs Committee, that I must have realised that a £10 million contract included arms. But in fact such contracts, not including arms, were an established feature of the region. In particular, the Nigerian-led ECOMOG forces which were occupying Liberia, and which we believed might be going on to invade Sierra Leone, received their supplies, training, transportation and logistic support from the United States government via a company called Pacific and Atlantic Engineering. Their role specifically excluded the provision of weapons. Their funding, totalling some US$40 million a year, included contributions from the German and Dutch governments.

_____

12*http://www.publications.parliament.uk/pa/cm199798/cmselect/cmfaff/1057/8111018.ht m*

I presumed that Spicer was indicating a prospective contract with Kabbah that would be similar in scope to the Pacific and Atlantic contract, and took that to be what he meant when he kept emphasising the term "non-lethal".[13]

Nonetheless, I felt worried by my meeting with Spicer. He had refused to clarify Sandline's ownership, and his repeated questioning on the possibility of sending arms to Sierra Leone led me to think that he was looking to add arms to training in the future. All in all, I had found him not straight. I therefore nipped three doors along the corridor to see Ann Grant, and told her that, having met Spicer, I was worried about his intentions and didn't trust him, and that I proposed to tell the Department to break contact with him. Ann agreed with my proposal, and I went immediately to let Tim Andrews and Linda St Cook know of my decision.

Spicer later claimed that he informed the FCO at our meeting that he was exporting arms, and that the FCO (i.e. I) gave approval. But both Tim Andrews and I were to make formal, independent statements to Customs and Excise in which we both stated that Spicer had emphasised that he was exporting non-lethal equipment. We both also independently stated that, when Spicer raised questions over arms exports, Tim Andrews read him the Resolution to show that any arms exports would be illegal. John Everard had minuted that Spicer had told him that he was supplying medical and communications equipment "and nothing higher profile".

Yet much of the media and most of the political establishment preferred to take the unsupported word of a mercenary – that he had told us about supplying arms - against all three of us.

Why would that be?

Well, the Conservative Party saw the "Arms to Africa affair" as their first real chance to hit the Blair government – still only seven months old – with a scandal. They desperately *wanted* Spicer to be telling the truth and the FCO to have connived at breaking the law, preferably with ministerial knowledge. Conservatives were comforted in this view by the fact that Tim Spicer was a public schoolboy and a former Lt Colonel of a Guards regiment. He was a gentleman, and socially very well connected,

---

13Spicer gives a quite different account of this meeting. See Tim Spicer, *An Unorthodox Soldier*, pp198-200

with friends in the royal family. Such people never tell lies, while John Everard, Tim Andrews and I were all irredeemably middle class.

This struck me forcibly when I was talking to a friend of mine, an officer in the Ministry of Defence. I told him that Spicer was not telling the truth when he said that I had approved of the shipment of arms. My friend (I believe it was Colonel Andrew Jocelyn, but it may have been another) winced and said "But he's godfather to one of my children." To many influential people in Britain, the idea that a senior Guards officer might lie was unthinkable – it struck at the root of their entire belief system.

Support for Spicer from Conservatives was predictable. But I had not realised that influence would be exerted on behalf of Spicer from 10 Downing Street. Our policy on Sierra Leone was to seek a solution by peaceful means. I am sure that was what Robin Cook favoured; I discussed it with him several times. But in No. 10 and in parts of the FCO, particularly the United Nations Department, they were starting to formulate the Blair doctrine of radical military interventionism that was to lead Tony Blair to launch more wars than any other British Prime Minister[14].

A fundamental part of this new Blair doctrine was to be the ultimate privatisation – the privatisation of killing. Mercenary troops were seen as having many advantages for quick aggressive campaigns in third world countries. Regular government forces had been configured to fight huge battles against other regular forces. Mercenaries were more flexible and less constrained by regulation.

If you consider what "less constrained" really means in terms of shooting up civilians, it is remarkable that this was viewed as an advantage. Still more remarkably, this policy of military intervention in the developing world had many adherents in DFID, where it was being promoted under the slogan that "Security is a precondition of development".

The "Sandline" or "Arms to Africa" affair has been presented by its proponents as a noble attempt to restore democratic government to Sierra Leone, hampered by pettifogging bureaucrats. In fact, it was nothing of the kind, but a deeply squalid plot to corner the market in Sierra Leone's blood diamonds.

14See John Kampfner; *Blair's Wars*

It was, in the baseness of its motivation, absolutely typical of white mercenary operations in Africa for the last fifty years.

The architect of the Sandline plot was Rakesh Saxena. Then 47, Saxena was a remarkable character. A self-professed leading international Marxist analyst, he had a (ahem) controversial career in banking, takeovers and derivatives trading. He was, at the time I joined the Africa Department, detained on bail in Vancouver while fighting extradition on fraud charges to Thailand. Saxena already had a long history of dealing in African blood diamonds, including in Angola where Executive Outcomes were "securing" the mines..

In Sierra Leone, Saxena planned to pull off a spectacular coup. He would speculate £10 million on arms and mercenary support to President Kabbah. In return, Kabbah would immediately give Saxena title to major diamond mining concessions with an estimated value of at least £70 million, plus promises of tax exemptions and preferred future access to diamond trading.

So the financier of the Sandline project was not the government of President Kabbah, but a millionaire businessman accused of fraud, who wanted diamonds. Saxena had made a hard business calculation, that for the £10 million he was risking Sandline could effectively restore Kabbah. It was the old story – trained white men to go in, shoot up a lot of Africans and grab control of key economic resources. That analysis characterises most – not all, but most – of the history of white intervention in Africa for the last five hundred years.

It was this contract, including the weapons, men and training which Sandline were to provide, and the diamond concessions and other deals which were to be given to Saxena, which the British High Commissioner to Sierra Leone, Peter Penfold, recommended to President Kabbah on 19 December 1997. By his own account to me, Penfold successfully persuaded Kabbah to sign. This is confirmed by Tim Spicer who writes "Kabbah had discussed our involvement in Sierra Leone with him [Penfold] before agreeing to the deal."[15]

Penfold then flew to London and had lunch as the guest of Tim Spicer and Tony Buckingham (of Executive Outcomes) on 23 December 1997.

15Spicer; *An Unorthodox Soldier, p193*

He then called into the FCO to pick up mail, and later flew to Canada on holiday. On 29 January Penfold returned to London, and again went straight to see Tim Spicer. Having seen Spicer shortly before leaving for Canada, why did Penfold need to see Spicer again immediately on his return?

In mid January 1998, Saxena was re-arrested by the Royal Canadian Mounted Police after being discovered in possession of a false passport, which they suspected he might use to jump bail. Saxena was therefore imprisoned by a Vancouver court, but continued to run the project from his jail cell.

I have struggled to understand Peter Penfold's motivation. The House of Commons Foreign Affairs Committee was to take the view that Penfold had exceeded his authority in giving full support to the proposed mercenary-led attack in Sierra Leone. But they concluded that his motivation was honourable. He believed the restoration of the democratic government, by armed force if necessary, was an overriding objective. The media portrayed Penfold as a heroic figure, the man in the middle of the action, fighting for democracy in the depths of Africa and being obstructed by the pettifogging bureaucrats back home. In short, the media treated him like General Gordon.

I am less sure. For one thing, Penfold deserved the praise he received from the Foreign Affairs Committee for winning the complete trust and confidence of President Kabbah. But Kabbah was not Sierra Leone. Penfold was undoubtedly popular with the Freetown faction around Kabbah. Religion is terribly important in West Africa and Penfold was – another parallel with Gordon – a charismatic Christian, who would lead Freetown church services with his guitar.

But in my conversations with him, Penfold never struck me as idealistic – and nor did idealism come over in his appearance before the Foreign Affairs Committee. What then was his motivation in getting so deeply involved in the Sandline project as to introduce it to Kabbah, and to appear so intent on reporting to Sandline in London?

I think in considering this question of Penfold's motivation, it is essential that we remember that the Sandline contract was the opposite of a noble venture. It involved tens of million pounds worth of blood diamonds in return for support by hired killers, with the financial backing of an alleged fraudster, in jail in Canada and on the run from the Thai authorities.

After I had concluded my meeting with Spicer on 19 January 1998, I had walked him to the door of the building. A gloomy premature dusk was already gathering over a cloud shrouded London, and little dust devils were whirling in King Charles St, driven by a biting cold wind that looked as though it portended a storm. As I shook Spicer's hand, he looked up at me and met my eyes – something I suddenly realised he almost never did.

"You won't deny this meeting happened, will you?" he asked.

I was taken aback by such an extraordinary question. What on earth did he mean?

"No, of course not. Why should I?"

The remark added to my distrust of Spicer – in my experience, those who suspect without provocation that others may be dishonest, are seldom exactly straightforward themselves. When you are naturally truthful, it hits you like a slap in the face if someone suggests that you may not tell the truth. The remark reinforced my feeling that there was something rum about Spicer, and on return I told Ann of my decision to tell the Department not to have further contact with him.

But I cannot pretend that Spicer was more than a minor cloud on my horizon. His proposed training for the Kamajors seemed to me a sideshow, simply a chance for Sandline to make a bit of money. The real question was if and when the vastly more capable Nigerian-led, US-supplied ECOMOG force on the Liberian border would move against the Sierra Leonean junta.

I comforted myself that, with any luck, I might never hear of Spicer again.

3
Almost Gabon

Meantime, I was delighted to be going out to West Africa again.

As is customary in the FCO, I flew out on a "familiarisation visit" to get to know the territories for which I was responsible or, in my case, to update myself. Given the number of countries for which I was responsible this was going to take several visits. On this first trip, I was going to Nigeria, Cameroon and Gabon. Nigeria was a given, because it has the largest population and greatest total wealth in Africa, while Cameroon is next door and an important Francophone state. I was to visit Gabon because it was taking a six month turn as a member of the UN Security Council and there were a number of issues on which I was briefed to ask for support. We did not have an Embassy in Gabon, and nobody from the British government had visited Gabon for some time.

Nigeria is a fascinating country. I served in Lagos from 1986 to 1990, and in my time there two personal friends of mine had been murdered by armed robbers in separate incidents, and a third deliberately poisoned in his office and left crippled. You were obliged to live behind so much of razor wire, iron bars and armed guards that it was like locking yourself in your own prison. Nigeria is a country where society has gone horribly wrong, to the extent that a whole nation, speaking some three hundred different languages and dialects, has been tarnished by the brush of criminality. But it has to be faced squarely that there is real cause – Nigerians are responsible worldwide for a high proportion of internet fraud, and of social security and identity fraud in the UK. You cannot safely walk the streets of Lagos at night.

This is all so different from Accra in Ghana, where anyone can and does stroll around the bars and restaurants at night, that it is different to imagine that the two cities are only ten hours drive apart. Given that both have very similar British colonial backgrounds, it is difficult to avoid the obvious conclusion that vast oil wealth has poisoned Nigerian society. But it is more complicated than that. The colonial authorities in Ghana made less changes to local customary law and to the local institutions of chieftaincy, which in Ghana still play an important role, particularly in the allocation of land. These institutions have contributed to Ghana's continuing social cohesion.

On any rational analysis, the primary practical impact of the government of Nigeria is to shift economic resources from the naturally wealthy South to the naturally poor North. The entire government machinery can be envisaged simply as a pump, with the flow of resources going only Northwards.

There are different mechanisms for transporting the economic resources North. One of the most important has been import licences. In an economy that historically has been ludicrously controlled and mismanaged, the ability to import everything from palm oil to motor cars has been awarded by government to a chosen few. Import licensing has overwhelmingly favoured Northerners, with the sugar and salt monopolies of the Dangotes and the Dantatas being one of the more egregious examples.

Northern control of the military has meant Northern control of government, as for most of its independent history Nigeria has been under military dictatorship. Over a fifty year period Nigeria has probably been the most corrupt country in the World, and as those pulling the levers of power have been Northerners, the effect of this has been the funnelling Northwards of many hundreds of billions of dollars of Nigeria's looted oil wealth. These overtly corrupt mechanisms (as opposed to the legal but still disastrous mechanism of import licensing) include plain looting of the Treasury by military dictators, massive corruption in award of government contracts, and a massive web of patronage.

It is not in the least that southern Nigerians are averse to employing any of these tactics. It is simply the case that the more martial North has been able successively to dominate military governments.

There is currently a fashion in development circles, and particularly within DFID, for aid to African armies and other military institutions. The argument runs that security is a necessary precondition of development. It is also argued that such training inculcates respect for democracy in African armed forces. The best riposte to this British doctrine of neo-militarism is to note that the large majority of Nigeria's rapacious stream of military dictators, and the senior coup plotters who supported them, have been trained at Sandhurst at British government expense.

Sandhurst has been responsible for educating those who generated untold repression and economic ruination in Africa. Of the immediate problems facing me, General Johnny Paul Koroma, who had initially overthrown President Kabbah in Sierra Leone in the military coup of 1997 and still led a powerful force there, was a Sandhurst man. The appalling General Sani Abacha, then dictator of Nigeria, had also been trained by the British government, at MONS in Aldershot and the infantry college at Warminster.

General Abacha had seized power in a military coup in Nigeria in 1993, after the military annulled the elections won by Chief Abiola. He had closed down the media, banned political parties and murdered thousands of opponents. He came to international opprobrium after executing the novelist (and my friend) Ken Saro Wiwa, as well as imprisoning for "treason" Abiola and former President Obasanjo.

Nigeria had been expelled from the Commonwealth and subjected to a variety of international sanctions. Abacha had retaliated against British interests, notably banning British Airways from the country. This was a stronger move than it sounds, for Nigeria was British Airways' most profitable route.

France sought to benefit from the freeze in Nigerian/British relations by cultivating Sani Abacha strongly. The French intelligence services were even paying personal bribes to Abacha to maintain the ban on British Airways.

For those who really know Africa, that is not shocking. In twenty years inside experience, I never saw French policy show any interest whatsoever in human rights or even economic development. French policy in Africa has been motivated entirely by short term commercial or financial gain, usually for individual French politicians or interests connected to them, rather than for France as a whole.

It is also worth noting that many British commercial interests supported Abacha. The annulment of the election results and transition to Abacha was handled by Ernest Shonekan, head of Unilever Nigeria and a long term ally of military dictators, as well as one of the most personally unpleasant men I have had the misfortune to meet. Abacha's killing of Ken Saro Wiwa, and of hundreds of others who protested at the appalling pollution and labour conditions in the Niger Delta oil industry, was in the interest of Shell and other oil giants.

Shell had certainly been making corrupt payments to then President Ibrahim Babangida when I was in the Commercial Section of the British High Commission in Lagos in the late 1980s, and I see no reason to suppose they had fundamentally changed their practices. These included personal payments to local police and military commanders who carried out on the ground the brutal suppression of dissent in the Niger Delta.

I found Abacha's Nigeria a sad and solemn place, with a new element of fear – people were scared to be seen with you, and were continually looking over their shoulders as we talked. Before Abacha, dictatorship had been rather sporadically applied with little sense of an all-pervading state. I used to call Babangida's Nigeria a dictatorship tempered by inefficiency. The feel of Abacha's Nigeria was much more oppressive.

One person who was certainly not going to be intimidated was Bola Ige, the vigorous lawyer, human rights activist and politician. Together with Frances Macleod, who accompanied me for the Nigeria leg of my trip, I visited Bola in his house in Ibadan. He made us tea with his own hands and we sat on comfortable chairs in his living room, which was strewn with books. Abacha had announced the introduction of "democracy" with five political parties created by himself – Bola memorably described them as "The five fingers of the leper's hand." He was blunt in his cataloguing of the persecution of political activists, and the astonishing rate of corruption. He was a comforting presence, so rational and secure.

After Abacha's death, Bola was to become a crusading anti-corruption Attorney-General of Nigeria. That is why they gunned him down and killed him, at about the spot where he now stood bidding us a warm goodbye.

Otherwise my visit to Nigeria was uneventful. In Abuja I stayed with our good and forthright High Commissioner, Graham Burton. My chief memory of the visit is how very old my Nigerian friends looked, and my worrying I too must be ageing fast.

From Nigeria I flew on to Yaounde in Cameroon. At Lagos airport there was the remembered chaos as it turned out more people had boarding cards than there were seats on the plane. Everyone had been checking in with astonishing quantities of luggage, and still managed to arrive at the gate with more hand luggage each than my total worldly goods.

Having made it onto the plane, we sat on the tarmac for over an hour while an astonishing number of textile-wrapped bundles were crammed into the cargo hold. Once the plane lumbered along the runway, it seemed to pick up speed far too slowly, and it ran out of tarmac and bumped at speed over a couple of hundred metres of rough grasses before slowly pulling itself into a very shallow climb. I wondered how we would get enough height to get over the major mountains on the Nigeria/ Cameroon border. I was being squeezed into the aisle by the massive lady sat beside me, who was several times wider than her seat and dressed in bright yellow cloth. She was waving a handkerchief in the air and singing hymns loudly. I decided to exercise my facility of being able to sleep in almost any position and circumstance, and re-awoke as we bumped along the Yaounde tarmac.

In Yaounde I saw a session of President Biya's pet parliament, and then travelled by car up to Bamenda to visit Cameroon's English speaking community. President Paul Biya is yet another of those African tyrants, having ruled with an increasingly ruthless hand since 1982. There are two additional factors in Cameroon which make Biya's reign particularly obnoxious. One is internationally well-known, the other distinctly not. They are the desecration of Africa's greatest remaining rain forest, and the repression of Cameroon's English speaking communities.

Beating around the country by Land Rover, I stood on the main road into Douala from the East, and counted timber lorries for a period of half an hour. I only counted those great lorries bearing logs of more than eight feet in diameter, to give a rough indication of primary forest. In just half an hour I counted 53 such lorries. They did not stop coming day or

33

night. Cameroon has regulations on the number of trees per hectare loggers may take from the primary forest, but these are commonly ignored, as are forest reserves, amid massive collusion between loggers and ministers. Among the disastrous effects is the tiny and ever declining population of the last surviving mountain gorillas.

You probably knew all that. But few people know of the repression of Cameroon's English speaking communities – indeed few people seem to know Cameroon has English speakers.[16] In fact they amount to about 15% of the population.

The British colony of South Cameroons was joined to Cameroon in 1961. The population have regretted it more or less ever since. Though English and French are joint official languages of Cameroon, in fact there is massive discrimination. This includes the closure and deprivation of resources of English schools and colleges, the paucity of government expenditure in the English areas and the denial of government jobs and patronage to English speakers. Then there is a long catalogue of torture, imprisonment, beatings and killings, with the gendarmerie having free reign in the English speaking areas.

Dictators are often popular in Africa through their personality cults, but President Biya is genuinely hated – so much so that in 1992 he managed to lose the Presidential election to an English speaking candidate, John Fru Ndi. The military then moved in on the Electoral Commission in typical African fashion, and the result was changed so Biya could be declared winner. There followed a wave of government violence and repression aimed particularly at the leadership of the English speaking community.

For example, the senior magistrate in Bamenda, Justice Forbin, was beaten to death by gendarmes. English language journalists were particularly targeted.

16Except in Washington where, extraordinarily, English Cameroonians have a firm position in the yellow cab trade. I was astonished when taking a taxi to give a talk at the Brookings Institute, to be asked by the African cab driver if I was *the* Craig Murray. I had given a Washington radio interview on the folly of the war in Iraq; a Cameroonian cabbie had recognised me as the man who came to Bamenda and tried to help, and had radioed his colleagues. For the remainder of that trip they ferried me around without payment, which must be the highest of accolades.

Driving now through the beautiful hills to Bamenda and Ndu I met human rights and journalism organisations and was horrified by the tales of systematic torture, many evidenced by physical injuries I was shown. I then had dinner in the home of John Fru Ndi, who was charming and gentlemanly. There was a small group of his key supporters present, every one of whom had been beaten and imprisoned, and every one of whom had a relative killed.

The really sad thing about this trip was how desperately glad they were to see me, and how desperately proud they were to be associated with the UK. They felt British as fervently as the citizens of Gibraltar, and they were genuinely puzzled that the UK had shown almost no interest in their plight and done nothing to defend them.

It is indeed a disgrace that we have done nothing. The major reason is that Paul Biya has the strong support of France and its Presidents, and we do not view the South Cameroonians as worth an argument with France. I was determined to try to do something about this; but sadly the Sandline affair was about to crash on my head and effectively end my chances.

The other point about the English speaking region of Cameroon, is that it is one of the most beautiful places on God's earth. Rolling green hills, fringed with fragrant stands of rubber and eucalyptus, their thin willowy trunks often reminding me of silver birch in the Scottish highlands. Streams run crystal clear, and low huts made of packed red laterite and thatch carry the smell of years of accumulated aromatic wood smoke. The people are proud and straight-backed. The sunsets are tinted with rose, and in the mornings there is a nip in the crisp, clear air.[17]

We headed down to Victoria on the coast, now known as Lembe. It is a ravishing spot where the lower slopes of Mount Cameroon sweep majestically into the sea. It also has the remains of a magnificent botanic garden, founded over a century ago by the Royal Botanic Gardens at Kew, and still retaining links to it. On this visit I met some young British volunteers who were enthusiastically researching different native varieties of cane. Apparently there was a world shortage of rattan, as Malaysia and Indonesia increasingly turned forest into palm oil and rubber plantation. They saw great potential for Africa, which had many varieties of

---

[17]Gerald Durrell has captured it all beautifully in *The Bafut Beagles*.

cane little exploited commercially, to fill this void through cultivation in secondary forest. Most of the suitable cane plants are protected either by barbs or sharp spines, and I remember that, as they enthused about their canes over lunch and a beer, their palms were swathed in rough bandages.

I next moved back to Douala, where I had dinner with our delightful French female honorary consul and her husband, and was impressed by the sheer scale and relentless activity of the docks, as well as horrified by the enormous quantities of virgin lumber, including vast rafts floating downstream.

Then I was due to meet the Gabonese foreign minister and visit that country. The Gabonese foreign minister was doing me the singular honour of flying to Cameroon to meet me. He was coming in on the Air Gabon flight, then returning on the same plane with me. I waited in the VIP lounge, and once the plane landed, I dismissed the British Embassy driver to return to Yaounde. The Gabonese foreign minister was only going to be in Cameroon for two hours, but nonetheless there was a guard of honour and military band to meet him.

These ceremonies over, he came bounding into the VIP lounge, a short, bouncy man with a wide grin, wearing an expensive silk suit. The lounge provided champagne for us and we fell to gossiping, mostly about African political leaders. We got on very well and really became very comfortable, while the champagne kept flowing. I noted the time for the plane to depart had come, and he commented it must be late. More champagne followed, then a flustered African in an open-necked white shirt came crashing into the VIP lounge, went down on one knee before the Minister and blurted out.

"I am sorry sir – the plane sir. I am sorry sir – it's gone."

Air Gabon had gone without us, while we sat drinking and chatting in the VIP lounge. The poor minister was utterly crestfallen and kept pronouncing himself desolate. I kept telling him not to worry, but I was pretty stunned myself, particularly as the plane had taken my suitcase off to Gabon, leaving me with the papers in my briefcase and the clothes I stood up in.

After his aides made a few phone calls, the minister was decanted into a large Mercedes and driven away. Fortunately I still had my wallet, and I went off in search of a taxi. It was already evening, and I set off with the taxi on a tour of Douala's hotels. Unfortunately, Douala was hosting a major conference of Francophone states and absolutely all the hotels were completely full. After searching for over two hours I still had nowhere to sleep.

I instructed the taxi driver to return to a large modern hotel situated on a bluff overlooking the city. We had tried it earlier with no luck, and I now asked whether there had been any cancellations. The answer was no. But I had returned there because I had noticed it had a casino, and had decided that as I couldn't find a bed my best option was to stay awake all night there.

The casino was much like any other, with banks of machines near the entrance and the roulette and card tables at the back. Seated at them were a few locals, a few wiry, heavy-smoking French expatriates, and the usual expostulating Chinese and Malaysians. As I wanted to play for some hours I went to the blackjack table. It is the best game for losing slowly and steadily, which over any period of time is the best you can sensibly hope for from a casino.

My ability to keep track of the cards in the shoe and reckon the odds was rather impeded by the champagne I had drunk, and as usual I turned down the free drinks.

I was winning slightly, and after a few hours was looking around the room and enjoying myself. A number of prostitutes were working the room, one of whom was a dark haired European lady, perhaps in her mid thirties, wearing a long pink silk dress with a white embroidered floral pattern and a split high up one side. She had dark hair and strong but not unattractive features. She would seat herself next to players at the tables and then attempt to open up conversation. About 2.30 am she finally got round to trying me. She glided on to the stool beside me, placed her hand on my shoulder and her lips by my ear, and she murmured the immortal words:

"I am wearing purple knickers".

37

I was perched at the blackjack table on a high stool, and I literally fell off it laughing.

She was a bit offended by this, but still continued to try to chat me up. She was Portuguese. I explained that I could find nowhere to stay because of the conference, and suggested that I would happily pay to sleep with her, provided she had a bed and I didn't have to have sex. Unfortunately she didn't have a bed, or at least only one that her husband was in, and nor did she seem a particularly nice or interesting person, so I soon indicated definite disinterest and she wandered off to a group of Frenchmen. But still, she had the greatest opening line I have ever heard.

The next day Air Gabon came back with my suitcase, and I managed to get a flight back to London. I never have made it to Gabon.

4

The Sandline Affair

On my first day back in my London office, Tim Andrews mentioned that Peter Penfold would be in that afternoon. I had by now heard a lot about Penfold, most of it good, and was keen to meet him. I spent the morning with my head down, working my way through the paperwork which had accumulated while I was away. Shortly after lunchtime I went to ask Tim something. I found Penfold in Tim's office, in gleeful mood, holding forth in a loud voice to Tim and Linda, who sat at their desks.

Penfold wore the regulation pinstripe suit and had put down a fawn raincoat on a chair. His shoes looked new, mirror bright and unmarked. He looked a bit flushed, and I thought he had enjoyed his lunch. He had iron grey hair, roughly cut as though with a razor blade. The newspapers were to describe him as "Beagle-faced". I am not sure what that means, exactly, but he had dark bags under his eyes and a deep vertical crease in each cheek. It gave him a rather mournful look, that belied the high good spirits of his voice. He was gesturing expansively as he spoke. As I walked in, he glanced at me in some annoyance at the interruption. Not knowing who I was, he carried on with his flow of words, his eyes occasionally flitting to me with a wary look.

"So I persuaded him to sign it!" Penfold was saying gleefully: "Kabbah would never have done it on his own – he's much too cautious. But Kabbah trusts my judgement. Kabbah said that if anyone else had brought him the contract, he wouldn't have signed. Kabbah said that directly to me. But because he trusts me, he signed. It's great! Now we are going to get the Kamajors organised, get the junta out, and we'll all be back in Freetown again!"

Tim and Linda looked from Penfold to me, and I decided to introduce myself:

"Hello, Peter. I'm John Everard's replacement, Craig Murray. I wonder if you would mind stepping into my office for a small chat?"

We walked through the connecting door into my office. Peter Penfold had been forced to quit his Freetown embassy when the military junta took over, as Freetown had become lawless (although in fact the Embassy was not looted and very loyal local staff continued to guard it). In evacuating British residents from Freetown, Penfold had displayed great personal courage. As Tim Andrews had told me, at one time a Sandline employee was defending the hotel in which the British citizens were gathered with a heavy machine gun mounted on the hotel roof, while the Royal Navy organised the evacuation by ship's helicopter.

Normal UK doctrine is that "We recognise states, not governments", and our major criteria for dealing with a government is that it has effective control of its territory. But, in what was intended as an example of our new ethical foreign policy, we had continued to recognise President Kabbah and his dwindling band of supporters as the legitimate government of Sierra Leone. Kabbah had gone into exile in Conakry, the capital of Guinea. Peter Penfold had therefore set up his "Embassy" there, in a hotel room, with no communications facilities except the hotel's dodgy telephones and fax. I should mention Penfold's long-suffering and hardworking deputy, Colin Glass. Colin was a bearded old hand with a beer belly who looked like he would be more at home in the rugby club bar that a diplomatic conference. Colin kept the show on the road.

Leading Penfold into my office, I did not sit behind my desk but motioned him to the settee, drawing up a chair beside him.

"It's good to meet you," I opened. "I've heard a lot about you."

"All good, I trust?"

"Pretty well, yes. Everyone says you played a very cool hand in the evacuation."

"I did my duty, no more."

"Well, not everybody does that."

"Thank you."

"I hope you had a good holiday? It must be difficult for you in Conakry."

"Pretty good, yes. Thank you."

I decided to come to the matter in hand.

"I had Tim Spicer come and see me a couple of weeks ago."

"Really?" Penfold's eyes brightened and his nostrils slightly flared. He leaned forward, perched now on the edge of the sofa. He sensed that I might be an ally. I was to disappoint him.

"He told me he was hoping to conclude a contract with Kabbah to train the Kamajors prior to an offensive against the Junta."

"Yes, yes."

"Look, he has every right to do that. It's perfectly legal business. But we didn't ought to be involved. Our policy is to seek a peaceful solution."

Penfold glared. He had a very mobile face and his eyes suddenly looked red-rimmed.

"Pah! Do you think the junta will simply go away? Now the AFRC are in cahoots with the RUF, they're entrenched. It's alright for you to talk of a peaceful solution. How does that help Kabbah?"

"Well, ECOWAS is really in the lead here. You know, our policy is to support moves in the UN for regional organisations to take responsibility for conflicts in their region. If ECOWAS can't get a solution, then they will have to go to the UN Security Council for a resolution enabling the use of force by ECOMOG in Sierra Leone."

"All that could take years."

"Not necessarily. I think it might only need a few weeks. But we are still looking to support moves to a peaceful solution."

"Well, if you think there's any point in negotiating with a mob of murderers."

I decided it was time to come to the point.

"Listen, I heard you tell Tim and Linda that you advised President Kabbah to sign the Sandline contract."

Penfold jutted out his lower lip: "Yes, I did."

"I really don't think that was wise. Sandline are a mercenary company."

"They have done good work in Sierra Leone."

"And Spicer talked of a possible Kamajor offensive. We are supposed to be looking for a peaceful solution, not restart the civil war."

"But where is your peaceful solution?"

"Look, I see what you mean. But if it comes to force, it has to be the UN and blue hats. And we have to address the causes of the rebellions"

Penfold got angry now:

"Causes! They have no causes! Is our policy, or is it not, to restore the democratically elected government of President Kabbah?"

"Yes, it is."

"Then I am the High Commissioner and I must be allowed to pursue that policy."

"But you cannot think that the Kamajors, even with Sandline, can take the whole country from the AFRC and RUF?"

"They don't need the whole country."

"So we will just be back into civil war?"

Penfold went silent for a while, then raised his head and looked me hard in the eyes.

"Craig, have you ever been to Sierra Leone?"

"No, I haven't."

"I am sorry, but you really don't know what you are talking about. And I believe I am senior to you. I will bid you good day."

Peter then left my office with a controlled slowness.

Once he had gone, I went next door to see Tim and Linda. They were giggling somewhat, as voices had been raised and they had heard much of the conversation. Linda looked up at me, blue eyes under long dark lashes.

"So you've met Peter, then."

"Interesting man. I am really worried that he advised President Kabbah to sign the Sandline contract."

"He said he gave it to him" added Tim.

Tim Andrews was interesting. A comfortable looking dark haired man in his early forties, much attached to his wife and family, he was genuinely horrified by the atrocities of the RUF and had taken them very much to heart. His natural sympathies lay on the side of anyone who wanted to use force against the RUF. I am sure he felt my desire to understand what caused the RUF to be liberal poppycock. But Tim was dead straight, and a good man to have around when the crisis broke.

I was genuinely very worried. Spicer had spoken of his Kamajor contract as a prospect. Penfold was now telling us not only that it had already been signed, but that it was he who presented it to President Kabbah and advised him to sign it. The prospect of a potentially extremely bloody renewal of civil war by a Kamajor offensive was alarming. But I was also very worried by the media and diplomatic implications.

If the media knew that a British High Commissioner had encouraged the signing of a mercenary contract in Africa, there would be a media storm given the context of "Ethical foreign policy". Still worse, we had been encouraging the negotiating efforts of ECOWAS. If ECOWAS knew that, at the same time, we were going behind their back to seek a military solution excluding ECOMOG, especially one involving white mercenaries, there could be repercussions that would affect British interests elsewhere in West Africa.

So I went straight to Ann Grant's office to tell her. Her secretary, Julie, said that she was in a meeting with her boss, Richard Dales, the FCO's Africa Director. I decided that he would need to know eventually, too, and that I had better not delay as the story could hit the media any time. So after a brief word with Richard's secretary, I entered his very grand and capacious office, full of mahogany tables and bookcases and all the trappings that had remained in place since this room ran part of the British Empire.

Richard was a plump, short man in his early fifties, with black hair swept to one side above brown spectacles. He had a small mouth, usually pursed, and he was meticulous in both dress and speech. He had plummy tones even by FCO standards. He was holding a bone china teacup and saucer as I entered. Richard was seated opposite Ann, who was talking animatedly, dark eyes flashing from under her wiry hair. I entered the room from behind him and he looked round querulously as he heard me.

Before he could expostulate, I said quickly.

"Listen. I've just learnt something that I think you need to know. You remember Tim Spicer told me that he hoped to get a contract from Kabbah to train and support the Kamajors? Well it's already signed. And it is Peter Penfold who gave it to Kabbah and urged him to sign it."

There was silence for a moment as this was digested. Ann gave me a look of support. Then Richard asked:

"How do you know this?"

"Peter just told me."

"Is he still around?"

"No, I believe he just left."

"Thank you, Craig."

"If the media get hold or ECOWAS find out..."

"Precisely. Thank you, Craig. Ann and I will discuss this."

I was dismissed. I turned on my heel and went back to my office. I started to read reports on Togo, Ivory Coast and Gambia and look over draft responses. An hour or so later Ann popped he head around my door and said:

"Craig , I have asked Peter Penfold to come in and see me tomorrow. Would you mind sitting in with me? I may need you to confirm what he told you."

Peter Penfold came in the next day in defiant mood. Having slept on it, he was more than ever convinced that he was in the right, and he was determined to battle his corner. He plainly resented control from the London department, and appeared to dislike Ann, who was his line manager.[18] It was an extremely tense and sometimes heated meeting between them. I dislike conflict and found it a bit embarrassing to be there. Penfold growled a lot and Ann was magnificently furious and plain spoken. Ann told him he was not entitled to have advised Kabbah to sign the Sandline contract. Penfold replied that he had advised Kabbah "in my personal capacity".

The account that Ann gave of this meeting to the Foreign Affairs Committee inquiry was rather guarded, but I think something of the flavour still comes through from her evidence there:

---

18 Of course, there is irony in my position in this, given the events of *Murder in Samarkand*. The issues and motivations in the two cases were however entirely different.

Ms Grant: I had asked Craig to be present and where I wanted to hear, firstly, Mr Penfold's side of the story from his own mouth and to make clear as his reporting officer and the guardian of the policy, if you like, in London exactly what I thought and I did that in the course of the meeting. It was as Craig recalls. There was some heated and quite lengthy debate about whether or not it was open to Mr Penfold to give advice to a head of state to whom he was accredited in a personal capacity. I said that I did not accept that he could do so. I thought that when he gave advice he should always bear in mind his official status and that President Kabbah would do the same. If he was giving advice to President Kabbah, President Kabbah would assume that advice had the backing of the British Government.

Dr Norman Godman MP: Can I ask a quick supplementary. In terms of the relationship between this professional diplomat and the President, what do you understand by the term a "personal opinion"?

Ms Grant: Well, as I tried to explain, in my view if you are giving advice on policy of any kind to a head of state or government or a minister in another government and the relationship of that person to you is one of High Commissioner accredited to that country, my own view is that you cannot have a personal opinion. I remember Mr Penfold arguing back that actually President Kabbah had listened to him particularly because of his personal regard for him and his personal relationship which we understood was very close. I said he could not know that. He could not know how President Kabbah was responding and he had to assume and behave as if all his communications, however informal, in whatever difficult circumstances, were in his capacity as British High Commissioner.

Dr Norman Godman MP: So can I infer by that it would appear that Mr Penfold had developed, if you like, a relationship that took him beyond that of the professional representative with the President? Was he acting as a personal advisor to the President in terms of Sandline and HMG?

Ms Grant: I was seeking to ensure by that conversation and by other conversations we had had of a gentler nature before that that relationship did not develop in an improper or a damaging way. I made it very

45

clear what I thought were the proper limits and conveyed those to Mr Penfold and expected him to observe those limits."[19]

In the course of his meeting with Ann Grant, Penfold made a number of comments which surprised me. He said that he had told Tim Andrews and Linda St Cooke all about the contract when he called into the office just before Christmas. I could not understand why Tim had told me nothing about this before my meeting with Spicer, or subsequently. Penfold also said that he had written an account of his 19 December meeting with Kabbah, and posted it to Ann before he left for Canada. Ann was adamant she had never received any such letter. She requested Peter Penfold now to write a full account of his dealings with Kabbah over the Sandline contract, and give it to her.

After the meeting was over, we quizzed Ann's PA Julie as to whether any letter had been received from Penfold. None had. I then checked the registry log, in which the clerks entered all incoming letters except junk mail, and then entered the replies. There was no incoming letter from Peter Penfold registered. Tim Andrews and Linda St Cooke were both equally mystified. And they looked completely blank when asked whether Penfold had briefed them on the Sandline contract shortly before Christmas. Linda said he had come in, on 23 December, but he had only picked up some mail and used the telephone. He hadn't said anything much to them at all.

I tried to get on with other work, but remained very uneasy about Sierra Leone. A search did not bring up any letter from Peter Penfold, and I was having some difficulty in believing he had posted it – or even written it. The House of Commons Foreign Affairs Committee enquiry was to make it very plain that Ann Grant had the same doubts:

Sir John Stanley MP: **Are you prepared to say that that letter was never received in the FCO?**

Ms Grant: **As far as I am aware that letter was never received in the FCO.**

Sir John Stanley MP: **Do you accept Mr Penfold's version of events that he actually wrote it and posted it?**

19*http://www.publications.parliament.uk/pa/cm199798/cmselect/cmfaff/1057/8111019.ht m*

46

Ms Grant; **All I can say is that I never received it.**

Sir John Stanley MP: **But you are happy to accept Mr Penfold's version of events that it was written and posted?**

Ms Grant: **I see no way of proving or disproving that.**[20]

For a senior FCO official to refuse to accept the word of a British High Commissioner, when invited to do so by a parliamentary inquiry, is pretty extraordinary. Long before this enquiry, it was already clear to me that the situation was unworkable and had huge potential for causing great embarrassment to Ministers. I could only see one sensible course of action. So I sat down on the morning of 3 February 1998 and wrote a minute to Ann Grant and Richard Dales, recommending that Peter Penfold be sacked as Ambassador, or recalled, as they say in the FCO.

In writing my minute I was well aware that, the FCO being a very hierarchical organisation, this was much more likely to boomerang back and hit me than to be effective. But I felt the Department was sleepwalking into big trouble with nobody getting a grip. I minuted that there was a dichotomy in our policy, with Mr Penfold favouring a military solution while the Department was promoting a peaceful one. Penfold's advice to Kabbah to hire mercenaries was a real mistake, while his account of meetings nobody else recalled and of letters going missing in the post was peculiar. The best thing was to take firm action and recall him; stuck in a Conakry hotel, he was not able to do much good anyway.

I was right to expect that this would rebound on me. The same afternoon Richard Dales walked into my office. This was not his usual style at all, he rather summoned people. He closed the door behind him and sat down across from my desk. He was plainly rather angry. This showed in his tones being even quieter and more measured than usual.

"Yes, Craig," he began, "Ann passed your minute on to me. Neither she nor I agree with your recommendation."

He passed me back my minute. He had written a manuscript note on the top:

"There is *no* dichotomy in our policy. Our difficulty lies in getting Mr Penfold... to follow it."

---

[20]*http://www.publications.parliament.uk/pa/cm199798/cmselect/cmfaff/1057/8111018.ht m*

He continued talking softly:

"You know, it is very unusual for a Deputy to recommend the recall of a Head of Mission." He stressed the word unusual, as though it were a terrible sin to do something unusual. "You know Peter Penfold is a brave man. He did a good job in the evacuation of Freetown. Of course, I do know he has a tendency to freelance. Before he went to Sierra Leone he was the Governor of the British Virgin Islands. As Governor he was constitutionally independent of the FCO and quite rightly did not take instruction from us. I think the problem is that he has got used to that mode of operation."

"I see." It was my first and last contribution to this conversation.

"Now, Craig, I want you to understand this. You are not Peter Penfold's manager. I will look after Peter Penfold. Understood?"

Richard stood up and walked out. I had received a very English bollocking.[21] But in retrospect, I am convinced I was right. If Penfold had been quickly and quietly removed, the whole Arms to Africa scandal could have been pre-empted. There might have been minor media interest at his removal, but even if the press had found out why, nobody could have argued that the British government had approved of illegal arms shipments. It is hard now to remember how massive the Arms to Africa scandal was – it was front page news for months.

I saw it coming and tried to stop it.

But just two days later, the whole Sandline question seemed to be overtaken. On 5 February the ECOWAS force rolled in to Sierra Leone from Liberia. The timing took us completely by surprise. By 10 February they had retaken Freetown, and had restored President Kabbah to his palace. They were establishing control over the coast and pushing the RUF back into the hinterland. They had largely dispersed the Armed Forces Ruling Council, with its leaders and a few units joining RUF forces. Sandline had played no role in the successful invasion. The Sandline contract seemed now quite redundant, and I breathed a sigh of relief.

---

21 *http://www.publications.parliament.uk/pa/cm199798/cmselect/cmfaff/1057/8111014.ht m*

48

These were very busy times indeed in the Department. The ECOMOG invasion of Sierra Leone was arguably illegal. FCO Legal Advisers did not accept the argument that ECOMOG had been invited in by President Kabbah, as he was not in effective control of his state. The general view of the international community was that a security council resolution was needed to legalise the position and put ECOMOG – which contained some highly undisciplined Nigerian units with a reputation for rape and looting – under some form of UN supervision. This was made more complicated by the fact that Nigeria insisted an ECOWAS mandate was sufficient and no UN resolution was needed. As always when dealing with the Security Council, I was having to work both in UK time and in New York time, and my working day started with an 8am commute in to London from Gravesend, while I was not getting home again until after midnight.

This was in fact not especially unusual in the FCO, where long hours were very common, and the fact that I did not usually arrive in the office until 9.30am brought occasional grumbling from Richard Dales. Meetings in the FCO were often scheduled for 9am or even earlier. But I feel it is important to work with your own biorhythm, and while I will work until the early hours with no problem, only in real emergencies have I ever got to work before 9.30am, and once there will read the paper and potter around, not actually really doing anything until 10am, by which time my cerebral cortex has started sparking again.

The rest of West Africa had not gone away. One visitor I received in my office was Stella Obasanjo, General Olesegun Obasanjo's young wife. I was pleased to see Stella Obasanjo and deeply committed to getting Olesegun Obasanjo out of jail. Not only was he the most high profile of Abacha's political prisoners, but he is, on a personal level, an extremely nice man. After taking over as military President of Nigeria in 1976 he had announced that he had only done so in order to end military rule, and to return the country to democracy and civilian rule within three years. Commendably – indeed astonishingly for an African military ruler – he had done just that, and had then left politics to become a farmer.

He had put a great deal of money into developing a huge chicken farm at Otta, a couple of hours drive from Lagos. I used to visit him there in the mid 1980s while I was in charge of agriculture at the British High Commission in Lagos. There was no doubt about his genuine commitment to farming. Unfortunately EU and US dumping of produce, and a ludicrously overvalued Naira had combined to kill off Nigerian maize production, and the vagaries and bureaucracy of importation into Nigeria meant that he was constantly losing tens of thousands of birds through running out of foods and vaccines. In addition, he had employed family and village connections in all the key positions; they were robbing him blind. So the farm was something of a money hole. But he was passionate, cheerful and persistent.

He was also unfailingly hospitable and gracious to the young Second Secretary who came out to talk farming and politics with him. At our first meeting he handed me two live chickens to take home with me. He just leant down and swooped them up, clutching them by the legs. They lay limp as though stunned, just bundles of white feathers, surrounded by an aura of insects buzzing golden in the sun. He handed them to me and I grabbed them from him by the legs, my soft hands touching his strong hardened ones as we exchanged grips. Once I had the chickens, they immediately came to life. Flapping their wings, arching their bodies and stretching up their necks, they pecked viciously at my hands as I fled back to the Land Rover. The driver saw my distress and quickly opened the back door so I could throw them in. The General rocked with laughter, his ample frame shaking beneath his large white tunic and crumpled blue cloth hat. I returned meekly.

"You look like you need a whisky" he said.

Yes, I felt passionately that we needed to get the old General out of jail. Once Abacha went, it seemed to me that Obasanjo would be essential to any possibility of holding Nigeria together, given the degree of Southern resentment that had been building up.[22]

I feel deeply that one should never rejoice at the death of another human being, however bad. But sometimes in practice it is difficult, and I could not help but feel a lightness in my step at the death of General Abacha. The most repressive of Nigeria's appalling stream of military

---

22Whether Nigeria ought to be held together is a quite different question, that I shall be discussing in a further book.

dictators, he had murdered numerous political opponents, and pillaged Nigeria's oil wealth at a rate probably unequalled by any dictator in history. We reckoned he stole over $7 billion.

I have never understood why anyone wants to steal that much money. If you have one billion dollars, that is already more money than you can possibly spend. Why go on and on stealing? Is it some kind of addiction?

One of the things Abacha liked to spend his money on was high class hookers, and he died in bed with three of them, from a heart attack brought on by a substantial overdose of Viagra tablets.[23] Contrary to rumour, I am quite certain that MI6 had no part in his death – he did it himself.

That day I was having a drink with Andrew Mackinlay MP in the Strangers Bar of the House of Commons. Tony Lloyd, then Minister of State responsible for Africa, was across the room in earnest conversation with someone. I was not sure if he had heard of the death of Abacha, so I caught his eye, gave him a quizzical glance and a tentative thumbs up. He broke into a huge grin, gave a thumbs up back, and raised his glass. He called across the room to me:

"The only good dictator is a dead dictator!"

The bar was quite full, and there was a general noise of assent followed by a lot of animated chatter. The death of Abacha had evidently cheered up the House of Commons. Towards evening I started getting phone calls from old friends at excited parties all over Nigeria, shouting against the noises of enjoyment.

No amount of money can possibly compensate for that many people, across continents, being happy when you die.

Sierra Leone seemed to have reached a stalemate. President Kabbah was back in Freetown, but much of the hinterland was still controlled by the RUF. ECOWAS were now promoting again a negotiated solution, but in a desultory sort of way. I had a little more time to deal with the other twenty countries on my patch. I stayed away from Penfold, as Richard

---

23I had an eyewitness account of his death within a day. I won't give the details for fear I would relish them, but his staff did not exactly rush to help or ease his passing. I quipped that it would take days to nail down the coffin lid, which I still think was rather good.

Dales had instructed me, and matters affecting Penfold were kept away from me. On 2 February Penfold had, as instructed by Ann Grant in her heated meeting with him, written to Ann an account of all his dealings with Sandline. I was not given this until 23 February.

That minute by Peter Penfold of 2 February was interesting for several reasons. It put in writing his claims that he had informed Tim and Linda about the Sandline contract before Christmas, and that he had posted a letter to Ann Grant about it before New Year. But it also downplayed his role in assisting Sandline. Penfold had obviously had time to think about it, and his minute did not say he had advised Kabbah on 19 December to sign the contract, only that he had discussed it with him. That was directly contrary to what he had said on 29 and 30 January to Tim, Linda, Ann and me. This rather fazed the Foreign Affairs Committee inquiry, whose chairman, Donald Anderson MP, was to hit the nail on the head by asking:

"Can we infer from that that the minute of the High Commissioner of 2 February was a sanitised and rather self-serving version of what he had told you earlier in your meeting?"

But the key new point in the Penfold minute was that it plainly stated that the Sandline contract included the supply of arms. That confirmed my suspicions. Sandline were acting, plainly and simply, illegally, and Peter Penfold knew that they were, yet had encouraged President Kabbah to go along with it. There was therefore the additional and major complication for the government that, whatever his attempts to cover up now, Penfold was by his own original account and his numerous contacts, deeply implicated with Sandline in an illegal business transaction.

I thought it over and decided to do nothing. Richard Dales had warned me off interfering with Penfold, whereas the Sandline contract was hypothetical now as it had been overtaken by events. Once more, I allowed myself to hope that I would never hear of Sandline again.

That hope lasted for less than a week. Ann Grant was away in Africa, and I received a letter addressed to her from Lord Avebury, the highly distinguished veteran human rights campaigner. He enclosed a six month old press cutting from the *Toronto Globe and Mail*, dated 1 August 1997. The article outlined the full detail of the Sandline plan, focusing on

Saxena's involvement. It specified that the deal included the supply of arms.

I was rather relieved that, with Lord Avebury's involvement, the Sandline affair was now known outside the confines of the Foreign and Commonwealth Office. I had been stymied by Richard Dales, but the truth looked like it would come out. Now that Lord Avebury was involved, the affair could not be hushed up. I handed the Avebury letter and the press cutting to Linda to fax on to Customs and Excise. As the allegation involved a criminal breach of sanctions, I suggested that Customs and Excise should investigate.

There followed a lull of several weeks, and again I got on with my work. Then, on 29 April 1998 Andrew Hood, Robin Cook's Special Adviser, walked into my office and turned my life to turmoil. Special Advisers are Party officials paid for by the taxpayer. There are far too many of them under New Labour. I have no idea why the taxpayers don't baulk at maintaining a vast apparatus of young party hacks.

On a personal basis, Cook's Special Advisers, Andrew Hood and David Mathieson, were very pleasant and well motivated. Hood was a tall and strong young man with short dark hair and an olive complexion. He had in his hand a letter from S J Berwin & Co, Sandline's solicitors. Berwin complained that Customs and Excise had raided Sandline's offices, which I was glad to hear. But I was astonished to learn that Sandline were claiming that I had given them approval for arms exports. That was, as I told Hood, the very opposite of the truth. I had rather warned them off.

You may think me naive, but I absolutely hadn't seen it coming. It did not occur to me for a moment that Spicer would claim I had given agreement. That is partly because I had not anticipated encountering an outright lie, and partly because I did not see how the lie could possibly work.

It seemed to me that the evidence that I had not given approval was overwhelming. First, I had a witness in Tim Andrews. Second, I had been so much against Penfold giving approval to Sandline that I formally recommended that he be recalled for it. Third, it was I who had called in Customs and Excise to investigate.

I really did not see how anyone could disbelieve me when I said I had not given permission. When, for political purposes, substantial political and media interests chose to accept Spicer's account and very publicly to brand me a liar, it was a terrible blow to me. I don't think anyone had ever seriously doubted my word before.[24] Usually my problems in public life have come from excess of honesty.

Andrew Hood asked me why I hadn't briefed Ministers on calling in Customs and Excise, and I explained about Penfold's involvement and Richard Dales' warning me off. Andrew's concern was to protect his Minister. He thought that Sandline would pretty quickly go public with the "Matrix Churchill defence."[25]

He was right in this. On Sunday 3 May the Sunday Times ran the front page headline "Cook Snared in Arms for Coup Inquiry." Cook was New Labour's most vulnerable target – his messy marriage break-up, with tales of his drinking, and new young wife had given him a full year of media abuse. The hacks were cynical about ethics of any kind. Given Cook's claims of an "Ethical foreign policy", if he could be personally linked to the illegal supply of arms, the press would have a huge ginger ministerial scalp. Cook was perhaps the most popular in the Labour Party of Blair's potential rivals, and was deeply opposed to Blair's neo-con tendencies. It was whispered in Whitehall that Alistair Campbell in No.10 had encouraged the media's targeting of Cook.

So the Sunday Times leaped on the briefing Sandline gave them. When I saw the story, I telephoned Ann Grant. It was a bank holiday weekend, but realising the urgency we both travelled in to the FCO that Sunday to prepare briefing for ministers and lines for the press. The media line was most difficult, as there was a formal legal investigation in progress, and we could not deny Penfold had been involved if asked.

24Except in my love life. I cannot justify it at all, and I would never lie to gain an advantage in any other aspect of my public or private life, but I have always taken the view that all's fair in love, while not taking that view in war. I just don't mentally characterise lies to cover infidelities as lies. I realise that is indefensible – but I also believe it is a very common flaw among otherwise honourable people. Human beings are complicated and it is not possible fully to disentangle the rational from the emotional. Some of the most admired people in history had convoluted love lives that must have involved lies. There must be a book in that somewhere.

25In the Matrix Churchill case a few years earlier, businessmen accused of exporting arms to Iraq in breach of sanctions had indeed been operating with the secret connivance of the FCO and MI6.

We had believed the Sandline contract had become obsolete following the ECOMOG invasion, so we were surprised by the Sunday Times' report that thirty tons of weapons had been landed and seized by the Nigerian army. Our immediate worry was that Tony Lloyd, the junior minister responsible for Africa, was due to be appearing before the House of Commons Foreign Affairs Committee on the morning of Tuesday 5 May, the day after the Bank Holiday. Ann and I prepared a very detailed briefing pack for Tony Lloyd. Being a Sunday we had to do all the typing, printing, photocopying and binding ourselves. It took until nine in the evening before we had finished.

The briefing advised Tony Lloyd to stress that a Customs and Excise investigation was in progress, and that this investigation had been initiated by the FCO. He could also add that no Minister had any foreknowledge or given any approval to arms shipments. If pressed further, he could state that officials in the FCO knew of a contract to train and provide non weapons logistics to the Kamajors, but did not know of any supplies which would breach the UN arms embargo.

It was early evening before I telephoned at her home Tony Lloyd's Private Secretary, who had recently come to the FCO from the Department of Trade and Industry.

"Hi, it's Craig here, Craig Murray. The briefing material on Sierra Leone is all now ready. Where do you want it sent?"

"Thanks awfully, but I don't think we need it now. You can just send it for the box on Tuesday"

Every afternoon the minister's box – those large bright red dispatch boxes you have seen on television – was closed with papers for him to study that evening or the next morning. The Private Secretary filtered what, from the mound of material received into the minister's office, did or did not make it into the box.

"But that will be too late" I expostulated. "He is appearing before the Foreign Affairs Committee first thing Tuesday morning. If the brief is in the box he can't see it before Tuesday evening."

"Don't worry, Sierra Leone isn't on the agenda for the FAC."

"I know that. But with this allegation all over the front of the Sunday Times, do you think that they won't bring it up?"

"Then the Minister will refuse to discuss it."

"What? Are you kidding?"

"Look, he doesn't need it until his box on Tuesday."

"For goodness sake, speak to him. Has he seen the Sunday Times?"

"I have already spoken to him. He doesn't want the briefing."

I went to find Ann, who was taking copies to the offices of Robin Cook and the Permanent Under Secretary (PUS). I told her what had happened, and she was aghast. She called Tony Lloyd's Private Secretary again. This time I heard only Ann's side of the conversation:

"Look, about this briefing.... Are you sure? Can't you speak to him again? Look I know he doesn't like to be disturbed, but this is an emergency. Well, can't I at least meet him at the Commons and put a copy in his hand just before the session, just in case? Well if he's adamant, but I protest."

Ann looked at me and shook her head in bewilderment.

Tony Lloyd is one of the nicest men ever to become a minister. But he was already renowned in the FCO for treating his weekends as sacrosanct. He would leave Friday lunchtime for his Manchester constituency, and not be back until Monday lunchtime or even Tuesday. His Friday box closed at 11am sharp, and if a piece of work missed it, there was no chance of a ministerial approval for at least four days. It is fair to say that this caused a lot of angst in the FCO, with its pressure of work and tight deadlines. Whether he was devoted to his family, or his constituency work, or both, I don't know. But it was a major failing for a Minister.

John Kampfner, in his excellent biography of Robin Cook, rightfully pinpoints Lloyd's "woeful" performance before the Foreign Affairs Committee as the moment that "the floodgates opened" and the Sandline affair moved from an easily managed press story to a huge scandal. The MPs on the FAC had a large number of legitimate questions they wanted answered. Had ministers approved of the illegal supply of arms? Were the FCO employing Sandline? Had officials helped Sandline?

All Tony Lloyd could do was plead he knew nothing at all about it. That was so unbelievable from a Minister, two days after the story had appeared on the front page of the Sunday Times, that everybody decided he must be desperately hiding a major scandal. The Conservative Party and the media all smelled blood.

Kampfner states that on that Tuesday after the bank holiday: "Lloyd took the early train to London from his Manchester constituency that morning. He arrived at the committee room ludicrously under-prepared. Nobody – from his private office, from the news department or from Cook's own office – had thought of briefing him about the latest details of the affair. Consequently Lloyd got a mauling..."[26]

The truth is that of course briefing Lloyd was top of the agenda for Ann Grant and I – there were no two more politically aware civil servants in Whitehall. We had come in on a bank holiday Sunday to do it. It was Tony Lloyd who refused to accept the briefing and thought he could get away with not discussing it at the FAC. It is hard to believe anyone could have such poor political antennae.

Tony Lloyd is now Chairman of the Parliamentary Labour Party.

So now Arms to Africa led every news bulletin, and every journalist I knew (and there were scores of them) was hassling me for the inside story. It was made very clear to us very quickly that we were not to speak to any media, but to refer all inquiries to News Department. But it is not that easy – a number of journalists were both good friends and important professional contacts, and I had to keep my relationship with them sweet. When I was at the centre of the biggest news story for months, to have simply refused to talk would undoubtedly have damaged relationships. So I told a few, quietly and off the record, that it was completely untrue that Ministers had approved the supply of arms, and that no minister had any involvement in Sandline's contract. Beyond that they could dig all they liked. It was certainly completely untrue that I had approved the supply of arms, whatever Sandline might claim.

As it became clear that Sandline's principal defence was that I had given approval of the supply of arms at the 19 January meeting, I found colleagues started to treat me with suspicion. My telephone stopped ringing, and I was no longer copied in on telegrams and minutes. It was as though I had been sent to Coventry and it was very unpleasant. This

_____
26John Kampfner: *Robin Cook*, pp237-8

was formalised shortly afterwards when a new unit headed by Rob Macaire was set up, in effect to do my job. I was not suspended from duty but just left with nothing to do all day.

Tim Andrews and I were called in on the Saturday following Tony Lloyd's disastrous FAC appearance to see Robin Cook, officially to brief him on our meeting with Spicer. In fact, I have no doubt that Cook wanted to look us in the eyes and judge for himself whether we were telling the truth. It was a very hot day. Arriving for a two o'clock meeting, we were told to come back in an hour, so we walked around the lake in St James' Park. People were sunbathing on the grass or sleeping in deckchairs. Small children ran around chasing ducks.

We returned to wait in the capacious suite of Cook's private secretaries' offices. We waited, and we waited. Meantime Cook was holding a series of other meetings, with Andrew Hood, with Sir John Kerr, the Permanent Under Secretary and Head of the Diplomatic Service, and with FCO lawyers. Eventually we were called in after being kept waiting some three hours. That was not unusual for Cook, who never valued anyone else's time, and had once famously kept Princess Diana waiting in similar fashion.

Robin Cook was seated in an armchair as we entered, drinking tea. He was short and wiry as he stood up to greet us, his neat ginger hair slightly receding from a tall forehead, and his tightly clipped beard flecked with grey around the jowls. He walked over to a long mahogany table, polished to a mirror like finish, and sat down, motioning us to sit across the table from him. This was surprisingly formal – every other time I had briefed a minister in their office it had been on the sofas and armchairs – but it did mean that we actually sat much closer.

Over the years I have read a vast amount about Robin Cook, but I have never seen anyone comment on his most striking feature – his eyes. Within that famously gnomic face and speckled complexion, he had the most beautiful eyes of the clearest china blue. They were extraordinarily piercing; you felt they could search right through you. It would be very difficult for anyone to lie when those eyes held your gaze. He did that too – hold your gaze. He held eye contact for much longer than British people normally do, inviting trust. It was somehow very difficult to look away from those eyes before he broke your gaze.

Tim and I outlined to him what had happened at the meeting of 19 January with Spicer. When we told him that we had informed Spicer that it was illegal to send arms to any party in Sierra Leone, he broke into a grin, and when Tim told him that we had actually read Spicer the relevant part of the Security Council Resolution, Cook was ecstatic. He picked up the letter from Spicer's solicitors:

"So you are telling me that the contention that you gave approval for this arms shipment is completely untrue?"

"Completely untrue, Secretary of State. He didn't even mention the arms shipment, just a hypothetical shipment by someone else."

"And you never, on any other occasion, gave approval for a shipment of arms?"

We both replied that we never had. Robin Cook turned to his saturnine Private Secretary, John Grant, who was lurking somewhere behind us.

"Did you get all that, John. You know, I feel confident that I can believe Mr Murray and Mr Andrews. So now our only problem is Mr Penfold and what he's been up to..."

We were ushered out by John Grant, who was notably more friendly than when we came in, now that his boss had passed judgement.

I had similarly been called several times to brief the Permanent Under Secretary, Sir John Kerr. I liked him a lot. He was from the West of Scotland, and had retained a strong accent. He had a guillotine mind and swore like a trooper. He immediately treated me with great confidence – he was rude about Robin Cook, with whom he had just had an argument on an unrelated point, at our very first meeting. Personally I liked Cook, but then Sir John saw vastly more of him than I did. I felt the rough edge of Sir John's tongue once or twice as the media story grew and grew; when I admitted to him that I had given some off the record comments to journalist friends that Ministers definitely did not approve any arms shipments, he called me a stupid cunt, but in a friendly sort of way. (Nigel Sheinwald, then Head of News Department, managed to call me a number of things which were ruder still.) I also go to know quite well Nigel's deputy, John Williams, an experienced tabloid hack Robin Cook had brought in from the Daily Mirror. John was shrewd and supportive. I was to need the support, as almost all the media believed Spicer's version of the 19 January meeting rather than mine. After all, if I was telling the truth and the FCO had not approved the arms shipment, then the story would die. That couldn't happen - it was selling newspapers.

The Customs and Excise investigation was very quick, from our point of view. A team of officers led by a very friendly man called Cedric Andrews descended on us one morning. The registry and filing cabinets were sealed off, with yellow tape festooned across everywhere, like in the films. I was interviewed twice. I was not cautioned, but interviewed as a witness. I was interviewed about my meeting with Spicer, about the various meetings I had with Penfold, and what Penfold had said about his recommending the contract to Kabbah, and how he had backtracked a bit on this when asked to put it in writing. We drew up a written statement on all this, and I signed it. Tim Andrews and Linda St Cook went through a similar procedure, Richard Dales and Ann Grant were also interviewed, though I am not sure if they also swore statements.

Peter Penfold was back in the UK. He was interviewed separately. Both Penfold and Spicer were interviewed under caution, as suspects for having broken the arms embargo.

Then, suddenly, Tony Blair intervened. On 11 May 1998, without consulting the FCO, he gave a statement to journalists. Penfold, Blair declared, was "a hero". A dictatorship had been successfully overthrown and democracy restored. Penfold had "Done a superb job in trying to deal with the consequences of the military coup." All this stuff about Security Council Resolutions and sanctions was "an overblown hoo-ha".

I believe this episode is extremely important. In 1998 the country was still starry-eyed about Blair, but with the benefit of hindsight, this intervention points the way towards the disasters of his later years in office.

It is extraordinarily wrong for a Prime Minister to declare that a man is a hero, when Customs had questioned him two days earlier *under caution* over the very matter the Prime Minister is praising. It shows Blair's belief that his judgement stood above the law of the land, something that was to occur again on a much bigger scale when he halted the Serious Fraud Office investigation into British Aerospace's foreign bribes.[27]

But of course Blair's contempt for UN security council resolutions, and the belief that installing democracy by invasion could trump the trivia of international law, prefigures precisely the disaster of Iraq. As with Iraq, Blair was also conveniently ignoring the fact that Sierra Leone was left a mess, with Kabbah in charge of little more than Freetown.

In the FCO we were astonished by Blair's intervention, and deeply puzzled. Where had it come from? It differed completely from Robin Cook's views. Who was drafting this stuff for Blair to the effect that the UN and the law were unimportant? For most of us, this was the very first indication we had of how deep a hold neo-con thinking and military interests had on the Blair circle. It was also my first encounter with the phenomenon of foreign policy being dictated by Alistair Campbell, the Prime Minister's Press Secretary. The military lobby, of course, was working hard to defend Spicer, one of their own.

A few days later Customs and Excise concluded their investigations. A thick dossier, including documentation from the FCO, from the raid on Sandline's offices, and from elsewhere, was sent to the Crown Prosecution Service. The Customs and Excise team who had interviewed us told me that the recommendation was that both Spicer and Penfold be prosecuted for breach of the embargo.

The dossier was returned to Customs and Excise from the Crown Prosecution Service the very same day it was sent. It was marked, in effect, for no further action. There would be no prosecution. A customs officer told me bitterly that, given the time between the dossier leaving their offices and the time it was returned, allowing time for both deliveries, it could not have been in the CPS more than half an hour. It was a thick dossier. They could not even have read it before turning it down.

I felt sick to my stomach at the decision not to prosecute Spicer and Penfold. So were the customs officers investigating the case; at least two of them called me to commiserate. They had believed they had put to-

---

27If you have been following carefully, you will recall that it was in the interests of this same company, BAE, and its sale of Hawk jets to Indonesia, that Blair first overruled Cook at cabinet.

gether an extremely strong case, and they told me that their submission to the Crown Prosecution Service had said so.

The decision not to prosecute in the Sandline case was the first major instance of the corruption of the legal process that was to be a hallmark of the Blair years. Customs and Excise were stunned by it. There is no doubt whatsoever that Spicer and Penfold had worked together to ship weapons to Sierra Leone in breach of UK law. Security Council 1132 had been given effect in British law by an Order in Council. I had never found in the least credible their assertions that they did not know about it. I had personally told Spicer that it would be illegal to ship arms to Sierra Leone, to any side in the conflict. Penfold's claim never to have seen an absolutely key Security Council Resolution about a country to which he was High Commissioner is truly extraordinary.

But even if they did not know, ignorance of the law is famously no defence in England. Who knows what a jury would have made of this sorry tale of greed, hired killers and blood diamonds. But I have no doubt at all – and more importantly nor did the customs officers investigating the case – that there was enough there for a viable prosecution.

The head of the Crown Prosecution Service when it decided not to prosecute was Barbara Mills. Barbara Mills is a very well-connected woman in New Labour circles. She is married to John Mills, a former Labour councillor in Camden. That makes her sister-in-law to Tessa Jowell, the New Labour cabinet minister with a penchant for taking out repeated mortgages on her home, and then paying them off with cash widely alleged to have come from Silvio Berlusconi, the friend and business colleague of her husband David Mills[28], who according to a BBC documentary by the estimable John Sweeney has created offshore companies for known Camorra and Mafia interests. Tessa Jowell and David Mills are close to Tony and Cherie Blair. Blair is also a great friend of Berlusconi, despite the numerous criminal allegations against Berlusconi and his long history of political alliances with open fascists.

Did any of those New Labour relationships of Barbara Mills, the Director of Public Prosecutions, affect the Crown Prosecution Service's decision not to proceed with the case, and to take that decision in less time than it

28http://www.independent.co.uk/news/people/david-mills-the-networker-467627.html

would have taken them to read the dossier Customs and Excise sent them?[29]

Barbara Mills was to resign as Director of Public Prosecutions later that year, after being personally criticised in his judgement by a High Court judge who ruled against the Crown Prosecution Service for continually failing to prosecute over deaths in police custody.[30] That has not stopped the extremely well connected Dame Barbara from being appointed to a string of highly paid public positions since then.

With Spicer and Penfold exonerated, the heat was now squarely on me. Robin Cook had announced an independent investigation into what lessons could be learned, to be conducted by Sir Thomas Legg and Sir Robin Ibbs. Cook had now lost control, and with No 10 driving, the "Independent" inquiry was a complete stitch-up – the first in a long line of Blair whitewashes that were to include the Butler and Hutton inquiries. The inquiry found that Ministers were, of course, blameless, and so was Spicer, who had been led to believe he had permission to export arms to Sierra Leone, including by me.

This was screamingly untrue. Fortunately the House of Commons Foreign Affairs Committee had decided, against strong pressure from No. 10 and the New Labour Whips' Office, that it would conduct its own inquiry.

I was told that I was too junior to testify, but I insisted. I received very strong support in this from Anthony Laden, the head of my trade union, the Diplomatic Service Association. Robin Cook and Sir John Kerr supported me, while No. 10 resisted. The committee itself, of course, very much wanted to interview me. In the end, it was agreed as a compromise that I could accompany Ann Grant when she gave evidence. I was not permitted to include any of the evidence that I had given to Sir Thomas Legg (who had largely ignored or discounted my evidence and Tim Andrews' evidence, preferring Spicer's). I was however allowed to submit a statement of where I disagreed with the Legg report, and under question-

---

29Ironically, Barbara Mills' current position is as Adjudicator of Customs and Revenue.

30*http://news.bbc.co.uk/1/hi/uk/417079.stm*

ing tell more or less the whole story. [31] In my memorandum to the FAC I wrote of the Legg report:

"I found some of the conclusions ... unjust, inexplicable in terms of the evidence given, and deeply offensive and depressing."

It was good to be able finally to give my version in public, but I did not get to do this until 10 November 1998, by which time the media circus had moved on. The story had had astonishing "legs", as the media call it – it made big front page headlines from May right through to early November, when Spicer and Penfold gave their evidence to the FAC. But I didn't have their glamour, being viewed as just a pen-pusher, and stood already condemned following the Legg report. While my memorandum to the FAC was only two pages long, it was obvious when I came before the committee that only one member had bothered to read it.

Still, Ann and I were grilled by the committee for over five hours in total, and I think that most of the truth got out. I was helped by the fact that Tim Spicer had not won many friends on the committee with his attitude.

I have said that when I met Spicer I found him very evasive about who owned Sandline, and how the Sierra Leone deal was financed. Sandline had been involved in a failed operation in Papua New Guinea. In line with all such mercenary operations, the aim was to secure a physical resource for a Western company – in this case a copper mine for Rio Tinto Zinc. Spicer had been arrested in Papua New Guinea, and had given evidence to a subsequent enquiry in Papua New Guinea that Tony Buckingham was the Chairman of Sandline. The FAC reminded him of this, and Spicer now attempted to retract:

Mr Spicer: **Perhaps I can cover that point by saying at the time I gave that evidence I was not really completely conversant with the structure. It was my view that if you like Mr Buckingham was the person I would turn to in the event of wanting some advice and support, and I may have referred to him as the Chairman but he is not the Chairman of Sandline.**

Donald Anderson MP (Chairman): **Who is?**

---

31 *http://www.publications.parliament.uk/pa/cm199798/cmselect/cmfaff/1057/8111009.ht m*

Andrew Mackinlay MP: Who is? Come on, tease us.

Mr Spicer I have already agreed to provide you, or at least ask those investors who own Sandline to provide you, with a note of the corporate structure.

Andrew Mackinlay MP: But you told the Papua New Guinea inquiry who it was. You now say it is erroneous. Can you tell us, give us all the other stuff but satisfy us this morning: who is the Chairman of Sandline?

Mr Spicer It is run on a day to day basis by me.

Sir Peter Emery MP: But you must know who your Chairman is.

Andrew Mackinlay MP: Come on.

Diane Abbott MP: You must know who the Chairman of your company is.

Mr Spicer As I have already said, it does not have a standard corporate structure. I run it on a day to day basis. It is owned by a group of investors who are formed into this group Adson Holdings. There is no Chairman as such.

Diane Abbott MP: I have to tell you that your description of Sandline as some kind of workers' collective does not really cut any ice at all with this Committee, nor are we persuaded that at one time you knew who the Chairman of your company was but now you do not. I have to say, Mr Spicer, that it does leave the Committee speculating as to why it is so important to you to draw a veil over the ownership of Sandline.

Mr Spicer: I am not attempting to draw a veil. I have said that I would ask whether the owners could supply the details of the corporate structure to the Committee. I cannot do any more than that.

Donald Anderson MP: When was Sandline incorporated?

Mr Spicer: Some time in the middle of 1996.

Donald Anderson MP: And you have been employed since?

Mr Spicer: Yes.

Donald Anderson MP: Are you saying that you have not taken the trouble to find out the Chairman and the other officials?

Mr Spicer: There is only one if you like senior official in Sandline and that is me. I have always made that very clear. The investors do not wish to have their identities revealed.

Diane Abbott MP: **I bet they do not.**[32]

When I eventually gave my evidence to the House of Commons Foreign Affairs Committee I was given firm instructions on what I was and was not allowed to say. It was made very plain to me by Sir John Kerr that I was giving evidence on behalf of the Secretary of State, not on behalf of myself. I was therefore to stick to the FCO line. I was also not to be drawn into speculation or comment. In particular I was not to mention that Peter Penfold had been in Canada between his two London meetings with Spicer. And I was not to call Spicer a liar.

The latter was especially difficult. Tim Andrews and I on the one hand, and Spicer on the other, were giving diametrically opposite accounts of our meeting. Tim Spicer claimed he had told us he was shipping weapons to Sierra Leone, and that we gave approval. Tim Andrews and I said that he had made no mention of shipping weapons himself but rather stressed that he was sending non-lethal equipment, and we had explained to him it would be illegal for anybody to send weapons to Sierra Leone.

Now plainly, both those accounts cannot be true, and such fundamentally different accounts of the key point of the meeting could not be accidental. Somebody has to be lying. But instructed not to say so, I had to resort to verbal contortion before the Foreign Affairs Committee:

Dr Norman Godman MP: **Now, you have also said that Mr Spicer has not been telling the truth. We, in the west of Scotland, might call him a bit of a chancer, but what you are suggesting here is that he is a liar.**

Mr Murray **I do not want to get into—**

Dr Norman Godman MP: **Well, might I infer from this that he is a liar?**

Mr Murray **You can certainly infer that he is not telling the truth.**

Dr Norman Godman MP: **Well, I am not going to engage in a debate on semantics with you, but, as I said, there is a profound contradiction there...**[33]

32*http://www.publications.parliament.uk/pa/cm199798/cmselect/cmfaff/1057/8110310.htm*

33*http://www.publications.parliament.uk/pa/cm199798/cmselect/cmfaff/1057/8111014.htm*

In the end, the committee split perhaps predictably on party lines with the Conservatives choosing to believe Spicer, the Labour and Liberals choosing to believe Tim Andrews and I. So the official report failed to exonerate me.

By that stage I was getting used to it. I seldom think about it nowadays; but when I do, as now, my burning anger and resentment returns to me.

Worse of all, the Blairites were already promoting the idea that the key lesson to be learnt was the need to regulate – by which they meant make legal – mercenaries, or private military companies, as we were told we were now to call them. Astonishingly, the British government had immediately adopted the terminology "Private Military Companies". Unlike the term "Mercenary" which occurs in the Hague and Geneva conventions and has legal force of long-standing, "Private Military Company" was a new term invented by the PR company Pearson working for ... Sandline! It had no history or legal force, but already in 1998 the British Government adopted Sandline's own bought-in euphemism.

The British army employed mercenary regiments of Gurkhas, the argument went, and Spicer's operations were no different. Provided the employer was a legitimate government – any government – mercenary activities operated from the United Kingdom should be legal. There was much more of this argument – in the post Cold War world mercenaries could bring valuable flexibility and reduce costs. There was even support from within DFID, where the fashionable doctrine of the moment, another Blairite concept, was that security was a necessary precondition for development – a handy excuse for invading pretty well any poor country you feel like. A white paper was written proposing the legalisation of mercenaries. They were to be employed in Iraq on a scale unprecedented in history.

Now, of course, Tim Spicer is an extremely rich man. Hundreds of thousands of people have died in Iraq, including thousands of British and American soldiers, but some people have made huge amounts of money from the war. These include of course arms manufacturers (Tony Blair's old chums British Aerospace actually wrote in their 2006 annual report that profits were up "in the Land and Munitions division because of heavier than expected ground fighting in Iraq and Afghanistan"). Other suppliers to the military, and engineering and logistics companies like Bechtel and Halliburton have also made a killing – an appropriate phrase. Big oil companies have profited from the huge leap in oil prices the war has caused, and are increasingly taking over Iraqi oil resources. The Iraq war is, of course, the most spectacular example recently of Western invasion of a developing state to secure mineral resources – and as always, the mercenaries are there.

Tim Spicer has made a fortune out of the Iraq War. There are at least 40,000 western mercenaries operating in Iraq, protecting Western personnel and of course oil and other mineral installations. Tim Spicer now runs Aegis, the latest incarnation of the Executive Outcomes and Sandline crew. This is all on a much bigger scale than Sierra Leone – Aegis has many contracts in Iraq, but one of their Pentagon contracts alone is worth US $293 million.

Tim Spicer, Tony Blair's favourite mercenary, whose company is now called Aegis Services, now has more hired killers working for him in Iraq than there remain troops of the British Army there. Aegis have gained something of a reputation for being aggressive and trigger happy in shooting-up local civilians, just as Executive Outcomes did in Africa. The "Aegis trophy video" that was posted on their website by one of their employees, shows the shooting up of civilian cars in Iraq by Aegis. I really do recommend you to look at this. You can find it at:

http://video.google.com/videoplay?docid=499399687545634893

If that link is down, "Aegis trophy video" is a pretty easy internet search. For me, the really scary thing about this video is that it was the subject of a formal United States Army enquiry, which says that the incidents shown were "Within standard operating procedures", as laid down by the US army, which in effect give Aegis the right to shoot up any car approaching them, in case it is a car bomb. Usually, of course, it turns out to have been someone taking the kids to school. Aegis themselves put out a statement that "There is no evidence of any civilian casualties as a result of the incidents." [34]

Please do look at the video.

34*http://www.aegisworld.com/article.aspx?artID=5*

Jack Straw, whose 1997 election expenses were 50% met by a Director of British Aerospace, was as ever in the forefront of those banging the drum for military interests. As British Foreign Secretary he was to declare:

"States and international organisations are turning to the private sector as a cost-effective way of procuring services which would once have been the exclusive preserve of the military...The demand for private military services is likely to increase...The cost of employing private military companies for certain functions in UN operations could be much lower than that of national armed forces".

Interestingly in the light of the Aegis trophy video, Tim Spicer has long been an advocate of shooting civilians in case they have bombs. In West Belfast in 1992, commanding a battalion of the Scots Guards, he had decided upon an aggressive approach, in his own words "to carry the war to the enemy"[35].

Operating under Spicer's command, soldiers shot and killed an 18 year old Irish Catholic, Peter McBride. He was shot in the back when he ran away when challenged - a response that was probably prompted by the aggression Spicer's men had shown in Belfast "carrying the war to the enemy". McBride was found to be unarmed; he was not on any wanted list and not believed to be a member of the IRA. He was just a young father who panicked when confronted by aggressive soldiers.

Almost uniquely, the case was so blatant that two soldiers, James Fisher and Mark Wright, were actually tried and convicted of McBride's murder. Spicer was outraged. He writes in *An Unorthodox Soldier* "They believed, and the evidence suggests they had good reason to believe, that they were about to come under attack." At least the man is consistent: that is precisely the excuse for the shooting up of Iraqi citizens in the Aegis trophy video. In Belfast, a civilian court did not agree that an unarmed young man running away could reasonably be construed as about to attack.

In Iraq, of course, Aegis do not have to answer to civilian courts.

In Ghana, our scholarly Deputy High Commissioner, Iain Orr, had suffered a heart attack and was not going to be able to return to his post. We needed to find a replacement quickly, and by now I really was feeling

---

35 Tim Spicer, *An Unorthodox Soldier*, p.111

fed up in London. So I suggested myself. Ann Grant was taking over as Director of Africa Command from Richard Dales, and she was keen. Sir John Kerr was helpful. I left AD(E), and was due in Ghana in January 1999.

First the FCO asked me to help out for a few weeks on the Administration Restructuring Team, which was conducting a review of the FCO's support services. The acronym was ARRT. I can't remember what the second R stood for, but it was designed to make it sound as if we were not solely a cost-cutting exercise, which of course we actually were.

The head of the team was Peter Collecott, undoubtedly the most nakedly ambitious man I have ever met. We were told to indulge in "Blue skies thinking". On the first day in our stark white attic room, I produced an organogram of all the support departments of the FCO, on a long whiteboard, then amended it to my proposed new structure, with an estimate of jobs that could be shed. When the final report was eventually produced three months later, it conformed almost 100% to my starting organogram.

There is indeed a great deal of waste in the FCO, but most of it is found in the top of the office in London. Between the Heads of Department and the Permanent Under Secretary there are two levels of Director, and one of those levels needs to be abolished, just as was done in the Treasury. However I was being tasked with shedding jobs among clerks and translators.

There were indeed some remarkable quaint survivals from a more comfortable age – the FCO had an in-house team of upholsterers, for example, based in Milton Keynes. I can understand intellectually that activities which are that far from the core activity are best outsourced. But there was something soul-destroying about searching out the ancient organisation's surviving Gothic nooks and crannies, only to eliminate them. I was also constantly on the receiving end of lectures from Peter Collecott for being too honest, or "open" as he called it. I went visiting parts of the organisation we were looking to "Restructure", and explained what we were doing. We were looking to shed some 400 jobs. The FCO however was hopeful we could achieve this without anyone noticing.

Of course, our activity had not in gone unnoticed anyway. A friend of mine in the trades union Unison told me that very early one morning they had sent a small group to snoop around our attic. They had studied my organogram on the whiteboard, which they recognised as the master plan. But unfortunately they had reported back that it was written in code. In fact, it was in plain English – it was simply that they could not decipher my very bad handwriting!

While I was in AD(E), every second Friday lunchtime we had a get-to-gether between the two deputy heads of Africa Department (Equatorial) and the single deputy in Africa Department (Southern). We would discuss pan-African issues and policy coordination, and work out resource allocations. In time honoured FCO fashion, these meetings were held in the basement of the Red Lion pub on Whitehall, and we would each buy a round. I never otherwise drank during the day – in fact throughout these months I hardly ever drank at all, I was too busy.

As was also the tradition, I was invited to the first get-together after I had left AD(E). As no successor had been appointed yet, there were still three of us and we drank three pints each. So it is fair to say I was not entirely sober. But neither was I drunk, and I returned to my desk and was typing up a report on the integration of language services. Another team member, Ian Whitehead, was with me. Suddenly Peter Collecott came in, and strode up to my desk.

"I hear you've been in the pub at lunchtime!"

It was an accusation.

I looked up, surprised.

"Yes" I replied mildly.

Collecott looked at me intently, as though he expected me at any moment to wrap my trousers around my head and sing "Lili Marlene."

"Are you capable of work?"

"I seem to be doing some."

"Come to my office."

Three of our four man team sat in one room, while Collecott had his own room next door.

"I don't approve of drinking at lunchtime."

"Oh."

"Do you think you should go home?"

"No."

"Don't do it again."

Ian gave me a sympathetic smile as I returned to my desk. I liked Ian a lot; he was a greatly experienced diplomat, who was currently recovering from a heart attack. If he had a higher opinion of Peter Collecott than I did, he hid it well.

"Jumped-up prick" I said. Ian grinned.

A short while later, I was off to Accra.

5

Deputy High Commissioner

Accra is an astonishing city. With no real centre and very few high rise buildings, it essentially consists of two hundred square miles of middle class suburban housing. There are shanty areas like Nima and shabby areas like Nungua, there are markets and shopping centres, but the overwhelming impression is of tens of thousands of really rather nice villas and bungalows, linked by many hundreds of miles of neat well tarmacked streets.

It is absolutely not what people expect of Africa, and it underlines the fact that Ghana, more than any other African country, retained its higher educational facilities, has a reasonably balanced economy, and an urban social stratification recognisable to Western eyes. It has prosperous skilled working, lower middle and upper middle classes. There are less extremes of wealth in Ghana than anywhere else in Africa. There is not one billionaire, and nobody starves.

Of course, there still is poverty, and in particular people still die of malaria for want of the knowledge and finance for a three dollar cure. Social and economic circumstances are such that it ought to be possible to eliminate this evil in Ghana, but it has not come yet.

But the overwhelming first impression that greets a visitor to Accra is of quiet prosperity, order and spaciousness. There is also a tremendous bustle of economic activity. Everyone is hustling, working, striving to make a living and get the next step up the economic ladder. Many people have two or three jobs. And every inch of roadside space supports somebody trading. They may start with a plank on two concrete blocks, with a few sweets, cigarettes and drink packs on it. They progress up to a table and stand, with the addition of biscuits, mobile phone chargers and cuff links. The next step up is a little wooden tin roofed shack, then part of a converted cargo container, finally progressing to the fully blown shop. It is a seamless progression, and the total value of the goods available in the street trade of Accra must amount to many tens of millions of dollars. I chose a twenty yard strip of road at random and walked along it counting the different items on sale, giving up somewhere over three hundred. There were CDs and silk ties, lighters and exercise bicycles, guitars and bobble hats, televisions and peanut butter, condoms and local spirits. A self-employed Ghanaian is a tremendous bundle of entrepreneurial energy. It is however extremely difficult to kindle that energy when they work for someone else.

We had family history in Ghana. My father, Bob Murray, with his youngest brother Tommy, had lived and worked in Kumasi for five years in the mid-1960s. They had done well there, owning a timber yard business producing parquet flooring, which was then very fashionable in the UK. They had also been involved in electricity distribution from the great Akosombo hydro-electric scheme which had created Lake Volta. About three hundred miles long and covering ten per cent of Ghana, it is the World's second largest man-made lake.

Before departing for Accra, I went to visit my mother and father at their small home in Incheswood, between Culloden and Inverness. My father was quietly pleased that I was going to Ghana in as exalted a role as British Deputy High Commissioner – though like many Scots, he seemed to object in principle to praising his children. I recall in 1982 when I phoned from Dundee breathlessly to tell him that I had just learnt I had been awarded a first class honours degree. He had replied: "Aye, well some folk have PhDs".

When I told him I had been accepted into the diplomatic service, he told me to watch out for all the poofs. I knew that a well of deep affection underlay those words – but the well remained concealed.

Fiona, the children and I now spent a couple of days walking on the moors with him. Jamie was ten and Emily four. My mother was carefree and laid-back as ever. It was a really happy couple of days, despite the very cramped sleeping arrangements. We sat in a pub one evening, the children overjoyed to watch the dolphins gambolling in the Moray Firth.

(Moray is precisely the same word as Murray, and pronounced exactly the same, just a spelling variation). My father turned to me with a serious look on his face:

"Craig, you'll be spending time in Kumasi. The Ashanti are a very attractive people. If you see any good–looking girl, age about thirty, light-skinned, whatever you do, don't touch her – she could be your sister!"

And his laugh roared out over the Firth.

My father had lost everything in Ghana when his companies were nationalised after a coup – I believe the coup by General Acheampong, although I never asked him exact details for reasons I shall explain later. My father had made good friends with the regional minister in Kumasi. In the coup a howling mob had come to drag the minister out to goodness knows what fate. My father had smuggled out the minister's teenage daughter, hidden under a tartan car rug in the back of his Land Rover. He had driven right through the riot, leaning his head out of the driver's window, waving his passport and shouting "British tourist! British Tourist!"

At least that was the story as he told it. I might not have given it too much credence had I not met the lady herself when she visited my father in the mid-80s.

This was a very sad parting, because my father had been diagnosed with lung cancer. A number of operations had failed to clear it and, although he seemed ruddy and hearty, we all knew he hadn't got long to go. He was still more full of life than ten ordinary people. He had a charisma that could hold a room and even now, poor and ill, he was automatically treated as very important everywhere he went. It was just something about his presence. But It was all fast burning out.

As we arrived in Accra on British Airways, we were first out the plane door as it opened and I was pleasantly surprised. In Lagos, you are greeted by a blast of warm, sickly sweetness. The humidity there is like being wrapped completely in hot wet blankets, and the smell of sewage and decay is everywhere. In Accra, while there is a welcoming warmth, the humidity is gentle on the skin and there is a dull, slightly smoky smell that is not unpleasant. There was nobody from the High Commission air-side to meet us and no VIP lounge, but the formalities were pleasantly conducted. Ghanaians queue meticulously, while officials are beaming and helpful. A High Commission Landrover was waiting to take us to our new home, Devonshire House.

Built for the Duke of Devonshire, a former colonial governor, Devonshire house has grounds as imposing as the title, and looks fairly large, but that is illusory; the long frontage obscures the fact it is only one room deep. Built to Colonial Office specifications in the frugal post-war period, if you strip away its verandahs it resembles nothing so much as a three bedroomed council house. The reception rooms had been extended several times, leaving a distinctly odd assortment of pillars and beams breaking up the space. But it is a lovely family home, it has a guest wing, and the gardens really are on a scale that befits a Duke. Accra never wobbles more than a very few degrees either side of 30 degrees Centigrade, all year round, day or night. It has the same rainfall as London only concentrated into a couple of brief rainy seasons. So the entertaining could almost all be outdoors. We fell in love with the varnished mahogany, ceiling fans and mosquito nets at first sight (while immediately putting in a requisition to extend the air conditioning).

We were greeted by a rather macabre sight. The car had pulled up short of the house's portico, because squarely in the middle of the parking space sat a large, strangely marked rock. On close inspection, it was difficult to be certain if it was rock or wood. Apart from some deep incisions its surface was much smoothed, and I surmised had been in the sea. It was very heavy – I bent to lift it out of the way, and I could scarcely budge it. I could not work out what it was – my best guess would be a very large calcified or even fossilised bunch of palm fruits.

It transpired that it had been the cause of Iain Orr's heart attack. My predecessor had found it on the beach, and had been fascinated by it. He had decided to take it home to investigate what it was. Lifting it from the back of his Landrover, he had suffered a heart attack. The object lay where it fell, because the staff were scared to move it, thinking it jinxed. This must have been a strongly held superstition as it was bang in the way of the front door, and the removals firm had packed and taken away Iain's possessions since. Fiona, Jamie and I rolled it away round the side;

that seemed to symbolise the new spirit of our family taking over the house.

My boss was the High Commissioner, Ian Mackley. Ian was a bull of a man, both in appearance and attitude. Overbearing and irascible, he laboured under a continual disappointment that his career had not ended in a more distinguished posting than Accra. He did not try to hide this – indeed he continually referred to it. He had previously been Deputy High Commissioner in Australia, and he had hoped one day to be High Commissioner there. Instead he had been put in charge of Training Department – about which he was particularly resentful – and then sent to Accra.

He was a complex man who at times could exhibit an attractive degree of self-knowledge. He would repeatedly joke about becoming "Twitter and bisted". But then he would just go back to being bitter and twisted again. His wife Sarah was a large, jolly hockey sticks sort of woman. Her social status was rather too important to her. She was considerably younger than Ian. She had been the secretary he divorced his wife for.

Ian adopted an anti-intellectual persona, which was peculiar as he was in fact very bright, well read and well travelled. But he preferred the company of what the English call rugger buggers and the Americans call jocks. He didn't so much wear his learning lightly, as attempt completely to conceal it. He attributed the failure of his career to reach the heights he felt he deserved, to discrimination against him by the upper class types who dominated the senior ranks of the FCO. He may well have been right in this. My problem was that he identified me with those upper class types, in fact quite wrongly.

It did not help matters at all that, pretty well as soon as I arrived in Accra, I was sent away to Lome, the capital of Togo. I was to be the UK representative at the Sierra Leone peace talks between the RUF rebels (who still controlled much of the hinterland) and the government of President Kabbah. Now our High Commission also covered Togo, so my doing this did not remove me from Ian's territory. But he was not in my line of command on these peace talks, and he resented it. When the instructions first came from London, he called me in to his office. When he was angry his broad face went very red, and now it was scarlet. He grumpily said that he would give his assent, but that as he was not involved, he could give me no credit for this work in my annual appraisal. On the other hand, if my work in Accra suffered because I was away in Togo, that *would* be reflected in my appraisal. He wanted that clearly understood.

I said OK, and in fact I was delighted to be involved in the peace talks, because I felt Sierra Leone was unfinished business. I especially wanted to resolve the problem without resort to force, by Spicer and his mercenaries or by the British Army. It had been the biggest problem in my career, and I had walked away from it unresolved. Now I had the chance to be back in the thick of it.

A situation where you are bringing those who have committed acts of terror into government always leaves a queasy feeling and poses a knotty moral dilemma.[36] But ultimately the only way to resolve violent conflict is to reconcile interests. It is a story as old as war. The atrocities in Sierra Leone were so stark and horrible as to sharpen the relief of the moral dilemma. Sitting across a table, smiling and talking with a man who has, personally, with those hands now clutching his pen and his whisky glass, lopped the limbs off children and other helpless human victims with a matchet, is a hard thing to do. But butchering your live victims' limbs with your own hands, is only more horrific in its immediacy than planting a car bomb, or bombing an Iraqi town from the air in your invulnerable jet. The results are exactly the same. If there is a moral difference of real importance, it is lost on those civilians ripped apart.

So on 28 April 1999 I made the three hour drive from Accra to Lome for the start of the peace negotiations. I was looking forward to seeing Lome again, for the first time in ten years. In the late 1980's it had been a haven of order and luxury. The Sarakawa hotel on the beach had been simply superb, with service and cuisine that would have rated five stars anywhere. Lome had teemed with expats, and the city, which was tidy, bustling and prosperous, exuded a very French glamour and sophistication that was poles apart from anything Lagos or Accra had to offer. That was, of course, the time that great delegations from the then European Eco-

---

36There have been numerous academic articles published on the Sierra Leone peace talks and Lome peace accords, most of which bear little relation to what really happened. Much better are the many vibrant Sierra Leonean internet portals. See for example http:// *www.sierra-leone.org/slnews0499.html*

nomic Community (EEC) met there to negotiate the Lome trade agreements with their former colonies. That in itself vouches for the degree of luxury in 1980s Togo – senior Eurocrats are not inclined to slum it.

I left Accra's neatness and sped East along the cost road towards Togo. I was trying to teach the High Commission drivers to drive the way I liked. Ghanaians have a mortal fear of potholes. If they are speeding along the road and one appears, no matter how big or small, they will stand on their brakes as hard as they can, slowing the car radically until their front wheel, locked, thumps down into the pothole, possibly after skidding and slewing all around the road in a desperate attempt to avoid it. If they have plenty of notice that the pothole is coming, they will do this in a more controlled way, changing down to five miles an hour and then either driving carefully around, or bumping down through, the pothole. As there might be scores of potholes per mile, this causes severe traffic delay.

Based on my experience all round Nigeria, I was trying to teach the High Commission drivers that, with very few exceptions, if you kept the wheels running and your speed up, you could skim across the potholes almost without noticing them. Only unusually large and fierce ones might cause a bump and even deflection, but again this was much easier to control if you didn't brake harshly.

The drivers found this counter-intuitive. The coast road ran straight and true for a hundred and fifty miles through low salty scrublands to Aflao and the Togolese border. The surface was basically good, running straight as a Roman road as it rose and fell over a series of undulations. Potholes tended to be concentrated at the bottom of each dip, where the water had gathered. They would show up as fierce red gleams in the dark grey asphalt, as we sped down the road towards them. The driver Joe had started to get the hang of my new technique, but now and then he would suddenly panic just before reaching a pothole. He would either slam on the brakes or veer alarmingly, sometimes right off the road. Then he would turn round in his seat and beam at me:

"Sorry sir! I have to get used!"

Speeding through the town of Viume, I was struck by the extraordinary vividness of the banks of pots displayed at the side of the road. It is common in villages for their local production to be offered for sale in this way, and the road is often lined with metalwork, furniture, food, wood carvings or other offerings from that particular locality. But these pots were so striking I asked Joe to stop, and reverse back to them.

The pots were essentially all vases or plant pots, in a variety of sizes and shapes of great elegance and simplicity. But they were finished in the most extraordinarily vivid colours, including many different shades of shimmering metallic finish, giving an effect much like oil on water. Some had striking patterns, ridged or incised. I was so struck that not only did I immediately buy four, but I asked to see the potter.

I was taken to a hut where I met an inarticulate young man wearing only torn khaki shorts. His dark torso was extraordinarily well defined and gleamed with sweat in the sunlight. Unfortunately he didn't seem to speak much English, and did not seem to understand when I asked to see the kiln.

I was then taken off to the low built hut of the local chief. It was made of concrete building blocks and consisted of two rooms, with dirty louvre windows and mesh doors. But the chief, who appeared very old, was extremely welcoming and professed himself delighted to have a British visitor.

He told me that there had been an important pottery at Viume, "for centuries", because of the excellent clays found by the banks of the Volta. But in 1943 the famous British potter Michael Cardew had been sent there to improve the quality of production, and to teach local potters. He had lived in Viume for six years. His pottery had been kept running by his pupils, and the tradition still survived. The chief noted sadly that Cardew had wanted to improve domestic African pottery production, and had worked on everyday items like cooking pots and drinking vessels. But now all that was produced in his style were plant pots for the tourist and expatriate markets. The chief added casually that "it was Clem Atlee's idea that Michael should come." Ghana regularly throws up these surreal moments when, seated in the most African of surroundings, the conversation becomes not just typically English, but the typical English of a 1950s Sussex drawing room.

I thanked the chief, and received another pot in return for my gift to him of a bottle of Johnnie Walker. It was a remarkable tribute to the colonial authorities' improving spirit that, slap in the middle of the Second World War, they were appointing an official Pottery Officer to Viume. Still more extraordinary that it should be someone who even then was recognised as a major ceramic artist. I suspect the vast majority of people who pull up their four wheel drives to buy a vase at Viume have no idea of the existence of Cardew. But his remarkable influence still lives on.[37]

At Sogakope we crossed the bridge over the mighty Volta. There is something wild in the spirit of a great African river, something I feel when I look at the Niger or Volta or Congo, that I just don't feel when I look at the Danube or Missouri or even the Syr Darya. African rivers have a mischief to them – it is nothing measurable, the Volta here being regulated by a great dam. There is a great thrill in crossing any African river, even on a bridge.

Amid the crowds and the clamour as we emerged on the Togolese side of the border, there was one thing in Togo that clearly had not changed in the past ten years: the scooters. We were immediately buzzed by myriad scooters, trailing us like seagulls around a fishing boat, diving across the front of us as though determined to go under our wheels. You could live in Accra from one month to the next without ever seeing a scooter, but in Togo they were everywhere, their T-shirted riders calling out to passers-by as they dodged around the city, short-skirted girls riding pillion, adjusting their hair as they cling on with their knees, and everybody smoking.

Otherwise I was to be much disappointed by Togo. Lome had regressed rapidly to an advanced state of decay in the ten years I had been away. The Togolese customs post at Aflao, which had seemed much more modern than its homely, wooden Ghanaian counterpart, appeared to have lost its shape under layers of dust and grime. Once into Lome, which starts immediately at the border, it seemed that not a lick of paint

37There is a video of Cardew throwing a pot at http://www.youtube.com/watch?v=kS7JEKMgZFQ

or a pane of glass had been added or renewed in the entire city. Now nature seemed to be bent on return. There was much more greenery than there had been ten years ago, mostly bursting out in places it wasn't wanted. Street lighting seemed a thing of the past. The wonderful Sarakawa hotel, where I remembered champagne breakfasts, dancers imported from the Moulin Rouge and sumptuous banquets on the sands, was now dark and deserted, many of its windows smashed.[38]

Togoland was initially a German colony. In 1914, in arguably the first German setback of the First World War, the British authorities of the Gold Coast and the French of Dahomey (modern Benin) acted with surprising speed to take Togoland. Flags from the German Governor's residence are displayed at the Suffolk Regiment's museum in Bury St Edmunds and the Ghanaian Military Museum in Kumasi. Eventually Britain incorporated the Western part of Togoland into the Gold Coast, now Ghana, and France kept the Eastern part separate as Togo. This splitting down the middle explains Togo's long thin shape.

Of course the division took no notice of existing cultural, ethnic or linguistic divisions. The Ewe people, for example, spread along the Southern portion of Eastern Ghana, Togo, Benin and Western Nigeria, their importance obscured by their division. In 1914 the boundaries were realloc-ated and the locals just had to get on with forgetting German and learning French or English, which they appear to have done with great alacrity. It always seems to me a great wonder – and not in a good way - that, one side of a completely artificial line, an African speaks French, smokes Gitanes and rides a scooter, while just across the line another man, quite probably his cousin, speaks English and is obsessed with getting the Manchester United score.

German presence has lingered more in Togo than in Eastern Ghana. Germany has a much larger Embassy than you would expect in a country of just six million people. There remains a small amount of striking German colonial architecture in the capital, and there are still a couple of ex-cellent German restaurants. But it is in some of the hunting lodges dotted

---

38It has since been refurbished and reopened as part of the Meridien chain, but is a shadow of its former self.

in the hills North of the capital that you can still close your eyes and imagine that you hear the German chatter as you breathe in the wood smoke.

Slashing colonial borders through tribal areas has had one delicious side-effect. Much of Ghana was proselytised by Scots Presbyterian missionaries. Many churches have great St Andrews crosses painted across their gable walls. These Scots protestants brought with them many of the cultural rites they mixed with their religion, such as Scottish rite freemasonry, which is very strong among Ghana's ruling classes, and even Orange lodges. There are over thirty Orange lodges in Ghana. They dress up in full regalia of orange sash, bowler hat and furled umbrella, and parade about to pipe and drum. The umbrella is a traditional symbol of chieftaincy and power in Ghana, which might be why they caught on so readily.

Every year a small delegation of Ghanaian Orangemen visits Belfast for the Orange parade of 12 July. What some of the more bigoted Ulstermen make of these strange comrades is an interesting question. I have little doubt what they would make of the Togolese Orangemen.

Orange Lodges being popular among the Ewe, and involving enjoyable dressing up and parading about, some of the neighbouring Ewe chiefs in Togo thought that they would like to have their own Orange lodges too. That is why I was to be astonished to see, on the streets of Atakpame in Togo's Plateau region, a full blown orange parade with perhaps eighty French speaking Orangemen strutting to beat of drum – walking behind choirboys in white surplices carrying a statue of the Virgin Mary! I asked the local schoolteacher if the Orangemen were protestants, and he replied that one or two might be atheists (by which I think he meant protestants) but of course, most were Catholics; this was Togo.

Africa has many marvels, but the Catholic Orangemen of Togo remain one of the funniest and most heart-warming sights I can recall. Africa still has a great deal to teach us.

On my first night at the peace talks, those of us who had already arrived convened for an introductory meeting. Apart from me there were three representatives of the Libyan security services, two of Charles Taylor's henchmen, three senior aides to President Eyadema of Togo and eight of the RUF delegation. Looking around the room at these hard eyed men, a sudden chill struck me.

I realised I was almost certainly the only person in that room who had never killed anybody.

6
Peacemaker

There is nothing that concentrates the mind more than being locked up in an African hotel with a bunch of assorted killers. I asked one of the RUF delegation, Colonel Isaac[39], how many people the RUF delegation had killed personally. He gave it some serious thought:

"At least a thousand between us", he said.

I don't think he was being boastful.

"But Isaac," I said cautiously, "you can't possibly have killed that many in the heat of battle. You'd all have been killed yourself."

"Oh, no" he replied, "most of them were prisoners. They were...prisoners." A long pause and he looked up at me. "That is wrong, isn't it?"

"Yes Isaac, that was very, very wrong."

The next day I paid my first call on President Gnassingbe Eyadema, introducing myself as the British representative for the talks. Eyadema was not just a brutal dictator, he was personally an extremely hard man. He had joined the French army, and fought in the brutal conflicts of Algeria and Vietnam, obtaining the rank of Sergeant. Returning to Togo, he became a member of the Presidential bodyguard, and in 1963 he personally murdered President Sylvanus Olympio as part of a coup that installed Nicolas Grunitzky as President. In 1967 Eyadema led a further coup against Grunitzky and installed himself as President. After 32 years he was still in power.

He had kept himself there by ruthlessness. He had murdered and tortured thousands of opposition figures. Only the year before in 1998 he had won re-election against opposition leader Gilchrist Olympio – the son of the President he had murdered. The ballot – which Eyadema "won"

39Name changed

52% to 48% - was heavily rigged, which Iain Orr had witnessed at first hand. Hundreds of Olympio's people were massacred during the campaign. Bodies were still being discovered in the bush. Just the week before I had arrived, a batch of bodies of more recent political victims had been washing up on the beach at Lome. Nobody could consider himself safe in Togo – in 1996 a German diplomat was shot and killed by Togolese security services.

It is a good example of the EU's moral blindness in international affairs that they had chosen Togo for their vast junkets to negotiate international trade treaties with the developing world. But Eyadema had always enjoyed the warm patronage of France, and been the friend of successive French Presidents. These relationships were based on blood diamonds, for which Eyadema was a major conduit and to which successive French Presidents were extremely partial. The webs of brutality and corruption that linked the dictators of la Francophonie with recent Presidents of France of all parties would make a fascinating book. Throughout Eyadema's rule, a battalion of French paratroops was stationed close to Lome airport ready to give him assistance if needed, and his vicious security services were controlled by French "Advisers". [40]

Over the next day or two, the rest of the key participants rolled into town. The Sierra Leonean government delegation was lead by the highly likeable Solomon Berewa, the Attorney General. Solomon was dignified but practical, and a pleasure to negotiate with. He was one of the few people there who was genuinely well-motivated. The UN representative was Frances Okelo, a Ugandan who was something of an aloof figure. He chaired the formal sessions together with Togo's Foreign Minister, Joseph Koffigoh, representing ECOWAS. In fact the formal sessions were meaningless, just occasional statements of position. All the real negotiating took place in corridors, hotel rooms, bars and restaurants. The United States sent Ambassador Joe Melrose, a grizzled old veteran Africa hand whose main interest was the stability of Liberia. He was a very good listener, a wise adviser and always helpful.

The negotiations were a grim game. The essential points of the peace plan were these. All fighting would cease immediately. There would be a

---

40Following Eyadema's death in 2005, his son Faure Gnassingbe is now President.

general amnesty, but not for "crimes against humanity." The RUF would disarm and enter the process, becoming a political party. There would be a government of national unity until elections a couple of years later. The RUF would have ministers in the government of national unity. They would get some funding to transform themselves into a political party, and help to develop their policy programme. They would get offices and office equipment in return for guns. There would be scholarships for their young leadership to be educated. The fighters would be disarmed and go into camps. There would be training programmes, and counselling for child soldiers. A percentage of the RUF fighters would be reintegrated into the national army.

This was an immensely complex negotiation. There were a huge number of practical points to agree upon, and then there were major ethical and legal questions at stake. Let me start by making a list on some of the practical points on which we had to reach agreement:

Amnesty – who would benefit from this, and who be exempted? Did the massacres and amputations carried out by the RUF constitute a "Crime Against Humanity"? If so, would the leadership or the actual killers be held responsible? And if everyone involved was held responsible, would that not make the amnesty in practice meaningless? Would trials be held in Sierra Leone or the Hague? Under international or Sierra Leonean law?

Remember the possible answers to these questions meant that the RUF delegation were negotiating for their very lives. While they were kept in luxury and under a safe conduct from the government of Togo, they were all too aware that they were in fact prisoners.

Disarmament – should only the RUF disarm? What about the Kamajors? What about the various factions of the Sierra Leonean army?[41] Would a bounty be paid for guns? How did you prevent it being used to pay for more guns? Who would fund this? Who would fund the disarmament camps and their education and training programmes? How many RUF fighters could be incorporated into the Sierra Leonean army? What

---

41 The Armed Forces Ruling Council was supposed to be in the talks alongside the RUF, but in fact played very little part and had more or less melted away.

kind of weapons could they be given? Should they be in distinct units, or dispersed in existing structures?

RUF as a political party - if the RUF was to be given funds, offices and training to enable it to become a genuine political party, who would fund all this? Would that not put the RUF at an advantage compared to established political parties? Who would monitor and supervise elections?

Power sharing – how many minister's should the RUF get? The RUF's opening position was eight, the Sierra Leonean government's opening position was two. Who would have key ministries in charge of diamonds and the army? Would President Kabbah choose RUF ministers, or could the RUF leader, Foday Sankoh, nominate them? What would Foday Sankoh's position be in a power sharing government? Could he be Vice President? What would happen if an RUF minister were indicted for crimes against humanity?

That is by no means an exhaustive list of the points on which I was trying desperately to broker and agreement. Many lives were at stake; there was at least one serious renewal of fighting in Sierra Leone during the talks. But also there were major areas of principle at stake, involving some very tricky moral dilemmas.

Was not this whole exercise an appalling appeasement, rewarding the RUF for their grisly campaign of murder and mutilation? Were we not just as wrong to be involved with the highly corrupt government of Sierra Leone, where beyond the formal written proposals on which ministries went where under power sharing, we were holding blunt and grubby talks about which politician or warlord got physical control of which diamond field?

On the RUF side, only their lawyer, Omrie Golley, was not guilty of multiple murder. For the agreement to stick, Sankoh and his top lieutenants would have to be given immunity. But one or two senior figures, and a large number of junior ones, would have to be tried and probably executed in Sierra Leone to appease the suffering population, while their colleagues went on to high office and riches. I was to find myself discussing with Sankoh which of his colleagues he wanted to nominate for the chop as scapegoats. Then there was a deeper, longer game that, after disarmament and power-sharing, after the elections, Kabbah's people and the party of James Jonah in Freetown might be strong enough to topple and execute Sankoh at last. That is if there were no further coup by the army, while nobody could predict what Sam Hinga Norman and his kamajors, or Charles Taylor of Liberia's militias, might do. Every participant in these talks was acutely aware of all of these permutations. We were playing a game of life and death for thousands in Sierra Leone, and in a very real sense for many of those around the table.[42]

Officially my role was very unclear. The negotiations were being conducted by the UN and ECOWAS. But in fact, as the former colonial power, everybody was looking to the UK to lead the negotiations, and that included both the Sierra Leoneans themselves, of all factions, and the Americans. Joe Melrose made it plain to me that the US was puzzled by the UK's failure to get a grip in Sierra Leone, the way the US had in neighbouring Liberia. Everybody was also looking to DFID as the only body able to provide substantial amounts of funding at short notice. This was to cause me real problems. We wrapped up agreement on the items patient step by patient step. For example, it was eventually agreed that the RUF would get six regional offices for its political party, and each would be provided with two computers and a photocopier. I was asked to try for funding for this. DFID outright refused to provide any funds specifically to the RUF. I recall trying desperately to call the Westminster Foundation for Democracy to ask them to give £40,000, before this particular hard won segment of the jigsaw of agreement evaporated before my eyes.

Secure communication with London was difficult. For the first week I was communicating by the hotel fax, and feeling sympathy for Peter Penfold's ordeal in Conakry. But after a week I drove back to Accra to pick up a bit of MI6 kit flown in for me from London. It was a satellite telephone and a laptop configured to MI6 and the FCO's secure communications network.

I could hook the laptop and satellite phone together and send an encrypted telegram back to the FCO. The FCO's cipher keys change daily and are normally held beneath numerous combination locks and steel

---

42A succinct and largely accurate account of these negotiations can be found at
http://www.c-r.org/our-work/accord/sierra-leone/lome-negotiations.php

doors in Embassy registries worldwide. I had them on a number of discs to insert into the laptop when transmitting. These were classified top secret, as anyone obtaining a copy would be a long way to decoding any secret British government communication worldwide.

I wrote "Swedish Porn", "Gay porn", "Donkey Porn" and similar titles on each disc with a DVD marker pen. I had nowhere secure to store them, so in the day I carried them in a single case inside my underpants. After sweeping my hotel room for bugs with another handy gadget I had been given (the room had an audio bug) I removed one of the foam rubber pillows on the bed from its case and cut a slit in it. At night I pushed the discs into the slit and sideways through the foam until they were well buried, then slept with my head on the pillow.

The satellite telephone was locked into a large metal briefcase, and the lid of the case became the satellite dish. This lid had to be pointed directly at the satellite. As there was a choice of one in South Africa and one in Spain, both were extremely low on the horizon in Lome. The only place I could get a signal was on the hotel roof - so I had to sneak up there, via the fire escape, at about 4am most mornings. The hotel Deux Fevrier is thirty six storeys high, and with the North Atlantic hitting the heat of Africa a few hundred yards away, it was pretty windy up there. Sometimes it would take a couple of hours to find the satellite and get the connections and encryption to work. If this all sounds very jolly, remember that the Togolese had shot and killed a German diplomat less than five years earlier.

About the third day I did this I returned to my room. The laptop battery was pretty drained. I put it on the desk to recharge, the cord stretched across the room to the nearest working power point. I put the discs into the slit in the pillow, turned out the lights, put my head on the pillow and quickly fell asleep.

I was awoken an hour later by a loud clatter. I sat up quickly, and without my spectacles saw a blurred figure lit by the corridor light as it opened the door and ran away. I leapt up and to the door, but by the time I got there the corridor was empty.

Somebody had entered the room and been approaching my bed when they tripped over the outstretched power cord and pulled the laptop onto the floor.

This was a bit worrying. That night I reported this to London. I did not want to make too much of it in case they simply pulled me out of the negotiations; but I did feel they might have found another member of staff to come and support me. So I stressed that there were plenty of possible explanations. It could, I wrote, have been a common thief or even "A prostitute with a pass key" – which was indeed something I had come across before in West Africa. But I was later to be reprimanded for this by Ian Mackley, who told me that John Kerr was appalled that I had used the term "Prostitute" in an official telegram, which would be seen by ministers (poor things).[43]

The immediate outcome was that I was instructed by the FCO to apply to the Togolese authorities for protection. I was assigned a Togolese government bodyguard, who was very nice and cleaned my shoes, but obviously hampered my activities. It took me a few days to negotiate him away again.

I had to play things with a high hand in order to meet everybody's expectations that the UK would play the leading role, when there was only me and I received very little in the way of instruction from London other than rather long-winded "Nos" from DFID.

It was taken as read that the Sierra Leonean government delegation would lean on the UK for support, and they duly did so, constantly. The great difficulty was to get the RUF to agree to a deal. There was little real danger that ECOMOG would do the hard fighting needed to drive the RUF from their home territories, and a return to guerilla terror tactics appealed to many of the RUF.

The RUF leader, Foday Sankoh, never left his suite on a high floor of the hotel. He did not attend negotiating sessions. People went to see him. Photos of him on the internet show a cheerful, tidy man in a little cloth hat and kaftan with a neat, clipped beard. In Lome, he didn't look like this at all. His beard was matted and had bits of what looked like twig

---

43 Sir John Kerr now states that he said no such thing. I am inclined to believe him – but I was definitely told he had objected.

and cloth woven into it. He smelled rank, and his clothes looked stained. He was incapable of following a logical argument, and I believe may have been illiterate – I certainly never saw him read or write.

Sankoh was obsessed with becoming Vice-President, which was necessary to "Clean Sierra Leone". On almost every other question he would reply "Dey no important". He usually spoke to me in pidgin, but I heard him interviewed much more rationally on the BBC. Solomon Berewa suggested to me he was "Playing mad, like Hamlet." I suspected he was on drugs – nearly all the RUF delegation were up to their eyeballs in cocaine most of the time. Sankoh lived with a young woman "Corporal Agnes" who seemed terrified of him, and he also had a constant stream of prostitutes taken to his rooms.

If the RUF were to disarm, they had to trust the peace deal would deliver the things they wanted – money and personal security. Once they were disarmed, they would be very vulnerable, and these people had lived whole lives by the gun where the unarmed were killed and mutilated. So to gain that level of trust in a few weeks was truly a formidable problem. To do that, I had to forge friendships with them. Remember, they were all mass murderers.

In these circumstances, you need to gain entry into their group, so they accept you socially and interact freely in front of you and with you. You have to become an accepted part of the scene, while not allowing yourself to be emotionally "captured" or others to perceive you as biased towards one group. That is a hard act to pull. To start, I needed an "in" to the RUF.

My "in" was to be Colonel Isaac, the young man I had started to befriend on my very first night in Togo. I made a point of greeting him in friendly fashion whenever I saw him, and especially in front of other parties. For someone in Isaac's position, unsure if the future was execution, friendly acknowledgement from the official representative of the British government was pretty heartening. I started drinking with him, and in the course of the next few nights I learnt his story, as he told it in morose and pained gobbets of memory. I don't think anyone had ever really asked him about this stuff before, and it was like exorcising a terrible substance from the depth of his soul.

Colonel Isaac thought he was nineteen years old.

The first people Isaac had killed had been his own parents, when he was just about eight. Charles Taylor's men had come to his village and raped his mother and sisters. They had killed both his older brothers, forcing him to watch as they clubbed them to death. Then they gave him a pistol and ordered him to shoot his father and mother in the head; otherwise they would do the same to his sisters. His father had cried and screamed, but his mother had begged him to do it to save his sisters.

Shooting his mother was easy; she closed her eyes and prayed quietly. He had been stunned when he pulled the trigger and her head exploded. Shooting his father was more difficult. He had always been so scared of his father, and he was confused to see him crying and begging. His shot took off the side of his father's head but didn't kill him. One of the fighters then plunged his hand right into his father's brain. Amazingly, for a few seconds his father had continued to speak.

"What did he say?" I asked gently.

"He say 'tell your mother'. Only 'tell your mother'."

The men then killed Isaac's youngest sister and took the other two as sex slaves. They killed one a few days later. After a few weeks some of the men left with his last sister; he never heard from her again. By then, Isaac was already a fully fledged fighter in the Liberian civil war: "I don go fo sojah" – I went to be a soldier.

Since then he had known nothing but brutality and killing. He made no distinction between fighting for Foday Sankoh in Sierra Leone and fighting for Charles Taylor in Liberia. To him it was the same struggle against the "Gnomes and ogres" who had cheated the people of the wealth of the country. He referred to all enemies as "Gnomes and ogres". I wondered where he had picked up the expression.

I thought I already knew a fair amount about African conflicts, but I was surprised to learn that, he thought aged about eleven, Isaac and about three hundred other boys had been put on a ship out of Liberia to go and fight for Unita in Angola. They had been packed into the hold of a cargo ship and quite a few died on the journey – he had been in charge of collecting bodies twice a day and throwing them overboard. In Angola the fighting had been murderous. Eventually they were declared victorious, and taken back to fight in Liberia again. Of that three hundred, only about forty made it back to West Africa.

Isaac was the product of the sores of Africa. He was a hardened killer, but he was also the little boy forced to kill his own mother. He caused me to think a great deal. Had Isaac been just two years younger, he would still have been a child soldier and there would be great concern to rehabilitate him. But now he had slipped past that category and into the adult killer range.

But had he ever had a chance? He was one of the middle ranking members of the RUF delegation. He really believed that now these peace talks were going completely to change his life, to wipe away all that hate and hurt. What Isaac wanted out of the peace talks was to go to College in the United States. I encouraged him to believe this could be possible. Despite the unthinkable things he had done, I believed Isaac was redeemable, and not only in the next world.

In fact, I also knew that the illiterate Isaac was definitely one of the people Foday Sankoh was indicating could be sacrificed by the RUF to stand trial.

Sankoh himself varied from day to day, but definitely was more often against a deal than for one. As he asked the BBC World Service "Did I fight a war for all those years just to get four ministers?" He was himself already sentenced to death in Sierra Leone. Unless the RUF delegation were strongly in favour, Sankoh would back out, so I continued to befriend Isaac and, through him, form relationships with the rest of the delegation.

In these circumstances it is fatal to be guarded. You have to display your own vulnerability in order to win trust. This means, in short, that you have to be blind drunk, or whoring, or singing raucously together. Shared secrets are the basis of trust, and I became accepted with the RUF as "a man". There are limits – I don't take hard drugs, and they were stoked up at least half the time. They continually offered drugs to me, and I had to laugh it off, usually countering by buying a whole bottle of Chivas Regal. I recall explaining to "Leatherboots", one of the more terrifying RUF commanders, that I didn't take cocaine because it stopped me getting it up. I had to grab at a couple of local girls to carry this off (letting them go again as soon as I could). It was also at times truly terrifying. They were violent and unpredictable, and would take to smashing up chairs, or throwing glasses at each other's faces, at no apparent provocation. The apparently scholarly Paolo Bangura, a former member of the AFRC, proved to be one of the more irascible.

I was extremely fortunate in having Solomon Berewa, the Sierra Leonean Attorney General, to work with. He was very shrewd and playing the long game, aware that once the RUF were disarmed the game would change. He was determined that the rule of law should be applied, but was also rational. I explained to him how I felt about Isaac. I suggested killers who had themselves been brutalised since early childhood could not be viewed as entirely responsible for their actions. He understood what I was saying.

There was one member of the RUF delegation for whom I felt no sympathy. Omrie Golley was a British national, whose father had been a Sierra Leonean minister. He had a legal practice on Kensington High Street, before (according to my briefing notes from the British intelligence services) being disbarred by the Law Society for embezzlement of a client's funds. He now operated out of Croatia, and had been popping up for the last couple of years as the official spokesman of the RUF.

Golley lived in great style in Lome. He had the entire top floor of a very pleasant French owned boutique hotel, complete with roof garden and pool. Omrie did the drafting and detailed negotiating for the RUF, reporting to Kabbah daily. One day he invited me to his suite to discuss the final draft of the peace deal. Once I arrived he made an excuse and left, leaving me for two hours in the company of his absolutely gorgeous Croatian wife, who was wearing just knickers and a negligee.

I don't think this was any kind of honey trap – the poor girl, apart from her deshabillee, behaved perfectly normally. She was bored and unhappy in Lome. She appeared completely ignorant of what was going on, and I believe genuinely had no idea that there was anything dodgy about her husband or disreputable about the RUF. It was a strange afternoon in a surreal period of my life.

For Isaac and some of his companions I felt sorry. A cruel fate had brought them here. Golley, however was different. He tried continually to ingratiate himself with me, posing as my fellow English gentleman in his pinstripe suits, talking of cricket and the Royal Family in his public school accent. But he very much had a choice, and was making money out of all this. He gave me the creeps, and I preferred the company of the Sierra Leonean, Togolese, Libyan, Nigerian and other assorted killers in our party.

At the start of the third week of the negotiations, I awoke one morning and had immediately to dash to the bathroom and sit there for an hour. The stomach cramps were very painful. My vision had taken on a yellowy tinge, and objects in my peripheral vision were circling around in a disconcerting manner. Once it seemed safe, I crawled back to my bed and took some imodium. About half an hour later I started to vomit.

I thought I recognised the symptoms; it felt just like the salmonella poisoning which Dr Handa had treated me for in Accra. The same treatment should work again. I called the driver to come up to my room.

"Joe," I said, "I am really sick. I need some hydration salts and some Noroxin. Let me write it down. I really think it's pretty bad and I need it urgently. Go quickly."

Half an hour later he was back. He was grinning at me and smirking in a way that did not seem at all appropriate for the gravity of the situation.

"Here you are, sir", he smirked, "Hope you get better soon."

I was mystified. Joe always seemed a very grounded, friendly and responsible person. Why this sudden callousness?

Anyway, the priority now was not Joe but my sickness. I pulled the medicine from the bag, and looked at the little white box of Noroxin. It was the same drug, only with a slightly different French spelling – Noroxine. And in its French packaging, it had displayed prominently on the front of the box: "Contre la syphilis".

No wonder Joe was giggling!

That night I hardly slept at all. I turned the air conditioning up to maximum and took the blankets off the bed, but I couldn't get cool, and felt like iron bands were being tightened around my head. The next morning my face looked strangely orange. My bodyguard Maurice was genuinely worried, and hurried me off to see "the white doctor."

We drove a short distance through the residential streets of Lome; everywhere the white paint looking like it had been rubbed off, revealing patches of light grey concrete. Vivid stretches of green vegetation were appearing on masonry, sprouting from gutters and downpipes, eating into roofs and thrusting strong searching roots into cracks in walls. We came to a building of a dirty sandstone colour, an open courtyard at the front with weeds growing between flagstones. An old copper coloured Peugeot 306 was parked diagonally across this space, its back window missing. From the top of the rear seats' cream coloured leather upholstery, a huge lime green praying mantis stood a motionless, angular guard as we approached. It is the only insect which visibly looks at you,

Inside and out, the whole building seemed the same dirty sand colour, and it was difficult to tell if any of it had ever been painted. We walked up three steps, and opened the much holed mesh insect screen closed across the front door, which stood ajar. The local receptionist recognised Maurice and we were shown straight through to a back room. The walls were lined with dark wood shelves from which yellowing periodicals seemed determined to escape, spilling in inexplicably frozen cascades. Behind a massive wooden desk heaped with cardboard files a small, ageing man sat in a large carved chair whose back rose above his head. He wore silver spectacles and a green corduroy jacket, rubbed at the elbows and cuffs. A thin clipped moustache rose above a smile of yellowing teeth. Evidently he had been expecting me, as he already knew my name.

"Monsieur Murray. Do you have fever? Vomiting? Diarrhoea?"

I nodded yes to all of these. The doctor didn't move.

"It's probably malaria" he said. "Go next door and see my young colleague for a blood test."

In the next room sat a younger Frenchman, perhaps in his early twenties. He wore a white shirt, the rolled up sleeves held above the elbows by gold elasticated bracelets. He had black chest hair curling over his shirt where it was open at the top, and about three days' growth of beard. At least it would have been three days growth for me – he looked like he might have produced it since breakfast.

As I entered, he motioned me to a chair placed against the wall, put down his magazine and stubbed out his cigarette. Getting up, he walked around his desk and motioned me to hold out a finger. He donned rubber gloves then took a microscope slide from a box, unwrapped it from its paper coverings and held it under my finger. As he prepared to prick my finger with something in his other hand, I saw what he was using and suddenly wrenched my hand away.

"Hang on!" I yelled in English, "Is that clean?"

He had been about to cut my finger with a sliver of broken glass. Looking annoyed by my outburst, he got up, looked at me, and pointedly shrugged his shoulders in a decidedly Gallic fashion. He carefully placed his piece of glass in a yellow bin, then started rummaging under his desk for something. He pulled out a small pane of glass, which incongruously brought memories flooding back to me of my grandfather's greenhouse, the strong smell of the tomato plants mingling with damp manure and rotting wood. The pane the young man now held had a substantial piece broken off from one top corner. He shrugged again, then quickly and expertly gave the broken pane a light knock against the side of his desk. Two or three small shards broke off and fell onto the desktop. He grinned, picked up one of these, and came back to me. He drew the glass shard across the top pad of my middle finger to draw blood, and I must say it hurt like hell. He then smeared my bloody finger across his glass slide.

I was returned to a waiting room, feeling still more dazed. Some half an hour later I was told I definitely did have malaria, and given medicine to start taking. I told Joe not to go back to the hotel but drive me straight to the border and back to Accra. From my experience of Togolese medical care, the sooner I was back in Ghana the better.

I was away for over a week. Paul Harvey, who had been the East African Deputy Head in African Department (Equatorial) while I was the West African Deputy, came out to take over. Paul continued the work I was doing and had the down to earth personality to win the trust and affection of all involved. By the time I returned, we had thrashed out an agreed draft peace deal on all of the major points. President Kabbah was under intense diplomatic pressure from Nigeria and the United States to agree.

Frances Okelo, Joe Melrose and I knew that there was no point in any deal if Charles Taylor did not sign up to it. He had the ability to send fighters to restart war in Sierra Leone, more or less whenever it suited him. We decided we needed to go to Liberia and present him with the draft. We also wanted to go to Freetown to see President Kabbah. He had not attended the talks, not being able to be seen to treat Foday Sankoh as an equal. Now we would go to him to add to the pressure for his agreement.

President Eyadema lent us his private plane. It was a small jet, equipped with massive swivel chairs in ivory leather for about six people. A stewardess plied us with vintage champagne. But there was something very disconcerting about the jet. As it flew, every minute or so it would shudder and buck, the tail twisting from side to side. I turned to Frances Okelo and asked him where they kept the parachutes. He was looking decidedly nervous.

We flew in to Freetown Airport. It said much for the lack of control of President Kabbah, and of ECOMOG, that the road from the airport was liable to RUF ambush. The only way in to Freetown was across the bay by UN helicopter. This was a huge old Russian machine, crewed by Ukrainians. I was strapped to a wall, perching my bum on a kind of ledge.

Our delegation of six was protected by about twenty Nigerian ECOMOG troops, who came in the helicopter with us. There were two heavy machine guns, manned out of the great open doors each side. The Nigerian troops were almost comically swathed in bandoleers, grenades, rocket propelled grenade launchers and guns of various calibres. There was a great crush in the helicopter and soldiers were hanging out, clinging on to struts.

It felt even less airworthy than Eyadema's plane, although I imagine it skimmed the water as a precaution against enemy fire, not because it could not get higher. Once in Freetown we decanted to a motley convoy of old vehicles, and thumped uphill to the Presidential palace. We threaded our way through a variety of whitewashed rooms, all empty of personnel and uninhabited looking, until we came to President Kabbah, sat alone in his office, behind an uncluttered desk.

Frances Okelo put the key questions to Kabbah. Would he be prepared to grant Sankoh a pardon and accept four RUF ministers in his transitional administration, making Sankoh vice-president? Why yes, replied Kabbah, provided his cabinet, the council of churches and civil society agreed. But would he be prepared to work for their agreement? Why yes, he said. Provided his cabinet, the council of churches and civil society agreed that he should work for their agreement. We were not going to get far with Kabbah, but at least we could give him a definitive text of the proposed agreement.

We left again for the old helicopter, then we took off again in Eyadema's juddering aircraft. Forty minutes later, we approached Monrovia airstrip. There were blast craters in the grass alongside the runway, and bullet holes in the crumbling concrete of the terminal building. This time we were squeezed into a minibus, with no air conditioning. As we travelled to Taylor's home through a nightmarish warscape, we were escorted by several pick-ups mounting heavy machine guns. About a dozen warriors were crammed into the load bay of each pick up. A few had neat new American military fatigues and boots, but most were in shorts and old shirts. A large number were children.

Entering Taylor's house through a large razor wire topped wall, past sandbagged artillery emplacements, the building itself had the air more of a large private house than an official residence. Entering on the ground floor, we went down a large spiral staircase to the living room, which was in the basement – presumably for protection from missile attack. It was a huge room, with several different levels. The astonishing thing about it was the sheer number of knick-knacks it was stuffed with. As well as far too much furniture, there were statues, paintings and vases everywhere.

A large number of these articles were gold and silver pieces, two or three feet high, of the sort that would be a table centrepiece for an army regiment or city corporation. It was the room of somebody who liked to spend their money in very expensive New York jewellers and furnishers, and had no style.

Taylor came in, dressed in a sharp, light grey, Italian silk suit. Monsters come in many guises and Charles Taylor both looked and sounded like a very bright New York lawyer, only more honest. He was slickness itself as he outlined, in his smart East Coast accent, his deep concern for his brothers and sisters in Sierra Leone, his outrage at the amputees, and his desire for peace and development. He said that he had never supported any party in Sierra Leone and had never had any links to any fighting there, while he had just secured firm control of Liberia's own borders and was acting firmly to prevent any cross-border mischief.

He flicked through the draft peace agreement, and said he would study it in detail. We could always rely on him to do anything to bring peace. Of course he would be happy to urge agreement on Foday Sankoh, but he had no influence there. He would also urge agreement on President Kabbah. But his efforts to help by securing the border would be very expensive for Liberia. Of course Liberia wished to play a very constructive role, but it was a poor country, and would need to be financially supported to do so...

It had not been an overwhelming success of a day, but it was a part of the process that had to be gone through, and at least nobody was openly opposing or obstructing the process. It would remain a case of ensuring everyone's self interest was served by securing a peace agreement. Altruism is in short supply in West Africa.

Our escort were noticeably nervous as we returned through the gathering dusk. Flames flickered in the city, and every now and then we heard gunfire, though whether in anger of celebration we could not tell. At the airfield our pilot was visibly agitated. With tropical swiftness, dusk turned to darkness as we climbed up the short flight of steps into the plane. Monrovia airport had no lights or beacon, or indeed electricity. We waited in the dark for half an hour. The distant sounds of gunfire seemed much more ominous as we sat helpless in our fragile little cocoon. By the light of torches, I could see men starting to roll an oil barrel down the railway. A further wait, then flames leapt up just beside us, and raced ahead of us. Then we lurched off down the runway, accelerating breathtakingly fast. We tore along the line of liquid fire, some of which clung briefly to our fuselage, and were up in the air. Climbing steeply, we pulled through the bank of heavy cloud and the gloom vanished as a bright silver moon shone on the crystal plumed castles just beneath us.

Our plane still juddered alarmingly, but suddenly felt homely and secure as we sped back to Lome. I fell asleep.

In fact, the plane was neither safe nor secure. Two days later, en route to Kara in Northern Togo, it fell out of the sky and was destroyed, killing our pilot and his crew.

The next few days consisted of diplomatic tidying up for us, with work to gain acceptance for the agreement being done in capitals. The only real question now was Foday Sankoh. He would indicate agreement one day, then denounce the deal to the media the next. He appeared increasingly unstable.

Jesse Jackson was flying in for the signing ceremony. His personal diplomacy had been key to initiating these peace negotiations, through a meeting he had held with Kabbah, Sankoh and Eyadema on 18 May 1999. In fact Jackson had caught the UK on the hop; the British government was wary of negotiations with the RUF and tended to favour the hard-liners in Kabbah's government who wanted a military solution. Jackson had been in Accra for an African-American summit, and had by force of personality swept up President Kabbah and forced him on an unplanned trip to Togo to meet Foday Sankoh. My own view was that Jackson's coup was brilliant – he had achieved a most unlikely ceasefire and the start of negotiations.

Nonetheless I was worried that Jackson's return at this stage would damage the extremely delicate agreement we had reached. I asked Joe Melrose why Jackson was coming back now; we had walked a knife edge to get to this point; the last thing we needed was any new factor. Joe grinned, shrugged, stubbed out a cigarette and said "Africa is high on the agenda of the Clinton administration. And it's got to look like it. Jackson's Presidential Envoy for Democracy in Africa. Liberia matters a lot to African Americans, and this shows progress on Liberia".

A young staffer working for Jackson had arrived a couple of days before the ceremony, to prepare the ground. I can't remember her name, but she looked like a Leanne. Very pretty, in her mid twenties, she knew nothing about Sierra Leone, little about Africa, and kept pestering us for details of what was going to happen, which we old Africa hands knew we would not get to know until it actually happened. Joe was keeping her at arms length, so she asked me whether I would be prepared to travel to the airport to meet Jackson off the plane, and come back in the car with him to brief him on the journey in.

The private jet pulled up outside the terminal building and Jackson, dressed all in black, appeared at the top of the steps, waving and pointing to the non-existent crowd. There were about six of us waiting there for him. I was thrilled to meet him – one of my political heroes. When I was introduced on the tarmac, he was looking around, craning his neck and not looking at me at all.

"Where's President Eyadema?" He barked the question at Leanne.

"He's waiting in the Presidential place sir. You'll see him this afternoon" she replied, her expensive poise disintegrating fast.

I sat with them in the back of a capacious limousine. He was still ignoring me, and still talking sharply to Leanne.

"Just what is going on here. Where were CNN? Where were NBC? What the heck did I fly all this way for?"

Leanne looked about to cry: "Well, I am afraid they don't have bureaux in West Africa sir. But there's someone from the New York Times in town."

"The New York Times! Damn! Hey girl, why do I pay you? This is not good. It's not good at all. I flew across the Atlantic for this? There had better be media at the signing ceremony, or...."

He seemed to see me for the first time.

"Oh, Ambassador...Murphy, isn't it? Tell me about this peace deal. I hope we're not pardoning human rights abusers?"

To avoid disappointment, never meet your idols. I believe Jackson genuinely wanted to help the people of Sierra Leone and Liberia. But even more so he wanted to be seen to be helping in the US, and he wanted good television images to do that. But he wasn't getting those, and he wasn't happy.

In fact, it was an even more distinguished visitor than Jesse Jackson who nearly upset the apple-cart, by not appearing. We were gathering for the signing, and I was seated quietly on a verandah outside one of Eyadema's gilded anterooms, when Foday Sankoh shuffled out and joined me. He had been tidied up a bit, his hair and beard clipped, and thankfully appeared to have had a good wash. His little blue pot hat was pulled even more firmly down on his head than usual, and he looked out at me quizzically from under it. For an incongruous moment he reminded me of Winnie the Pooh.

"Hello, Ambassador Murray" he said. "Can I call you Craig?"

He gave a shy smile, and then squatted down on his haunches beside me.

"I am worried" he said. He looked me straight in the eyes. "God don't come to see me today. He always come before ten o'clock in the morning. This morning, he don't come."

There was really not much I could say to that. I thought, tens of thousands of lives depend on the word of this lunatic. Christ!

"So I am thinking" Sankoh continued "Maybe God don't come because he don't want me to sign the agreement. Maybe God is angry about the agreement."

Sankoh had gone back on the draft agreement twice that month already; a third time could be fatal to the peace. I gripped the top of his arm.

"No, Vice President Sankoh" I said, using his proposed future honorific as a piece of bait. "I know what it means. God is very happy with you, and this piece of work is finished, so he doesn't need to see you today. He doesn't want to disturb your peace, and just wants you to go on and sign the agreement. I am sure that is what it means. I swear this by the Bible."

He returned my grip on a shoulder, and we just stayed there for what became a very tense couple of minutes. Then he stood up, shook his head, and started repeating to himself, chuckling gently:

"Ambassador Murray, Ambassador Murray, Ambassador Murray. You think Foday Sankoh is a simple Corporal. You think Foday Sankoh don't understand. I understand, I know exactly what is happening."

He laughed out loud. Then he exclaimed:

"And you are right. That is what God meant. I knew it already. I just check if you too are a man of God. God is strong in you, Ambassador Murray."

And he simply shuffled off. In history, we can never answer "What if"? Maybe my line in bullshit wasn't really needed. But it may have been the most valuable thing I ever did, because if war had re-erupted at that stage, almost certainly thousands would have died again before it could have been brought under control.

The signing ceremony went very well, washed down by a good deal of excellent vintage champagne, served in ringing crystal flutes with deep gold leaf around the rims. The Togolese had produced a very grandly presented document which was signed first by Solomon Berewa for the Government of Sierra Leone, followed by a beaming Foday Sankoh for the RUF, then by President Eyadema for ECOWAS and Jesse Jackson for the United States. After that came the representatives of Nigeria, Ghana, Ivory Coast, Libya and numerous other countries. Places had been found for the consultants and civil society groups to sign.

The British Government remained deeply ambiguous about the agreement, being grateful for the ceasefire but only very reluctantly accepting the need to bring the RUF into government. To mitigate the danger of press or public criticism in the UK, I was under strict instruction not to sign the document in any capacity. Given that we had done more than anyone to bring about this peace agreement, and it was undoubtedly already saving hundreds of lives, I felt sad about this.

After the signing ceremony, President Eyadema awarded medals to all the key participants. I was awarded Togo's highest order, becoming *Officier de l'Ordre de Mono*, named after Togo's major river.

Given that I oppose the honours system in the UK, and had three times rejected the offer of British honours, it was pretty strange to be accepting one from a brutal African tyrant. But it had been sprung on me and to refuse, on top of not signing the peace document, might have been taken as a signal that the British government did not support the peace deal. With Kabbah already facing massive criticism in Freetown from James Jonah and his faction for dealing with the RUF, I decided that it was best to go along with the general air of bonhomie, a decision later confirmed by the FCO.

So I stood in line as President Eyadema handed me a large scroll and a beautifully enamelled and jewelled little cross in a bright red box, from a top Paris jeweller. He beamed at me, enclosing my hand in his huge fist:

"Mr Ambassador, I create you an Officier of the Order of Mono. Well done. Very well done."

"Thank you. If I get two, is it the Order of Stereo?"

He released my hand and clapped his great paws on both my shoulders. He leaned his head in towards mine, still smiling but blood-shot eyes glaring balefully.

"Craig" – it was the first time he had used my name, I was surprised he knew it – "You should drink coconut milk. It will make you piss."

With that enigmatic advice, he stalked from the room. I was to meet him once more, about a year later, when George Opata and I went to Lome for the State Visit of President Jacques Chirac, and Eyadema personally invited us to drink champagne with him at 6.30 am. We reminisced about the Sierra Leone negotiations, and he showed me a bullet which had been dug out of his spine following a failed assassination attempt.

"They can't kill me. Eyadema is Togo" he declared. He beckoned us to leave, then as I reached the great gilt door of his audience room he called out to me again.

"Oh, Ambassador, did you every try that coconut milk?"

I laughed and waved. Those were the last words I heard from the late President Gnassingbe Eyadema.

Returning to Accra from Lome, I received a personal letter of thanks and appreciation from Robin Cook for my success in the Lome peace talks. It remains a much valued memento, not least of Robin Cook. The beautiful star of the Order of Mono got lost by the children in a dressing up game.

7

The Strange Attraction of Jeremiah Rawlings John

The peace accord we reached at Lome formally only lasted a year or so. But even a year's peace is a lot of lives saved, and the structures it set in place remained the foundation for subsequent settlements, particularly on disarmament. When fighting did break out again, we had the unusual development of direct intervention of the British armed forces. The additional structures they brought in – with British "Advisers" effectively officering the Sierra Leonean army, and a British head of the police force, with British officials effectively running the Sierra Leonean Treasury – amounted to no less in practice than a return of colonialism. In many ways it was a blueprint for future puppet administrations in Iraq and Afghanistan, and while undoubtedly there have been short term gains for the population of Sierra Leone, I do not myself believe that a return to the colonial model represents the way forward for Africa.

At last, I could return to my desk in Accra and concentrate on Ghana.

Ghana epitomises much of the best of Africa, but in so doing it only throws into sharp relief the tragedy of Africa. I started working on Africa in 1984. Ten years later, Africa was substantially poorer, in absolute not comparative, terms, than it was when I started. Ten years later, it was still poorer again and the rate of decline had accelerated. Today, Africa as a whole continues to get poorer and I have no reason to believe that ten years hence the poverty will not be worse than it is today. I hope we can harness the naive enthusiasm of those who marched to "Make Poverty History", and I detest the manipulative cynicism of Gordon Brown and the other politicians who tried to hijack the bandwagon. But I fear there is little real understanding in the West of just how difficult the task is.

Take Ghana. At independence in 1957, Ghana was a middle income country. It had then massive foreign reserves of US$417 million, which the colonial government handed over to Nkrumah (who squandered them inside three years). With a 1957 GDP per capita of over $300 per head , Ghana was significantly richer than Argentina, Brazil, Malaysia or Singapore.

Today all of those countries are massively wealthier than Ghana, each by factors of over ten. When I arrived in Ghana in 1998, Ghana was stuck more or less where it started with GDP of under $400 per head. Compare that to over $300 at independence thirty years earlier. Let me be plain. These are the actual figures – they are not uprated for inflation or comparison. If you translate that into real terms, national income per capita in Ghana is, even now, well below income at independence.

What does that mean to ordinary people? Well, my friend George Opata told me his uncle was a schoolteacher. On his schoolteacher's salary, they used to have a car – not a new car, but a series of old ones. Nowadays, the government in Ghana has just launched a campaign to give cheap Chinese bicycles to teachers as a reward for diligent service in rural areas. And those that receive them are pathetically grateful for these cheap Chinese bicycles. That is the difference in Ghana after fifty years of independence.

Don't worry, I am not going to tell you that this proves that the Empire was a good thing – that requires the shallow populism of a Niall Ferguson But nor is it true that colonialism is the cause of all of Africa's woes.

For more food for thought on this, go to the town of Nkroful and visit the birthplace of Kwame Nkrumah. The house is no longer there, but its very modest dimensions are marked out on the ground, and it brings home to you that this was a man from a very poor background in a poor village, who went on to become the greatest leader of the African independence movement, a symbol of black pride and respect and the driving force behind pan-Africanism.

Yet it is more complicated than that. It was the British who raised Nkrumah from that hut. They spotted his potential and recruited him for the colonial elite. They gave him a thorough schooling enabling him to go off to university in the United States. He applied the grounding the British gave him to win freedom and build a nation. And, in the nation he built, you realise as you look around Nkroful that nobody from that sad little place will ever get a good schooling or get to a good University again. Nkrumah dynamited the bridge behind him.

Nkrumah was not only post-colonial Africa's first independent Head of State, he was post-colonial Africa's first dictator and the model who blazed the trail of anti-democratic rule. In many ways he was the model for Mugabe, with a similar record of destroying both democracy and the economy. Mugabe studied in Ghana under Nkrumah and met his first Ghanaian wife there.

Nkrumah's Preventative Detention Act swept many of his opponents into jail with more gusto than the British had ever used. He closed down newspapers, banned trades unions and made strikes illegal. The great independence campaigner and journalist J B Danquah was imprisoned by Nkrumah for his writing and died in prison of kidney failure caused by the beatings he had endured.

In the United States and then in England, Nkrumah picked up the Marxism which was then being fashionably peddled by public school educated tutors from wealthy families. Finding it gelled well with his fierce, Oedipal anti-colonialism, Nkrumah was all prepared to kick start the destruction of the Ghanaian economy by unleashing Marxism upon it. A nation which had achieved quiet comfort through astute trading of the products of assiduously cultivated agricultural small-holdings, was to be dragged towards utopian prosperity by the application of grandiose schemes of central planning and massive industrial projects.

By 1961, having already squandered the reserves – equivalent to about $38 billion today – the British had left him, Nkrumah brought in the key instruments that were to wreck the Ghanaian economy. Import licences meant that the government controlled who could import goods. Allied to an over-valued exchange rate, these became a license to print money for government cronies and the Nkrumah government descended rapidly into massive corruption. The completely false "official" exchange rate, and the import license limiting who has access to it, became the chief instrument of economic corruption all over Africa – and is still so today in, for example, Mugabe's Zimbabwe. It became the method of choice for dictators to reward their key supporters. Having led the way in African nationalism, Nkrumah was pioneering the forms of economic mismanagement that were to destroy the economies of the continent and bring starvation and immeasurable suffering to billions. That is the "achievement" for which Nkrumah should truly be remembered.

Nkrumah also confiscated private foreign currency holdings, replacing them with government junk bonds, enforced a monopoly cocoa board purchaser and forced down the cocoa price to farmers, at the same time skimming off the Cocoa Board's revenues. He thus initiated the process by which Ghana's share of the World Cocoa market fell from 37% in 1957 to 17% in 1972.

Western commentators focus, quite rightly, on the disastrous impact that dumping of subsidised Western food produce on the African market has had on African farmers. The West has been culpable in Africa's plight in a number of ways. Of these, the worst has been in irresponsible lending to dictatorial regimes to finance grandiose capital projects, whose major object was generally corruption and which resulted in generations of debt for the poor Africans who received no benefit from them. Those who did benefit – massively - were the dictators, their cronies, and the bonus-quaffing Porsche driving bastards of the City of London.

But even greater damage was done by our dumping of cheap food on Africa. In both the US and Europe, the farm lobby carries disproportionate political clout and since the Second World War Western farmers have received huge sums from their countries' taxpayers' to produce vastly more food than their societies could absorb. Sometimes this meant it built up in storage mountains of beef or grain, but the major policy instrument for getting rid of the unwanted surplus was always the export subsidy. This did what it said on the box – large sums of money were given to Western farmers to produce food which was sold on foreign markets at subsidised prices.

Throughout the seventies, eighties and nineties, US maize and rice was being landed in Ghana at a price that varied between 40 and 70 per cent of its production cost. That drove the maize and rice farmers of Ghana into bankruptcy. The EU was landing in Accra subsidised beet sugar at one third the cost of its production. Sugar cane is vastly more efficient than sugar beet – without subsidy and protection sugar beet has never been viable. Sugar cane grows prolifically in West Africa, but the EU taxpayer spent billions in paying EU farmers to send beet sugar to West Africa. I watched first hand as the large Nigerian plantations of Bacita and Savannah Sugar were driven under by this, and many thousands made unemployed. This is fashionable analysis now, but I sent in 1987 from Lagos what may have been the first British government memo railing against the devastating effects of EU subsidy on African agriculture.

All of the above is true. It is now widely acknowledged, all too slowly Western policies are shifting and the NGOs indulge in some well-deserved flagellation of governments over the issue. But the truth is that an even bigger factor in the destruction of African agriculture has been the disaster Nkrumah first adopted – import licensing and the false official exchange rate. Agricultural commodities – wheat, rice, maize, barley, sugar and salt – were always the most sought after and profitable import licences. If the President's nominee has an import license for rice, that gives him monopoly access to import it at an official exchange rate that is one fifth of its true cost, and that rice already carries a US government subsidy – then what chance is there at all for the local producer? On top of which the President's mates obtain an active interest in driving the local producer out of business. This pattern too has repeated all over Africa.

So there are indigenous African factors of trade policy mismanagement which we tend to ignore. There is a further one equally important – massive tariff and non-tariff barriers limiting trade between African nations. If you manufacture almost any item in Ghana (except certain textiles), you can import it into the European Union free of duty. But, despite ECOWAS resolutions to the contrary, try and export it to a neighbouring state – say Togo, Ivory Cost or Mali – and you will face tariffs, impenetrable bureaucratic delay and unceasing demands for bribes. A manufacturer of slaked lime in Takoradi who sent regular supplies to gold mines in Ivory Coast, told me that in addition to formal tariffs there were eighteen different checkpoints along the route where bribes had to be paid.

Again, much of this comes down to the pernicious effect of import licensing. It would undermine your position as the monopoly import licensee of rice, if in neighbouring Togo their licensee could get his rice over the border into your country. So West Africa devoted vast resources to border protection between African states and to controls virtually impenetrable to trade. If you go to any of the major border checkpoints, beneath the hum, colour, bustle, stench and vibrant noise, the really interesting thing is to note just what a low volume of trade goods actually goes over. The killing of regional trade has been at least as devastating to African economic development as anything the West has done, depriving industrial producers of a critical mass of local market.

Africans have destroyed their own regional trade, for the protection of corrupt private interests. This has required no help from the West, and as we have no reason to feel guilty over it, has gone little remarked by Western analysts.

The result was a predictable disaster. But this was par for the course for all of Africa, as the Cold War powers fought out their proxy battles, funding murderous dictators here and murderous guerillas there, the Bible and the dollar pitched against Das Kapital and the Kalashnikov.

The British were nonetheless somewhat affronted when the CIA sponsored the coup that got rid of Nkrumah in 1965. But the military were to prove just as keen on nationalisation and expropriation as the Marxists. Ghana went through thirty years of ludicrous economic mismanagement, which I shall not outline in detail. But I must say something of Jerry Rawlings, who was to have a great influence on this, my story.

It is impossible to discuss modern Ghana without discussing the controversial figure of Jerry Rawlings, who by 1999 had been running the country for nineteen of the previous twenty one years. Flight-Lieutenant Rawlings had been sentenced to death following an alleged failed coup against the then military dictatorship in May 1979. Like Danton only more successfully, he used his trial to make populist speeches from the dock. A successful coup organised by others later the same year released him from jail. Rawlings became the head of the government and immediately organised the execution of a number of senior officers, including three ex-Presidents, Generals Acheampong, Afrifa and Akuffo. He unleashed a wave of terror against the middle classes which he called "house-cleaning." Many were "disappeared", and others jailed or beaten in this period.

Rawlings handed over to a civilian government for a few months, but then took power again in a further coup in 1981. It is beyond doubt that these first years of Rawlings in government unleashed political terror on Ghana that outstripped anything done by British colonial rule or by Nkrumah, or by successive military regimes, which had been comparatively genteel in their methods.

Rawlings' power and populism attracted fierce ideologues to his Provisional National Defence Council, including some of the Marxist base of Nkrumah's support, and some British anti-colonial intellectuals. His campaign against the middle classes in some ways resembled Mao's cultural revolution. People were terrorised for having quite small amounts in the bank, or two indoor toilets. Market women were stripped, beaten and sometimes killed for "Profiteering". All this was accompanied by populist rhetoric which did genuinely make Rawlings popular with the masses, plus a powerful appeal to his Ewe tribal base.

In May 2008, Rawlings was to declare that personally he only ever ordered the execution of three people, referring apparently to the former Heads of State. He claimed to be unable to restrain the "Righteous anger of the army and the people" that caused all the other killings. Few people believe him.

One brutality above all has come to symbolise those days of terror. On 30 June, 1982, three high court judges and a retired army major were abducted from their homes by soldiers in the night. Their partially burnt bodies were discovered at Bundase, some twenty miles away. The judges had been sitting to consider the constitutionality of Rawlings' regime.

The soldiers who murdered them were commanded by Amartey Kwei, one of Rawlings' ministers. In response to international outcry, Rawlings had Kwei executed, but not before Kwei revealed that he was acting under the instruction of Kojo Tsikata, Rawlings' right hand man. The squad that carried out the murders had actually been living in a house belonging to Rawlings, and they collected the keys to the Fiat truck they used for the operation from the home of Rawling's wife, Nana Agyeman Rawlings. The law is a greatly respected profession in Ghana, and of the many thousands killed under the Rawlings, these murders of judges caused the most shock.

Kojo Tsikata was still very much around when I arrived in Accra, in charge of national security and the most feared man in the country. But the orientation of Rawlings' government had changed. He had moved from being the protégé of Gadaffi to the pin-up boy of the IMF. Who was Jerry Rawlings, and how had this happened?

The Caledonian Society of Accra remains a thriving organisation, and I much enjoyed speaking at its Burns' Nights. Every year it elects a chieftain, and every year that chieftain has his name added on a new gold link on the chieftain's chain of office. The links are substantial chunks of gold, and after many decades the chain has become very valuable and very heavy to wear. One name appears twice as chieftain, in the late 1930s and early 1940's. That name is James Ramsay John. Rawlings believes John to be his father.

John was a Stirlingshire pharmacist who came out to Accra with the United Africa Company (UAC). He was known as "Dr John", but he was a chemist, not a doctor. But then Ghanaians kept calling me "Ambassador", and I was only a Deputy High Commissioner. Ghanaians are very polite.

"Dr John" had an affair with Rawlings' mother, Mrs Agbotui, who was a cook in the civil service. Jerry was born in 1947. Shortly before the birth, Dr John (whose Scottish wife was also in Accra) broke off the relationship with Rawlings' mother, because he believed his mistress was unfaithful. Dr John never acknowledged Rawlings as his son, though he did contribute money towards his education. On the one occasion Rawlings travelled to Scotland to see his father, John refused to meet him. John died in 1982.

A Ghanaian contact of mine who knew Rawlings' mother at the time said that she was a "very friendly lady", and that a more likely candidate for Rawlings' father was a Greek sailor he knew. But Rawlings' mother herself has never deviated from the view that Dr John is the father, and Rawlings appears to have followed her word.

Rawlings was sent to the prestigious Achimota School, one of a number of extremely good schools the British founded based on their own public schools, to inculcate a colonial elite. Rawlings was a poor student, but he did pick up his name there. The school told him his name was not Jeremiah Rawlings John, as John was not a surname. They registered him as Jeremiah John Rawlings, and Jerry John Rawlings he has been ever since. It is interesting to speculate if Dr John, who was picking up some or all of the school fee but did not accept Rawlings as his son, had a hand in the change of surname. In a school for the elite, as a fatherless child of an uneducated mother of dubious reputation, Rawlings must have had a difficult time at Achimota. Ghanaians are very snobbish. This is almost certainly the root of the extremes of class hatred he brought into Ghanaian politics.

An alternative story current in Accra is that the change of surname from "John" to "Rawlings" was imposed on him not at school, but on joining the Air Force.

Given an almost complete lack of educational qualification, strings must have been pulled to get Rawlings into the Ghana Air Force in the coveted position of Flight Cadet, and it would be interesting to know who stood behind him at age 19 to do this.

Rawlings was happy in the Air Force, his natural intelligence asserted itself and he was a talented pilot. As a young officer he was known around Accra for his flashy sports cars and flashier girlfriends. He was popular with British expatriates; nobody thought of him as a political figure. But resentments were seething underneath his debonair exterior.

Once in power, his poor absorption of formal education made him a prey to ideologues, be they promoting Marx or Monetarism. On his journey from one to the other, he kept with him most of the people who joined him early. His administration when I arrived therefore contained several anti-colonial ideologues who hated the British – some of them British, like Shirley Ababio and Valerie Sackey. His foreign minister, Victor Gbeho, was a very nasty little man, eaten up by spite.

I had not yet met Rawlings, or even seen him close up. Every day Ian Mackley would pass on to me those official invitations he did not want to take up – which was almost all his official invitations. He would either tell me to deputise, or ask me if I wanted to, depending on his view of the importance of the event. One on which he asked if I would like to go was the summer 1999 graduation ceremony of Ho Polytechnic. Jerry Rawlings was due to present the degrees. Ho was only about three hours drive North East; I decided to go.

Like Ian, the entire rest of the diplomatic corps had somehow managed to resist the invitation to the graduation ceremony. This was their loss, because it was fascinating. When I arrived into a riot of flustered academics, boisterous graduands and proud parents, nobody had any time for me as they were all overawed by the impending arrival of Jerry. I was left to find my own place.

The ceremony took place outdoors, in a courtyard between 1960's style school buildings, coloured panels alternating with rows of large windows. Rows of chairs for the students filled the centre of the space, facing a raised pavilion canopied in the Ghanaian colours of red, green and gold. The chairs for the students sat in the brilliant light of the Ghanaian sun; behind them was another raised area for the audience, with a corrugated iron roof supported by rough wooden beams, and rows of wooden benches sitting on the plank floor.

The chairs were already filling up with noisy and irreverent students, clad in American high school style gowns and mortar boards. They seemed all to be screaming at or wrestling with each other, in friendly fashion. On the benches at the back were crammed proud parents, the women swathed in improbable yards of cloth, with head coverings of many, many yards wrapped, curled and twisted around and up from their heads, rising towards the iron roof like improbable swathes of tropical plant growth.

I moved towards the back of the crowded rows of benches, but with the Ghanaian politeness and hospitality I was to meet again and again, people spontaneously and unanimously stood up, pushed, bustled and chattered until space had been made to squeeze me on to the front row.

I sat amid a happy, cheery crowd in the sweltering heat of the oven like space for a while, until suddenly motorcycle outriders came screaming into the area, circling the seats. The crowd stood and went absolutely ecstatic. It was like a goal being scored at a major cup final. Jerry Rawlings was walking in, and he was here, in the heartland of his Ewe tribe, the nucleus of his support, among his very own people. They went crazy for him – screaming, jumping up and down, ululating, waving their hands in the air. I was knocked forward and had to step down from the platform until the storm subsided a bit.

It was my first look at Jerry Rawlings. He was whiter than I expected, even knowing he was half European. A tall, strapping, barrel-chested man with a cropped beard and attractive smile. He had the ability to project, without the use of words, his personality to that entire crowd, including me. That quality is a strange thing, but very real. From my personal observation Thatcher and Mandela had it, but some you might think would – like Blair and Walesa – did not. It is a morally neutral force, being shared by Mandela and Mussolini. Where Rawlings stands in the moral spectrum is a complex question, but beyond doubt Rawlings had charisma by the bucketful. The aura he projected was strong, warm and comforting – in a word, paternal. His grin seemed entirely genuine. By contrast his tall, elegant wife, still beautiful, wore the falsest of grins and took her chair, flapping languidly with a fly whisk made from strips of the same bright green cloth as her dress.

I will never forget Rawlings' speech, not so much for its extraordinary content, as for the way he held his audience in the palm of his hand, played with them, and made them love him. This is what he said, working up punctuating cheers like a gospel preacher:

"Hi! Hi! Hi! It's great to see you! You're looking good! The young people of Ghana are looking good! Ghana is looking good! We are looking good! Alright!"

"Now education. Education. We need education. Education is necessary if we are to develop Ghana. Education is necessary if our young people are to take their place in the World."

"You know, here in Ghana a lot of people don't have education. Take Jesus. You know, here in Ghana, a lot of people think he really had that thing on his head. You know, you see it in the paintings. What do you call it? You know, that shiny thing above his head. What do you call it again? Halo? That's right, thank you. Halo! A halo! You know there are some people here in Ghana who think that Jesus really did walk around with a halo above his head!"

"But think about it. It can't be true! People would have noticed! If he had one of those things on his head, they would have noticed! Wouldn't they have written about it in the Bible? In the Gospels it tells us about his robe. Don't you think it would have mentioned that he had this amazing thing above his head?"

"Also, if people saw someone coming towards them with a strange thing like that above their head, they would be scared. They'd run away. Like it says in the Bible, when the shepherds saw the angels they were sore afraid. But does it say that when people saw Jesus they were sore afraid? Does it say they saw the Lord and ran away? No, it doesn't. It doesn't say that at all. So, you see that he didn't have one of those things above his head. He didn't have a ... a halo. The painters just put it in to show it's him. In a painting it's like a figure of speech."

"But here, even here today, here in Ghana, some people still think that he had that thing above his head, really, not just as a figure of speech. They are wrong to think that. They think that because they are ignorant. But it's not their fault they are ignorant. I say it's not their fault. They are ignorant because they never got the chance of good education. Now we are making sure that everybody gets good education. I am here today to support good education and the success of these great young people here in Ho. Because education is the future of Ghana. Thank you."

The crowd erupted again and roared for a good five minutes. I was gobsmacked. I didn't know what to make of it. It had been like top quality, surrealist comedy delivered by a master of timing in an extraordinary stream of consciousness. The central passages had been punctuated by screams of delight and collective guffaws of laughter. But what did Rawlings mean by it? How consciously was he being funny? Did he view the belief in the reality of haloes as a problem he must tackle, or had he just picked on it as a humorous example?

I was to discover that surreal conversation, but with an underlying shrewdness, had become Rawlings' hallmark of late, and nobody seemed confident as to his state of mind and health. Rawlings was, and remains, a profound enigma. It is important to remember that he introduced the practice of systematic political murder and violence into Ghanaian politics and for many years ruled by fear and destruction. Whatever he is now, that must not be forgotten.

Ian passed on to me another invitation, to attend the opening of an anti-corruption seminar hosted by the British Council. These can be dull and worthy affairs, and this one was no different in that everyone spoke politely about corruption as though it were an abstract and unavoidable evil, that descends at random, and certainly has no connection with present company.

After three or four waffling speeches by experts, I made my brief four minute contribution. I referred to a recent World Bank survey which pointed to a sharp increase in corruption in Ghana at all levels, I went on to say it was quite wrong to view corruption as an uniquely African disease, and noted that in most large scale corruption cases in Africa Western companies, including British companies, were involved.

The speech caused a furore. In particular the opposition media, both print and radio, picked it up as a major news item. "Your Government is Corrupt says British High Commission" screamed one full front page headline. The Ghanaian Foreign Minister, Victor Gbeho, called in Ian Mackley to protest. Ian was grumpy about the inconvenience, but broadly agreed with what I had said. I knew I would be supported by Ann Grant, and I had cleared the text of my speech in advance with DFID, who were the lead department on corruption issues. Indeed I had based my text and approach on a recent speech by Clare Short.

Nonetheless I found myself in very hot water because a British company felt their interests in Ghana could be damaged and decided to make a formal complaint in London. This resulted in a formal investigation into my speech and why I had made it. This was taken so seriously that it was conducted by the Permanent Under Secretary, Sir John Kerr, himself. It concluded with a formal letter from Sir John. He ruled that there had been no misconduct. I had been right to make the speech, which was in line with policy on corruption and had been properly cleared with DFID. However, he wrote me a formal letter of reprimand, stating that I should not have said that British companies were involved in corruption, as I could have damaged British interests. Sir John had in fact managed to reverse a snap ministerial judgement to withdraw me from Accra because of my anti-corruption speech.

I was outraged by this bollocks. How, with any credibility, could we condemn corruption in Africa if we refused to admit that British companies were sometimes involved? It lacked all intellectual credibility – "we condemn corruption, which is always the work of coons, wogs and dagoes". An anti-corruption policy which refused to recognise even the existence of British corruption was not worth the name.[44]

But at least Ghana now knew I had arrived.

44Sir John Kerr's attitude prefigured the appalling behaviour of the government over the BAE Saudi arms bribery scandal, where New Labour illegally attempted to subvert the rule of law and prevent investigation of over a billion dollars worth of bribes. Sadly the UK government no longer has any credibility on international corruption issues.

8

The African Queen

One morning I was sitting in the lounge at Devonshire House, with its fitted wool carpets and chintz sofas. I was drinking the tea that our steward, Nasser, had brought me. I heard movement in a corner of the room, and thought it must be Nasser cleaning there. But looking round, I saw nobody. Puzzled, I got up and walked towards that corner. Rounding a settee, I nearly stood upon a thin, green snake. About four feet long and just the thickness of your thumb, it was a bright, almost lime green colour. There was not much wedge shape to its head, which rather tapered from its neck. Its tongue was flickering toward me, perhaps a foot away, its head raised only slightly off the floor. I took a step backwards. In response it too retreated, at surprising speed, and zipped up the inside of the curtains.

I stood stock still and yelled "Nasser! Nasser!" This brought Nasser hurrying into the living room with Gloria, the cook.

"Nasser, there's a snake in the curtains!"

Nasser and Gloria screamed, threw their arms in the air, and ran together into the kitchen and out the back door of the house. This was not altogether helpful. I remained where I was to keep an eye on the snake, not wanting it to be lurking inside the house unseen. After a while the front door opened and somebody, presumably Nasser, threw in Nasser's scruffy little dog. The dog was normally banned from the house, and celebrated this unexpected turn of events by immediately urinating against the hall table. Then the dog too ran into the kitchen and out of the back door.

Abandoning my watch, I went out and recruited the reluctant gardeners and gate guards. They armed themselves with long sticks and came in and beat the curtains until the snake fell onto the floor. As it sped for cover under a sofa, Samuel the youngest gardener got in a solid blow, and soon everyone was joining in, raining down blows on the twitching snake. They carried its disjointed body out on the end of a stick, and burnt it on a bonfire.

Everyone identified it as a green mamba. I was sceptical. Green mambas are among the world's deadliest snakes, and I imagined them to look beefy like cobras, not whip thin and small headed like this. But a search on the agonisingly slow internet showed that indeed it did look very like a green mamba.

The important question arose of how it had entered the house. With air conditioning, the doors and windows were usually shut. Nasser seemed to have solved the mystery when he remarked that a dead one had been found last year inside an air conditioner. The unit had stopped working, and when they came to fix it they found a snake jammed in the mechanism. That seemed the answer; it had appeared just under a conditioner, and it seemed likely the slim snake had entered via the vent pipe, avoiding the fan as it crawled through the unit.

This was very worrying. If anti-venom was available (and we held a variety in the High Commission) an adult would probably survive a green mamba bite. But it would almost certainly be fatal to Emily, and possibly to Jamie.

A week or so later, I was constructing Emily's climbing frame, which had arrived from the UK. A rambling contraption of rungs, slides, platforms and trampolines, it required the bolting together of scores of chrome tubes. I was making good progress on it and, as I lifted one walkway side into position above my head, a mamba slid out of the end of the tube, down my arm, round my belly and down my leg. It did this in no great hurry; it probably took four seconds, but felt like four minutes. There was one terrible moment when it tried an exploratory nuzzle of its head into the waistband of my trousers, but luckily it decided to proceed down the outside to the ground. It then zig zagged across the lawn to nestle in the exposed tops of the roots of a great avocado tree.

Again the mob arrived and beat it to death with sticks. I persuaded them to keep the body this time, and decided that definite action was needed. I called in a pest control expert. I was advised to try the "Snake Doctor". I was a bit sceptical, equating "Snake Doctor" with "Witch Doctor", but when he arrived I discovered that this charming chubby Ghanaian really did have a PhD in Pest Control from the University of Reading. As Fiona had an MSc in Crop Protection from the same Department, they got on like a house on fire and it was difficult to get them away from cups of tea to the business in hand.

He confirmed that the dead snake really was a green mamba. We obviously had a colony. They lived in trees, and he advised us to clear an area of wasteland beyond the boundaries of our house, and build a high boundary wall of rough brick at the back, rather than the existing iron palings. He also suggested we cut down an avenue of some 16 huge mature trees along the drive. I was very sad, but followed this sensible advice. That removed the mamba problem from Devonshire House. But I continued to attract mambas on my travels around Ghana.

The second half of that first year in Ghana was to be almost entirely taken up with preparations for the State Visit of the Queen and Duke of Edinburgh in November 1999. A huge amount of work goes into organising such a visit; every move is staged and choreographed, designed for media effect. You need to know in advance just where everybody is going to be, who will move where when, and what they will say. You need to place and organise the media to best advantage. You need to stick within very strict rules as to what the Queen will or will not do. Most difficult of all, you have to agree all this with the host government.

I had been through it all quite recently, having paid a major part in the organisation of the State Visit to Poland in 1996. That had gone very well. The Poles regarded it as an important symbol that communism had been definitively finished. It was visually stunning, and at a time when the Royal Family was dogged with hostile media coverage, it had been their first unmixed positive coverage in the UK for ages. I had handled the media angles, and my stock stood very high in the Palace.

I am a republican personally; I was just doing my job. The Palace staff knew I was a republican, not least because I had turned down the offer of being made a Lieutenant of the Royal Victorian Order (LVO) after the Warsaw visit. I had earlier turned down the offer to be an Officer of the Order of the British Empire (OBE) after the first Gulf war.

Rawlings was delighted that the Queen was coming. He craved respectability and acceptance in the international community, which had been hard to come by after his violent beginnings. But he had turned his Provisional National Defence Council (PNDC) into a political party, the National Democratic Congress (NDC), and had fought elections in 1992 and 1996 against the opposition New Patriotic Party, which had an unbroken tradition running back to Nkrumah's opponent J B Danquah and his colleague Kofi Busia. There were widespread allegations of vote-rigging, violence and intimidation, and certainly in 1992 the nation was still too cowed to engage in much open debate. Even by 1999, social life was still inhibited by the fact that nobody except those close to the Rawlings would do anything that might be construed as an ostentatious display of life, while Rawlings had sustained and inflated the personality cult of Nkrumah still further (he is known as *Osagyefo,* "the conqueror".) Open discussion of the disasters Nkrumah brought upon Ghana was almost impossible. It is still difficult for many Ghanaians today, after decades of brainwashing. As Rawlings had gradually liberalised society, the increasing freedom of the media, particularly the FM radio station, was giving a great boost to democracy. But there was still much prudent self-censorship. The media was particularly reticent about investigating governmental corruption.

The NDC government was massively corrupt. There was one gratuitous example which especially annoyed me. A company called International Generics, registered in Southampton, had got loans totalling over £30 million from the Royal Bank of Scotland to construct two hotels, La Palm and Coco Palm. One was on the beach next to the Labadi Beach hotel, the other on Fourth Circular Road in Cantonments, on the site of the former Star Hotel. The loan repayments were guaranteed by the Export Credit Guarantee Department, and the time a British government agency designed to insure UK exporters against loss. In effect the British taxpayer was underwriting the export, and if the loan defaulted the British taxpayer would pay.

In fact, this is what happened, and the file crossed my desk because the British people were now paying out on defaulted payments to the Royal Bank of Scotland. So I went to look at the two hotels.

I found La Palm Hotel was some cleared land, some concrete foundations, and one eight room chalet without a roof. Coco Palm hotel didn't exist at all. In a corner of the plot, four houses had been built by International Generics. As the housing market in Accra was very strong, these had been pre-sold, so none of the loan had gone into them.

I was astonished. The papers clearly showed that all £31.5 million had been fully disbursed by the Royal Bank of Scotland, against progress and completion certificates on the construction. But in truth there was virtually no construction. How could this have happened?

The Chief Executive of International Generics was an Israeli named Leon Tamman. He was a close friend to, and a front for, Mrs Rawlings. Tamman also had an architect's firm, which had been signing off completion certificates for the non-existent work on the hotel. Almost all of the £30 million was simply stolen by Tamman and Mrs Rawlings.

The Royal Bank of Scotland had plainly failed in due diligence, having paid out on completion of two buildings, one not started and one only just started. But the Royal Bank of Scotland really couldn't give a toss, because the repayments and interest were guaranteed by the British taxpayer. Indeed I seemed to be the only one who did care.

The Rawlings had put some of their share of this looted money towards payments on their beautiful home in Dublin. I wrote reports on all this back to London, and specifically urged the Serious Fraud Office to prosecute Tamman and Mrs Rawlings. I received the reply that there was no "appetite" in London for this.

Eventually La Palm did get built, but with over $60 million of new money taken this time from SSNIT, the Ghanaian taxpayers social security and pension fund. Coco Palm never did get built, but Tamman continued to develop it as a housing estate, using another company vehicle. Tamman has since died. The loans were definitively written off by the British government as part of Gordon Brown's HIPC debt relief initiative.

That is but one example of a single scam, but it gives an insight into the way the country was looted. The unusual feature on this one was that the clever Mr Tamman found a way to cheat the British taxpayer, via Ghana.

I still find it galling that the Royal Bank of Scotland also still got their profit, again from the British taxpayer.[45]

So while the State Visit was intended as a reward to Jerry Rawlings for his conversion to democracy and capitalism, I had no illusions about Rawlings' Ghana. I was determined that we should use the Queen's visit to help ensure that Rawlings did indeed leave power in January 2001. According to the constitution, his second and final four year term as elected President expired then (if you politely ignored his previous decade as a military dictator). We should get the Queen to point him towards the exit.

Buckingham palace sent a team on an initial reconnaissance visit. It was led by an old friend of mine, Tim Hitchens, Assistant Private Secretary to the Queen, who had joined the FCO when I did. We identified the key features of the programme, which should centre around an address to Parliament. A walkabout might be difficult; Clinton had been almost crushed in Accra by an over-friendly crowd in a situation which got out of control.

A school visit to highlight DFID's work would provide the meet the people photo op, otherwise a drive past for the larger crowds. Key questions were identified as whether the Queen should visit Kumasi to meet Ghana's most important traditional ruler, the Asantehene, and how she should meet the leader of the opposition, John Kufuor. Rawlings was likely to be opposed to both.

The recce visit went very well, and I held a reception for the team before they flew back to London. Several Ghanaian ministers came, and it ended in a very relaxed evening. Tim Hitchens commented that it was the first time he had ever heard Queen and Supertramp at an official function before. It turned out that we had very similar musical tastes.

Planning then took place at quite high intensity for several months. There were regular meetings with the Ghanaian government team tasked to organise the visit, headed by head of their diplomatic service Anand Cato, now Ghanaian High Commissioner to the United Kingdom. We then had to visit together all the proposed venues, and walk through the proposed routes, order of events, seating plans etc.

45Only recently have Ghanaians felt able to talk about these things. See, for example, *http://www.modernghana.com/news/97469/1/JAK-writes-off-JJs-pals-119m-debt*

From the very first meeting between the two sides, held in a committee room at the International Conference Centre, it soon became obvious that we had a real problem with Ian Mackley. The High Commissioner had been very high-handed and abrupt with the visiting team from Buckingham Palace, so much so that Tim Hitchens had asked me what was wrong. I said it was just his manner. But there was more to it than that.

In the planning meetings, the set-up did not help the atmosphere. There were two lines of desks, facing each other. The British sat on one side and the Ghanaians on the other, facing each other across a wide divide. The whole dynamic was one of confrontation.

I have sat through some toe-curling meetings before, but that first joint State visit planning meeting in Accra was the worst. It started in friendly enough fashion, with greetings on each side. Then Anand Cato suggested we start with a quick run-through of the programme, from start to finish.

"OK, now will the Queen be arriving by British Airways or by private jet?" asked Anand.

"She will be on one of the VC10s of the Royal Flight" said Ian.

"Right, that's better. The plane can pull up to the stand closest to the VIP lounge. We will have the convoy of vehicles ready on the tarmac. The stairs will be put to the door, and then the chief of protocol will go up the stairs to escort the Queen and her party down the stairs, where there will be a small reception party..."

"No, hang on there" interjected Ian Mackley, "I will go up the stairs before the chief of protocol."

"Well, it is customary for the Ambassador or High Commissioner to be in the receiving line at the bottom of the aircraft steps."

"Well, I can tell you for sure that the first person the Queen will want to see when she arrives in the country will be her High Commissioner."

"Well, I suppose you can accompany the chief up the steps if you wish..."

"And my wife."

"Pardon?"

"My wife Sarah. She must accompany me up the steps to meet the Queen."

"Look, it really isn't practical to have that many people going on to an already crowded plane where people are preparing to get off..."

"I am sorry, but I must insist that Sarah accompanies me up the stairs and on to the plane."

"But couldn't she wait at the bottom of the steps?"

"Absolutely not. How could she stand there without me?"

"OK, well can we then mark down the question of greeting on the plane as an unresolved issue for the next meeting?"

"Alright, but our side insists that my wife..."

"Yes, quite. Now at the bottom of the steps Her Majesty will be greeted by the delegated minister, and presented with flowers by children."

"Please make sure we are consulted on the choice of children."

"If you wish. There will be national anthems, but I suggest no formal inspection of the Guard of Honour? Then traditional priests will briefly make ritual oblations, pouring spirits on the ground. The Queen will briefly enter the VIP lounge to take a drink."

"That's a waste of time. Let's get them straight into the convoy and off."

"But High Commissioner, we have to welcome a visitor with a drink. It is an essential part of our tradition. It will only be very brief."

"You can do what you like, but she's not entering the VIP lounge. Waste of time."

"Let's mark that down as another issue to be resolved. Now then, first journey..."

The meeting went on for hours and hours, becoming increasingly ill-tempered. When we eventually got to the plans for the State Banquet, it all went spectacularly pear-shaped as it had been threatening to do.

"Now we propose a top table of eight. There will be the President and Mrs Rawlings, Her Majesty and the Duke of Edinburgh, The Vice President and Mrs Mills, and Mr and Mrs Robin Cook."

Ian positively went purple. You could see a vein throbbing at the top left of his forehead. He spoke as though short of breath.

"That is not acceptable. Sarah and I must be at the top table".

"With respect, High Commissioner, there are a great many Ghanaians who will feel they should be at the top table. As we are in Ghana, we feel we are being hospitable in offering equal numbers of British and Ghanaians at the top table. But we also think the best plan is to keep the top table small and exclusive."

"By all means keep it small," said Ian, "but as High Commissioner I must be on it."

"So what do you suggest?" asked Anand

"Robin Cook" said Ian "He doesn't need to be on the top table."

I couldn't believe what I was hearing. Neither could Anand.

"I don't think you are being serious, High Commissioner" he said.

"I am entirely serious" said Ian. "I outrank Robin Cook. I am the personal representative of a Head of State. Robin Cook only represents the government."

I decided the man had taken leave of his senses. I wondered at what stage can you declare your commanding officer mad and take over, like on *The Cain Mutiny*? Anand was obviously thinking much the same.

"Perhaps I might suggest you seek instruction from headquarters on that one?" he asked. "Anyway, can we note that down as another outstanding item, and move on to..."

I don't know whether Ian secretly realised he had overstepped the mark, but he didn't come to another planning meeting after that, leaving them to me and the very competent Second Secretary Mike Nithavrianakis.

The most difficult question of all was that of meeting the opposition. Eventually we got the agreement of Buckingham Palace and the FCO to say that, if the Queen were prevented from meeting the opposition, she wouldn't come. But still the most we could get from Rawlings was that the leader of the opposition could be included in a reception for several hundred people at the International Conference Centre.

I had by now made good personal friends with several Ghanaian politicians. Among those who I could have a social drink with any time were, on the government side John Mahama, Minister of Information and Moses Asaga, Deputy Finance Minister, and on the opposition side John Kufuor, leader of the opposition, his colleagues Hackman Owusu-Agyemang, Shadow Foreign Minister, and Nana Akuffo-Addo, Shadow Attorney General. In the International Conference Centre the precise route the

Queen would take around the crowd was very carefully planned, so I was able to brief John Kufuor exactly where to stand to meet her, and brief the Queen to be sure to stop and chat with him. As he was the tallest man in the crowd, this was all not too difficult.

Once the Queen arrived and the visit started, everything happened in a three day blur of intense activity. Vast crowds turned out, and the Palace staff soon calmed down as they realised that the Queen could expect an uncomplicated and old fashioned reverence from the teeming crowds who were turning out to see "Our Mama".

The durbar of chiefs in front of Parliament House was a riot of colour and noise. One by one the great chiefs came past, carried on their palanquins, preceded by their entourage, drummers banging away ferociously and the chiefs, laden down with gold necklaces and bangles, struggled to perform their energetic seated dances. Many of the hefty dancing women wore the cloth that had been created for the occasion, with a picture of the Queen jiggling about on one large breast in partnership with Jerry Rawlings jiving on the other, the same pairing being also displayed on the buttocks.

After the last of the chiefs went through, the tens of thousands of spectators started to mill everywhere and we had to race for the Royal convoy to get out through the crowds. Robin Cook had stopped to give an ad hoc interview to an extremely pretty South African television reporter. Mike Nithavrianakis tried to hurry him along but got a fierce glare for his pains. Eventually everyone was in their cars but Cook; the Ghanaian outriders were itching to start as the crowds ahead and around got ever denser. But where was Cook? We delayed, with the Queen sitting in her car for two or three minutes, but still there was no sign of the Secretary of State or his staff getting into their vehicle. Eventually the outriders swept off; the crowds closed in behind and we had abandoned our dilettante Foreign Secretary. Having lost the protection of the convoy and being caught up in the crowds and traffic, it took him an hour to catch up.[46]

---

46 Gaynor Cook was with him on this trip. She was very pleasant and a bit shy, and I remember little more about her on this visit. When I saw Cook hang back to give the interview, for example, I do not recall her being with him.

Cook was an enigma. I had already experienced his famous lack of both punctuality and consideration when kept waiting to see him over the Sandline Affair. His behaviour now seemed to combine an attractive contempt for protocol with a goat-like tendency – would he have fallen behind to give a very bland interview to a male South African reporter? He was also breaking the tradition that the Foreign Secretary does not make media comments when accompanying the Queen.

When we returned to the Labadi Beach Hotel, there was to be further evidence of Cook's view that the World revolved around him. He was interviewing FCO staff for the position of his new Private Secretary. Astonishingly, he had decided that it would best suit his itinerary to hold these interviews in Accra rather than London. One candidate, Ros Marsden, had an extremely busy job as Head of United Nations Department. Yet she had to give up three days work to fly to be interviewed in Accra, when her office was just round the corner from his in London. Other candidates from posts around the World had difficult journeys to complete to get to Accra at all. I thought this rather outrageous of Cook, and was surprised nobody else seemed much concerned.

The port town of Tema, linked to Accra by fifteen miles of motorway and fast becoming part of a single extensive metropolis, sits firmly on the Greenwich Meridian. As far as land goes, Tema is the centre of the Earth, being the closest dry spot to the junction of the Equator and the Greenwich Meridian. You can travel South from Tema over 12,000 miles across sea until you hit the Antarctic.

There was in 1999 a particular vogue for linking the Greenwich Meridian with the Millennium. This was because of the role of the meridian in determining not just longitude but time. Of course, the two are inextricably linked with time initially used to calculate longitude. That is why Greenwich hosted both the Naval Academy and the Royal Observatory. The fascination with all this had several manifestations. There was a BBC documentary travelogue down the Greenwich meridian. There was a best-selling book about the invention of naval chronometers, *Longitude* by Dava Sobel, which I read and was as interesting as a book about making clocks can be. There were a number of aid projects down the meridian, including by War Child and Comic Relief. Tema and Greenwich became twin towns. And there was the visit of the Duke of Edinburgh to Tema.

I think this was the idea of my very good friend John Carmichael, who was involved in charity work on several of the meridian projects. It was thought particularly appropriate as one of the Duke of Edinburgh's titles is Earl of Greenwich – though the man has so many titles you could come up with some connection to pretty well anywhere. We could make it a new game, like six degrees of separation. Connect your home town to the Duke of Edinburgh.

Anyway, Tim Hitchens had warned me that the Duke was very much averse to just looking at things without any useful purpose. As we stood looking at the strip of brass laid in a churchyard which marks the line of the meridian, he turned to me and said:

"A line in the ground, eh? Very nice."

But we moved on to see a computer centre that had been set up by a charity to give local people experience of IT and the internet (providing both electricity and phone lines were working, which thank goodness they were today) and the Duke visibly cheered up. He was much happier talking to the instructors and students, and then when we went on to a primary school that had received books from DFID he was positively beaming. The genuinely warm reception everywhere, with happy gaggles of people of all ages cheerfully waving their little plastic union jacks, would have charmed anybody. We returned to Accra via the coast road and I was able to point out the work of the Ghanaian coffin makers, with coffins shaped and painted as tractors, beer bottles, guitars, desks, cars and even a packet of condoms. The Prince laughed heartily, and we arrived at the Parliament building in high good spirits.

There he was first shown to a committee room where he was introduced to senior MPs of all parties.

"How many Members of Parliament do you have?" he asked.

"Two hundred" came the answer.

"That's about the right number," opined the Prince, "We have six hundred and fifty MPs, and most of them are a complete bloody waste of time."

The irony was that there was no British journalist present to hear this, as they had all thought a meeting between Prince Philip and Ghanaian parliamentarians would be too boring. There were Ghanaian reporters present, but the exchange didn't particularly interest them. So a front page tabloid remark, with which the accompanying photo could have made a paparazzi a lot of money, went completely unreported.

On a State Visit, the media cannot each be at every occasion, as security controls mean they have to be prepositioned rather than milling about while the event goes ahead. So by agreement, those reporters and photographers accredited to the visit share or pool their photos and copy. At each event there is a stand, or pool. Some events may have more than one pool to give different angles. Each journalist can probably make five or six pools in the course of the visit, leapfrogging ahead of the royal progress. But everyone gets access to material from all the pools. The FCO lays on the transport to keep things under control. Organising the pool positions ahead of the event with the host country, and then herding and policing the often pushy media in them, is a major organisational task. Mike Nithavrianakis had carried it off with style and only the occasional failure of humour. But he had found no takers for Prince Philip in parliament, which proved to be fortunate for us.

I should say that I found Prince Philip entirely pleasant while spending most of this day with him. I am against the monarchy, but it was not created by the Queen or Prince Philip. Just as Colonel Isaac of the RUF was a victim of the circumstances into which he was born, so are they.

Had I been born into a life of great privilege, I would probably have turned out a much more horrible person than they are.

Prince Philip then joined the Queen in the parliamentary chamber. Her address to parliament was to be the focal point of the visit. I had contributed to the drafting of her speech, and put a lot of work into it.

The speech was only six minutes long (she never speaks longer than that, except at the State Opening of Parliament. Her staff made plain that six minutes was an absolute maximum.) It contained much of the usual guff about the history of our nations and the importance of a new future based upon partnership. But then she addressed Rawlings directly, praising his achievements in bringing Ghana on to the path of democracy and economic stability. The government benches in parliament provided an undercurrent of parliamentary "hear hears".

But there was to be a sting in the tale:

"Next, year, Mr President," the Queen intoned, "You will step down after two terms in office in accordance with your constitution."

The opposition benches went wild. The Queen went on to wish for peaceful elections and further progress, but it was drowned out by the cries of "hear hear" and swishing of order papers from the benches, and loud cheers from the public gallery. There were mooted cries of "No" from the government side of the chamber. I had drafted that phrase, and it had a much greater effect than I possibly hoped for, although I did mean it to drive home the message exactly as it was taken.

For a moment the Queen stopped. She looked in bewilderment and concern at the hullabaloo all around her. The Queen has no experience of speaking to anything other than a hushed, respectful silence. But, apart from some grim faces on the government benches, it was a joyful hullaba-loo and she ploughed on the short distance to the end of her speech.

Once we got back to the Labadi Beach Hotel, Robin Cook was com-pletely furious. He stormed into the makeshift private office, set up in two hotel rooms.

"It's a disaster. Who the Hell drafted that?"

"Err, I did, Secretary of State" I said.

"Is that you, Mr Murray! I might have guessed! Who the Hell ap-proved it."

"You did."

"I most certainly did not!"

"Yes you did, Secretary of State. You agreed the final draft last night."

His Private Secretary had to dig out the copy of the draft he had signed off. He calmed down a little, and was placated further when the Queen's robust press secretary, Geoff Crawford, said that he took the view that it was a good thing for the Queen to be seen to be standing up for demo-cracy. It could only look good in the UK press. He proved to be right.

The State Banquet was a rather dull affair. Ian Mackley's great battle to be on the top table proved rather nugatory as, in very Ghanaian fashion, nobody stayed in their seat very long and people were wandering all over the shop. There were a large number of empty seats as, faced with an invitation to dinner at 7.30pm, many Ghanaians followed their customary practice and wandered along an hour or so late, only to find they would not be admitted. This caused a huge amount of angst and aggravation, from which those of us inside were fortunately sheltered.

Mrs Rawlings had chosen a well known Accra nightclub owner named Chester to be the compère for the occasion. His bar is a relaxed spot in a small courtyard that features good jazz and highlife music, and prostitutes dressed as Tina Turner. It was a second home for the officers of the British Military Advisory and Training Team (BMATT). Chester himself was friendly and amusing, but amusing in a Julian Clary meets Kenneth Williams meets Liberace sort of way. Chester says he is not gay, (regrettably homosexuality is illegal in Ghana) but his presentation is undeniably ultra camp. It is hard to think of a weirder choice to chair a state banquet, but Chester was a particular pet of Mrs Rawlings.

Chester was stood on the platform next to the Queen, gushing about how honoured he was. His speech was actually very witty, but the delivery was – well, Chester. I turned to Prince Philip and remarked:

"You know, I don't think I've ever seen two Queens together before."

To give credit to Chester, I gather he has been telling the story ever since.

High camp was to be a theme of that evening.

Fiona and I accompanied the Royal party back to the Labadi Beach Hotel to say goodnight, after which Fiona returned home to Devonshire House while I remained for a debriefing on the day and review of the plans for tomorrow. By the time we had finished all that it was still only 11pm and I retired to the bar of the Labadi Beach with the Royal Household. The senior staff – Tim and Geoff – withdrew as is the custom to allow the butlers, footmen, hairdressers and others to let off steam.

The party appeared, to a man, to be gay. Not just gay but outrageously camp. The Labadi Beach, with its fans whirring under polished dark wood ceilings, its panelled bar, displays of orchids, attentive uniformed staff and glossy grand piano – has the aura of a bygone colonial age, like something from Kenya's Happy Valley in the 1930s. You expect to see Noel Coward emerge in his smoking jacket and sit down at the piano, smoking through a mother of pearl cigarette holder. It is exactly the right setting for a gay romp, and that is exactly what developed after a few of the Labadi Beach's wonderful tropical cocktails.

We had taken the entire hotel for the Royal party, except that we had allowed the British Airways crew to stay there as always. Now three of their cabin stewards, with two Royal footmen and the Queen's hairdresser, were grouped around the grand singing Cabaret with even more gusto than Liza. Other staff were smooching at the bar. All this had developed within half an hour in a really magical and celebratory atmosphere that seemed to spring from nothing. I was seated on a comfortable sofa, and across from me in an armchair was the one member of the Household who seemed out of place. The Duke of Edinburgh's valet looked to be in his sixties, a grizzled old NCO with tufts of hair either side of a bald pate, a boxer's nose and tattoos on his arms. He was smoking roll-ups.

He was a nice old boy and we had been struggling to hold a conversation about Ghana over the din, when two blokes chasing each other ran up to the settee on which I was sitting. One, pretending to be caught, draped himself over the end and said "You've caught me, you beast!"

I turned back to the old warrior and asked:

"Don't you find all this a bit strange sometimes?"

He lent forward and put his hand on my bare knee below my kilt:

"Listen, ducks. I was in the Navy for thirty years."

So I made my excuses and left, as the News of the World journalists used to put it. I think he was probably joking, but there are some things that are too weird even for me, and the lower reaches of the Royal household are one of them. I have heard it suggested that such posts have been filled by gays for centuries, just as harems were staffed by eunuchs, to avoid the danger of a Queen being impregnated. Recently I have been most amused by news items regarding the death of the Queen Mother's long-standing footman, who the newsreaders have been informing us was fondly known as "Backstairs Billy". They manage to say this without giving the slightest hint that they know it is a double entendre.

The incident in parliament had made the Rawlings government even more annoyed about the proposed handshake in the International Conference Centre reception between the Queen and John Kufuor. My own relationship with Ian Mackley had also deteriorated still further as a result of the Royal Visit. I had the advantage that I already knew from previous jobs the palace officials and Robin Cook's officials, and of course Robin Cook himself, not to mention the Queen and Duke of Edinburgh. All in all, I suspect that Ian felt that I was getting well above myself. As the party formed up to walk around the reception in the International Conference Centre, Ian came up to me and grabbed my arm rather fiercely.

"You, just stay with the Queen's bodyguards" he said.

I did not mind at all, and attached myself to another Ian, the head of the Queen's close protection team. I already knew Ian also. Ian set off towards the hall and started ensuring a path was clear for the Queen, I alongside him as ordered. Suddenly I heard Sarah Mackley positively squeal from somewhere behind me:

"My God, he's ahead of the Queen! Now Craig's ahead of the Queen."

If I could hear it, at least forty other people could. I managed to make myself as invisible as possible, and still to accomplish the introduction to John Kufuor. The government newspaper the Daily Graphic was to claim indignantly that I had introduced John Kufuor as "The next President of Ghana." Had I done so, I would have been in the event correct in my prediction, but in fact I introduced him as "The opposition Presidential candidate".

As always, the Queen's last engagement on the State Visit was to say farewell to all the staff who had helped. She gives out gifts, and confers membership of the Royal Victorian Order on those deemed to merit it. Only once in the Queen's long reign had she ever been on a state visit and not created our Ambassador or High Commissioner a Knight Commander of the Royal Victorian Order – that is to say, knighted him. Ian and Sarah were to become Sir Ian and Lady Sarah. This seemed to me to mean the world to them.

The day before, Tim Hitchens had turned to me as we were travelling in the car:

"Craig, I take it your views on honours have not changed."

"No, Tim, I still don't want any."

"Good, you see that makes it a bit easier, actually. You see, the thing is, we're trying to cut down a bit on giving out routine honours. The government wants a more meritocratic honours system. We need to start somewhere. So, in short, Ian Mackley is not going to get his K."

I was stunned.

Tim continued: "And as well, you see, it hasn't exactly escaped our attention that he has ...issues with the Ghanaians, and some of his attitudes didn't exactly help the visit. Anyway, if you were to want your CVO, then that would be more difficult. Ian Mackley is going to have one of those. So that will be alright."

No, it won't be alright, I thought. You'll kill the poor old bastard. For God's sake, everyone will know.

I wondered when the decision had been taken. The kneeling stool and the ceremonial sword had definitely been unloaded from the plane and taken to the hotel: that was one of the things I had checked off. When had that decision been reached?

We were lined up in reverse order of seniority to go in and see the Queen and Prince Philip. I queued behind the Defence Attaché, with Ian and Sarah just behind me. She was entering as well – nobody else's wife was – because she was expecting to become Lady Mackley. Tim was going to tell them quickly after I had entered, while they would be alone still waiting to go in. You may not believe me, but I felt completely gutted for them. It was the very fact they were so status obsessed that made it so cruel. I was thinking about what Tim was saying to them and how they would react. It seemed terribly cruel that they had not been warned until the very moment before they were due to meet the Queen. I was so worried for them that I really had less than half my mind on exchanging pleasantries with the Queen, who was very pleasant, as always.

If you refused honours, as I always did, you got compensated by getting a slightly better present. In Warsaw I was given a silver Armada dish, which is useful for keeping your Armada in. In Accra I was given a small piece of furniture made with exquisite craftsmanship by Viscount Linley. Shelving my doubts about the patronage aspect of that (should the Queen be purchasing with public money official gifts made by her cousin?) I staggered out holding rather a large red box, leaving through the opposite side of the room to that I had entered. Outside the door I joined the happy throng of people clutching their presents and minor medals. Mike Nithavrianakis and Brian Cope were Ian Mackley's friends, and they were waiting eagerly for him.

"Here's Craig" said Mike, "Now it's only Sir Ian and Lady Sarah!"

"No, it's not, Mike", I said, "He's not getting a K"

"What! You're kidding!"

It had suddenly fallen very silent.

"Ian's not getting a K, he's only getting a CVO."

"Oh, that's terrible."

We waited now in silence. Very quickly the door opened again, and the Mackleys came out, Ian with a frozen grin, Sarah a hysterical one beneath the white large-brimmed hat that suddenly looked so ridiculous. There was a smattering of applause, and Sarah fell to hugging everyone, even me. We all congratulated Ian on his CVO, and nobody ever mentioned that there had been any possibility of a knighthood, then or ever.

Personally I don't understand why anyone accepts honours, when there is so much more cachet in turning them down.

9

Democracy In Africa

One of the great things about our time in Ghana was the constant stream of visitors. Peter Hain, Robin Cook's new deputy minister for Africa, was one of the earlier ones. I was very pleased about this – Peter Hain's anti-apartheid campaigns had aroused the first stirrings of political consciousness in me, and influenced my decision to join the Liberal party in 1973, age 14. By the time I made my way on to the national executive of the Young Liberals, Hain was just about leaving, but we overlapped slightly.

We were giving a large afternoon reception for him to meet civil society groups. His Private office had sent us a long list of dietary requirements. He was a strict vegetarian who required a gluten free diet and was allergic to nuts. Fiona and Gloria had some difficulty in coming up with things that he could eat. We had been in meetings all day and arrived a little late for the reception, which was in full swing. The brightly dressed Ghanaian guests were lining up at the rows of barbecues, and sitting contentedly around circular tables across the lawn. A live band was playing. Gloria was hovering with her specially prepared food for Hain. He ignored this and strode up to a barbecue, picked up a skewer of meat, and bit into it. "Great" he said, grinning happily, then disappeared into a backslapping crowd. He remains very popular in Ghana from the anti-apartheid years.

The British Council had an excellent and energetic Director in Accra, James Peters. He had established a football programme for street children. They signed up to receive professional football coaching, and in return they guaranteed to stay off drugs and out of crime, and do a certain amount of community work every week. The scheme had been a great

140

success, and I had been very active in finding money to expand it. War Child were involved through my friend John Carmichael.

Peter Hain was a very good football player, as I remembered from games in my youth. He had professional trials.[47] So I had suggested to London he might like to take part in a charity football game between the children from the community football scheme and the High Commission. I conceived it as a fun event for which we could get sponsorship for the project from British companies. Peter Hain readily agreed.

We changed at Devonshire House, as the game was being held on one of the project's pitches in the shanty district of Nima, and there were no changing facilities. Arriving there, the first problem was the pitch. Although carefully cleared of refuse and approximately level, it consisted of red laterite without a single blade of grass. It was, quite literally, rock hard. It was studs off and trainers on, but a fine covering of red dust still made it very skiddy. The second problem was the opposition. Rather than the kids from the project, lined up against us were super-fit professionals, some of them on the fringes of Ghana's world class national squad.

Peter grinned at me. "This should be fun". I smiled nervously back. The last time I had seen Peter in a football game, I was helping to carry him off it. At the Young Liberal national conference of 1976 in Great Yarmouth we had played a game there on the lees. I was playing in defence against Peter, who was making an idiot of me, going past me at will. So I had kneed him in the bollocks, rather harder than I intended.

Now in Nima Peter and I were playing up front, and we spent the first five minutes chasing back, lungs bursting in the heat. I was going through that barrier you have to cross before you get your second wind. But I never got there.

Someone played a hopeful long punt out of defence. I got in front of and across my huge defender, trying to glance the ball through for Peter to run on to. But the defender was much bigger quicker and younger than I, and he came right though me. I went down heavily, and stuck out my right hand to break my fall. It was extended rigidly as it hit the rock

---

47Frank Keating, *Caught By Keating* ,p 92, Andre Deutsch, London, 1979

hard ground, and just at that moment the big defender landed across my arm.

I felt stunned as I picked myself up, but not in great immediate pain. I could tell something was very wrong. I could not move my left arm, and my left hand seemed to be hanging below the level of my left knee. Something seemed to be pushing on my shoulder and chest. I peeked inside my football shirt, and was stunned to see a bone sticking out of the left of my chest, above the nipple, not piercing the skin but showing white through it. This was definitely not good.

I stood in puzzlement. Play was carrying on, and I lifted my right arm for help, then involuntarily fell down again. This time it was Peter Hain's turn to help carry me off the field.

I travelled in an Embassy Landrover to the Trust hospital, Fiona with me. By now the pain had really started, and it was indescribable. Doctors will tell you that a dislocated arm is about as painful as anything can be, because of the great bundles of nerves travelling through the shoulders. It was excruciating in the most literal sense. It was the dislocation of the shoulders that made crucifixion such a terrible death. It has been used as torture forever – the drawn in hung, drawn and quartered, and the rack, were both to dislocate the arms. There is no worse pain, and I was suffering now. Supporting the arm, or not supporting the arm, both brought simply slightly different qualities of extreme agony. Every bump in the road was terrible to me.

By the time I reached the hospital I was literally out of my mind. I did not, for example, know who Fiona was. I was lain down on a trolley, while a surgeon was called. Although I learned later that Fiona had urged, begged, screamed, threatened and cried, the hospital had refused to give me any pain relief stronger than paracetamol until the surgeon arrived. I lay for four hours in the most appalling agony. I wish I could tell you that I became accustomed to the pain, but I did not, nor did I lose consciousness. The four hours seemed to me to last four months. If you were now to tell me I had to go through that again, or to surrender every single thing I own, including my clothes, books and the laptop I am now writing on, I would give you everything without a second's hesitation.

Eventually the surgeon did arrive, and I was thankfully put under. I awoke in a private room, in pretty well no pain. The only good thing about a dislocated shoulder is that, pretty well as soon as it gets put back, it stops hurting. But I discovered that I had my left arm attached firmly to my chest, simply taped there with what looked like several rolls of sticky tape wrapped right around me. It was to stay completely immobile like this for eight weeks, which was very inconvenient, especially as I am left handed. I had to invest in a number of floaty kaftans I could wear over my strapped arm.

There was one long term consequence. While having no sporting talent, I was always an enthusiastic player. My shoulder never did recover, and I have never been able to play active sport again. I had already decided I would be giving up football, and because of the weakness of the shoulder I have not been able to take up tennis or golf - Fiona had just bought me the clubs. When the accident happened I weighed 73kg. Within four months, I was 80kg and today am 88kg. I view that football game as the start of middle age!

We were able further to boost the community football project with another charity game, this time starring Bobby Charlton. He had come to Ghana seeking support for England's bid to host the 2006 World Cup. I have to say that he was still an astounding player at age 60 – his fitness levels and robustness were astonishing, and it was extremely good of him to get on the pitch for an obscure charitable cause. Large crowds turned up.

That having been said, I found Charlton very disappointing. He was the opposite of his gentlemanly image, being entirely self-centred and generally ratty and demanding throughout his time in Ghana. He was one of those heroes you wish you hadn't met, like Walesa.

On the other side of the equation, Roger Moore came out as a goodwill ambassador for UNICEF. Fiona and I hosted a small dinner party for him. He was charming and suave, just as you would expect, with a fund of brilliant stories beginning with lines like "One day Frank, Dean, Tony and I decided to play a trick on Marilyn..." But while he played the role of Roger Moore to perfection, there was much more to him than that. He was genuinely very well briefed about children's issues in Ghana, and was prepared not just to do the PR stuff, but to get his hands dirty helping out in refugee camps without a camera in sight. I was impressed by Roger Moore.

I was less impressed by Jamie Theakston. The BBC were filming an episode of *The Really Wild Show* in Ghana, looking at the endangered green turtle population near Ada. I had been very much looking forward to meeting Michaela Strachan, and was slightly disappointed to be getting Jamie Theakston instead. The Ghana Wildlife Society was yet another body I had been working closely with, so we did a large party for them and other conservation and environmental groups. We had music and dancing, and a great party atmosphere. A group of young volunteers had accompanied the BBC team, to help the newly born turtles to reach the ocean. But one poor girl became hysterical. A schoolteacher in her mid-twenties, her brown hair was dishevelled and streams of mascara had spread down her flushed pink cheeks. I took her off to wash herself in the guest wing, and sent someone to look for Fiona.

Her story was that Jamie Theakston had been sleeping with her on this trip, and that he had told he he was in love with her and wanted a continuing relationship. But now, on this last evening, he had told her before the party that he was moving on and did not want to see her again. The poor girl was totally distraught. Meantime, Jamie Theakston sat surrounded by young women, enjoying the adulation, and showing not the slightest concern for the girl he had just dumped and the state she was in. Not the most pleasant of people.

Much of my work focused on development and our assistance to the Ghanaian economy. This was in the doldrums because its two leading export commodities, cocoa and gold, were suffering from low export prices on World markets. Gold in particular was at an all time low in terms of the real dollar price. It had been hovering at around US$280 an ounce for a couple of years, and was there at the start of 1999. But by the summer of 1999 it had slipped down to just under US$250, and many gold mines could no longer produce profitably. But then suddenly at the end of September it leapt up to $300, and reached $325 before settling back to around $290 at the end of the year.

Obviously this volatility around low prices would be a problem for any gold mining company. But Ashanti Gold, the largest company in Ghana, got itself into trouble in ways that opened my eyes to much of the craziness of modern world markets, with their reliance on futures and derivatives trading, or betting as you and I might call it. It also told me a great deal about Rawlings and his government.

Ashanti Gold was the third biggest gold mining company in Africa and about the ninth in the World. It was traded on the London Stock Exchange. At Obuasi it had the third largest hole in the ground in the World in the shape of its open cast mine. But most of its remaining reserves in Ghana were now in deep mines, and becoming unprofitable at these very low prices. Ashanti's big hope for the future was a very valuable resource at Geita, in Tanzania, but that was at a development stage where money was still being pumped in, rather than taken out. So Ashanti was vulnerable in 1999.

Despite this, in the first half of that year, Ashanti was doing rather well, because of its hedge book. That is precisely the same as "Hedging your bets". What Ashanti was doing was buying financial instruments that amounted to a bet that the price of gold was going to fall. In effect, the more the gold price fell, the more money they made on their hedge book.

That may sound strange, but it is not stupid. If you are producing gold and the price drops, to offset your losses would be described by those doing it as insurance against a price fall, rather than a bet.

But Ashanti went at it so enthusiastically that they stood to make more money if the price of gold fell, than if it increased. When you think about it, that is not good for a gold mine. They might as well have given up the mining completely and just have taken the available cash to a casino.

Anyway, all went well until the autumn of 1999 when there was a sudden 20% jump in the gold price. Ashanti started losing their bets – in fact they lost $450 million worth of bets in three months. The share price plummeted and the company – which had already taken out large loans in the City of London to finance the Geita development – could no longer service its debt.

Ashanti sought to restructure its debt – which means put off payment – and to look for new loans. It also negotiated to reduce the payments on its hedge book, which means welsh on its bets. Then, at the end of January 2000, Rawlings intervened to try to drive Ashanti Gold into bankruptcy.

Ashanti had originally been part of the Lonrho group, but had been nationalised by a previous Ghanaian government. In his IMF phase, Rawlings had re privatised it, but with the Government of Ghana retaining a "Golden Share", which gave it a veto on the board.

In privatising Ashanti, Rawlings had not expected it would actually start behaving like a private company. Ghana still had many parastatal companies, and these all loyally, if often unofficially, contributed funds to the Rawlings family, to Rawlings' NDC party, or to its many offshoots such as the ubiquitous "31 December Women's Movement", which was run by Mrs Rawlings and used by her as a front to buy up many companies. Equally, the apparatus of the state had been used to make it very difficult for anyone to run their business who did not support and contribute to Rawlings. So the idea that the country's biggest company would stop paying over cash was highly antithetical to the Rawlings.[48]

The Chief Executive of Ashanti was Sam Jonah, a very tough old mining professional. The Rawlings had demanded a million dollars from him, ostensibly for election purposes. Sam had refused. Mrs Rawlings was now determined to regain control of Ashanti from Sam, and the financial crisis in the company seemed to provide the perfect opportunity. The long-term chairman of Ashanti, Kwame Peprah, was now Rawlings' Finance Minister. Rawlings obliged him to resign from Ashanti, as a company going bankrupt with the Finance Minister as Chairman doesn't look good. On 10 February 2000 the Ghanaian government then issued a strong statement attacking the board of Ashanti in no uncertain terms and making plain its refusal to agree to restructuring.

I was picking up from a wide variety of my contacts that Mrs Rawlings' view was that the gold reserves were in Ghana and would remain in Ghana. To drive Ashanti bankrupt would not lose the gold, only liberate it from interests hostile to the Rawlings. They could then bring Ashanti's gold reserves back under control, either through renationalisation or a more compliant private company.

48Taylor, AA, *Sam Jonah and the Remaking of Ashanti p182*

Ashanti was a major company. London banks and London investors stood to lose a great deal of money it if went under. At this juncture I received a phone call from Sir Leon Britten. He was leading the loan renegotiation efforts with Ashanti on behalf of the consortium of British banks. He was somewhat baffled by the very negative signals the government of Ghana was sending out about Ashanti. Surely a government could not be wilfully undermining the largest company in the country? I explained the political background to him, and advised him not to panic. We would have to bring the government round.

I next invited Sam Jonah round to Devonshire House for tea. I like Sam immensely. We discussed recovery plans, debt restructuring and the future of the Geita project in Tanzania. There was pressure on Ashanti to sell its interest in Geita to redeem some debt, but that would be to throw away enormous potential for the future. I then telephoned Sir Leon again and outlined Sam's plans. We also discussed widening the board of Ashanti with strong non-executive directors with good international political connections, and the need to seek support from the IMF in pressing Rawlings. Then came the difficult bit.

I called on President Rawlings at the castle, finding him moody and subdued. He launched a tirade against Ashanti's management folly of over-hedging. I cheered him up by agreeing with him that futures trading and the extent of speculative financial flows had become a danger to the real economy everywhere. But I said that the UK would take it very badly if the government of Ghana blocked Ashanti's restructuring and sent it into bankruptcy. A lot of British money was at stake, both loan and investment. Certainly the international community would react very badly if Ashanti were nationalised. We may have to reconsider DFID's aid to Ghana.

I had absolutely no authority to say the last, and DFID would have been horrified. But something worked, because in the next few days we got the restructuring package together without encountering a government veto. Ashanti recovered, and its share price more than doubled within a year. It went on to merge with Anglo Gold, with Sam Jonah becoming President of Anglo Ashanti.

I like Sam very much. He started underground in mining, as a shovel boy, and went on to a British university education as a mining engineer, before becoming arguably Africa's most successful legitimate business-man. He remains down to earth, and enjoys nothing better than drinking whisky or going fishing, both of which I have done with him.

Before leaving Accra I nominated Sam for a knighthood. I wanted to underline the fact that Africans are perfectly able to operate at the very highest levels of the corporate world, and that African businesses can be world class. On the rare occasions Africans are honoured in the West, it is usually in a context that portrays Africa as a basket case, concerned with famine, aid or political disaster. Sam for me personifies what Africans can be, and he did it by his own endeavours.

The story of his knighthood is an example of how difficult it is for Africans to win recognition. The first proposal I drafted was rejected by the Downing Street honours committee on the grounds they had never heard of him! I had to redo it, with citations from Lynda Chalker and the Financial Times.

Brian Page, our Consul, was one of several staff at our High Commission whose quiet competence and pleasant attitude made my life more enjoyable. He came in to see me one day looking particularly unhappy.

"James has been arrested" he said. James Peters, the excellent British Council Director, was gay. Homosexuality is illegal in Ghana, and James had been reported to the police by somebody who had tried to blackmail him. James was now in a cell at Asylum Down police station. I prepared to go there, and went to tell Ian Mackley what was happening. I found Ian very truculent:

"It's up to James to follow the law of the land", he said, "If he's broken it, he'll have to follow the consequences. I don't want to get in an argument with the government of Ghana about foolish behaviour."

I was shocked by Ian's lack of empathy, and the fact that he seemed to have no instinct to support a colleague. I suggested that the best thing we could do is squash the problem before it became a real issue.

A paradox of Ghana is that it is a kind and friendly society, and on a day to day basis homosexuality is tolerated. But fundamentalist Christianity has such a grip on the country that when confronted with the question of whether gays should be jailed, most Ghanaians would sadly say yes. Society works by looking the other way and never getting confronted with the question. If it became a high profile question – if the media got hold of the issue – then we would be drowned in politicians insisting that James be jailed. No prominent Ghanaian politician, even from those many who are members of the English bar, has ever dared to speak out against the persecution of gays.

So it was essential that I kept the matter of James' arrest inside Asylum Down police station. Once news got out, we were likely to be in trouble. I arrived at the run-down old colonial building, with its aluminium louvred windows and filthy net curtains, and was shown into an office to meet the Inspector. He mumbled on about this being a serious offence. It was extremely hot and uncomfortable in that mouldering office, and I wondered how James was faring in the cells down below. I explained that homosexuality was not a crime in the UK, and that what we had here was not a crime but a cultural misunderstanding.

The Inspector was in no hurry, and called for tea. We then chatted about the weather and cricket and football; he was anxious to demonstrate how Anglophile he was. We had been chatting for a good hour without any further mention of James. I felt that to press would not be productive. Then he started to get to the nub of the matter. His old car was irreparable and he needed a new one; and he was having financial difficulties with his son, who was studying in the UK.

He did not make any demands, he just set these out as open problems. I asked for more tea, and then it was my turn to get discursive, talking about my love for Ghana and the different places I had visited. We chatted on and on, and eventually I got on to saying what a happy relationship now existed between Ghana and the UK, and how nothing should disturb our friendship. We then had more tea, and started another round. Eventually, after over three hours, I left with James in return for a small sum given in friendship, and the case was dropped.

I should note that James thinks it was simultaneous behind the scenes work by a senior Ghanaian official, rather than my stint in the police station, which secured his release.

I took James back to his home, a lovely house which he had furnished beautifully. We sat and chatted over a cold bottle of Pinot Grigio. I had not really known James well before this event, but we became firm friends.

Ian Mackley, who had school age children, had returned to the UK for the Easter holiday. For the Easter weekend Fiona and I took Jamie and Emily to the Ankobra beach resort, past Takoradi, then over four hours drive from Accra. This is a beautiful place, the archetypal tropical paradise, with a long bay of pure white sand stretching along to distant rocks and breakers, the whole fringed by coconut palms and littered with playful crabs. The hotel only has some twenty rooms, and you could have acres of beach to yourself. We enjoyed ourselves hugely, running around with the children.

On Easter Sunday we were eating lunch in the resort's beach restaurant when I glimpsed a navy uniform with silver buttons. Looking up, I saw Buckman, a High Commission driver, coming towards me. Buckman was always cheerful, but now he looked sombre and I had a sinking feeling as I stood up to greet him. Something was very wrong.

As I stood up from the table, Buckman said "I am sorry, sir" and handed me a note. It said, very briefly, that my father had died. I told Fiona what had happened. I left with Buckman back to Accra, leaving Fiona to round up the children, pack and return with Peter, our personal driver. I returned to London on British Airways, leaving Accra at midnight that night, and took a connecting flight to Inverness. Ian Mackley had arrived back in Accra on the plane that took me out.

About a month earlier I had received a telephone call from my father to say that the doctors had given him just three months to live. The FCO paid for one leave journey per year back to London, but you could get a compassionate journey to attend the funeral of an immediate relative. I had written to ask them if I could get the journey in order to see my father one last time, rather than wait until he had died. The FCO had replied demanding a medical certificate to prove that my father was dying. He had gone to ask his Inverness GP for this, and the doctor had exploded:

"Bloody Hell! They trust Craig to represent the interests of the United Kingdom, and then they don't trust him when he says his father is dying! Do they think he would make that kind of thing up! These bureaucrats are bloody well sick!"

But he did write the certificate, and the FCO had agreed I could go to the funeral early. I had agreed with Ian Mackley I would leave once his Easter holiday was over.

My father had remained at home, but as the end approached been moved into a hospice on the banks of the River Ness. He had only been there one day when he suffered a massive heart attack and died instantly. Given the suffering caused by lung cancer, this was a good thing, although it robbed me of a chance to see him one last time.

I have no doubt my father loved me, though he was sometimes not good at showing it. This is not the place to write his detailed story, but some background is now needed. My father had come from a very poor family indeed – as poor as you can be with twelve brothers and sisters and an alcoholic father in the worst slums of Edinburgh in the 1930s. Forced to leave school and do manual labour aged just 13, he had struggled hard to free his family from poverty. He had not been the most present of fathers when I was a toddler. Nor had he always stayed entirely the right side of the law, and when I was five years old he had been obliged to disappear abroad. I saw him very rarely after that, totalling just a handful of weeks spread over thirteen years, then when I was nineteen and at university he simply returned to the parental home as though he had never been gone.

He had not seen me grow up, and his own father had not exactly been a good role model. He bonded better with my two younger brothers, who were still children and living with him after his return, but I felt he was often hostile to me. As I was at University and studying history, he also seemed worried I might be gay.

It took a long while for us to get to know each other and become friends. But we did eventually do so. About a year after he had returned, when things were at rock bottom between us, we had a huge argument in Aviemore, almost coming to blows. We both stalked off in different directions. Half an hour later, I was walking on a path through a conifer wood looking for my father to apologise. I saw him coming towards me on the same mission. For the first time in fifteen years we hugged, and we both cried. It was raining and we were surrounded by the dense smell of wet conifer. Pine needles crunched underfoot. The smell of pine still makes me want to cry in remembrance.

Things got slowly better after that, but I still never knew my father as well as I would have wanted. Now as I carried him in to the crematorium, high on a hill with breathtaking views over the Moray Firth, I was full of pain for all I had lost, had not valued at the time, and will never regain.

Back in Accra, I was astonished to be called in to his office by Ian Mackley and dressed down in no uncertain fashion. I had not prepared a briefing for him on his return (normally I would do a two page "While You Were Away" note, with documents attached). I had left my post without permission. That was a sacking offence.

"Ian," I said, "My father died." Besides, I told him, I had telephoned London to say that I was coming back – indeed they had bought the ticket for me.

Ian changed tack and said that I had deserted Accra without permission, to go to Ankobra. He was now talking complete nonsense – you don't need permission to travel within the country. We had over thirty diplomatic staff, so there were plenty of people to cope had a crisis arisen on Easter Sunday, which was unlikely. There were also plenty of people, including four First Secretaries, to brief him on what had happened while he was away.

The FCO is a strange place to work, and the nature of its staffing requirements in small overseas outposts makes it hard to eliminate bad management. But that particular attack from Ian Mackley, after the death of my father, was the nastiest and most vindictive I have ever encountered. I was much relieved when Ian left later that year and was replaced by the very pleasant Rod Pullen.

I now faced the biggest challenge of my diplomatic career so far. The Ghanaian Presidential and Parliamentary elections, due in December 2000, were fast approaching. All the signs were that the Ghanaian people might be preparing for a change of government. We were preparing to put in a major effort to ensure that the elections were free and fair. DFID were financing the greatest part of a programme run by the Electoral Commission of Ghana, to introduce photo ID cards to reduce the electoral fraud that had marred the elections of 1992 and 1996.

There would be one major change already. Rawlings was finally stepping down as Head of State, after a decade as military dictator followed by eight years of more or less constitutional rule. Rawlings' party, the NDC, was putting forward the Vice President, John Atta Mills, as its Presidential candidate. Mills was a pleasant academic who enjoyed Rawlings' trust. There seemed to be little doubt that Rawlings was prepared to hand over power to Mills; the question people were asking was, would Rawlings be dictating Mills' every move? The further question on whether Rawlings would be prepared to hand over power to the opposition NPP candidate, John Kufuor, was another matter. Most believed Rawlings would not be prepared to let the NPP win.

Remember, Rawlings had launched three coups, two of them successful. There had never been a democratic handover of power to the opposition in Ghana's history. Indeed, there had been extremely few democratic handovers of power to the opposition in Africa's history. Many were openly questioning whether democracy was suitable for Africa. In Ghana, the seasoned expatriates in the major Western corporations were arguing that we shouldn't worry too much about free and fair elections this time. Rather than provoke a crisis, we should let Rawlings hand over to Mills as a step towards eventual democracy.

I had other ideas.

The Ghanaian Electoral Commission had a massive task in providing some 11 million voters, the majority of them living in rural villages, with photo ID cards. The NDC had belatedly woken up to the threat that the photo ID cards posed to their ability to rig the election. In particular the process of issuing the cards was leading to a wholesale cleansing of fictitious or "Ghost" voters from the register, because non-existent voters could not turn up to have their photo taken. The exercise was to reveal and eradicate over a million fake names.

The NDC government had paid little attention to the plans to issue photo ID cards, which had been agreed between the Electoral Commission and the British and Danish governments. But as the Electoral Commission teams started to work their way around the country, with their Polaroid cameras and laminators, working region by region, they were setting up stall at every single polling station in Ghana – the scale of the logistical task was mind-blowing. District Chief Executives started to send in panicky reports about the purging of the registers and the NDC started work to undermine the photo ID card programme.

E T Mensah and Victor Gbeho made high profile speeches claiming that the photo ID cards were disenfranchising the rural voters because they had not reached every electoral district, and because insufficient information had been given to the electorate about the need to register.

The problem was, given the scale of the difficulties associated with such a massive exercise in a country with Ghana's weak infrastructure and dislocated public services, these claims had a distinct ring of plausibility. I decided that I needed to take over personal supervision of the process, both to see how it was really going, and to try to make it go better,

I therefore undertook a series of long up country trips with the ID card teams. The results were fascinating. In one village South East of Bolgatanga, the team were perplexed that they had issued only 82 cards but there were 1,200 people on the register. It was a typical northern village. The round huts were made of packed mud and thatched with millet stalks, while herringbone woven screens of the same material fenced the village into discreet living, livestock and food preparation areas. Dotted apparently at random around the settlement were beehive shaped mud structures, taller than me, in which grain was stored. The scent of dried dung hung in the hot, sticky air.

I squatted on a low wooden stool, set on the beaten earth floor of the chief's hut, and drank Schnapps with him. After ritual greetings and compliments, I discussed with him the curious case of the missing thousand from the electoral register.

The chief was the retired head of a teacher's training college, and understood precisely what was going on. I showed him the register and suggested that these voters possibly came from other, surrounding small villages. He laughed, and said that they were completely fictitious names. They had been added by the District Chief Executive's office. He declared himself delighted that the British government had come and was going to stop this cheating and bring back true democracy to Ghana. He then told me about his four children, who all lived in Manchester. He went to a deeply carved wooden chest, so dry and cracked and grey with age it seemed already well on its journey to dust. He rummaged under several striped local garments and produced a heavy, light blue football shirt, with a V neck and white edging. It had what looked a fading black stain across the front. That, he announced proudly, was Colin Bell's signature.

The chief's enthusiasm for the cleansing of the electoral register was genuine; it shone in the half light of that low, mud hut from his beaming, sweat pearled face. And it was an enthusiasm I found pretty well everywhere in Ghana. It was like a new dawn of hope; a thorough-going and all-pervasive enthusiasm for the democracy which people genuinely believed would not only cement their individual freedoms, but also end their economic woes. While slightly sceptical about the expectations, I found it nonetheless impossible to avoid being swept up in the enthusiasm, which was irresistible. The interest in politics was everywhere, and in the meanest village there would be a group of people under the banyan tree listening to the FM radio and arguing about the coming change. It was one of those rare moments of joy and expectation in human life, where a whole society feels that things can become radically better and fairer:

Bliss was it in that dawn to be alive

But to be young was very heaven.

In the West, tired of the venality and deceit of our politicians, we no longer much value our democracy and feel little empathy for our ancestors who struggled, fought and died to achieve and then protect it. It truly is a wonderful thing to see a people who have been abused and trampled, exercising for the first time their real power as a people over those who would govern them. In 1999 the sheer enthusiasm of the ordinary people of Ghana for democracy was truly inspiring and at times deeply moving.

FM radio was of vital importance in spreading the spirit of democracy –
indeed I would go further and say that the FM radio stations were the
most vital single factor in bringing real democracy to Ghana. Between
1996 and 2000 some thirty independent FM stations had been established
and they all featured the liveliest political debate. There was almost
nowhere in the whole country where an independent station was not in
range. In small villages you would find groups of locals seated under the
shade of the banyan tree, grouped around a battered old transistor and
discussing debt cancellation policy.

The Rawlings regime must be given credit for allowing the growth of
independent media. Ghana's lively, indeed quarrelsome, newspapers
were also a factor but by no means reached the depth of population or the
geographical spread of the radio stations. Again, I think that Rawlings
simply did not realise the transformational effect of the outburst of free
debate he was unleashing – until it was too late. I was to witness directly
a cack-handed attempt to shut down the FM threat once it was way too
late, on the eve of the election.

The direct impact of this intellectual ferment that I was now to discover
was that it was completely untrue that people did not know about the
voter ID cards. The FM stations had been broadcasting for weeks information about them and details of where and how to obtain them in each
electoral district. There was an extraordinary enthusiasm for the project,
explained only in part by the fact that in many places the large majority of
the people had never seen a photo of themselves, and getting one for free
was irresistible.

In order to be sure that the process was really reaching everyone, I visited the teams in the most remote parts of the country, including the un-
ruly lands of Upper East (where chieftaincy disputes were still being resolved by beheading), the NDC heartlands of Volta region where there
was hostility to the whole process, and the areas in the higher Western
reaches of the Volta known as "Overseas" because you could only pass
the swampy complex of creeks and reed beds by canoe. Everywhere I
went, I found orderly queues of people getting their photo ID cards,
many having hiked long distances to do so. The electoral officers were
carrying out their task with thorough-going diligence but also with flexib-

ility – where there was a problem, such as a shortage of film or laminated pockets, they would extend their stay if necessary. Such problems were surprisingly rare, due largely to the quite remarkable organisational skills of the Chairman of the Electoral Commission, Dr Kwadwo Afari-Gyan. I had only just met this wry, slim, chain-smoking and beer drinking bundle of energy, but was to come to have the most profound respect for him over the course of the next few months.

Travelling North West from the city of Sunyani, I visited the town of Tainano[49]. This had been a renowned market gardening centre, but had gone into a dreadful economic decline some ten years earlier following the collapse of its bridge in a storm. I arrived at the fallen bridge, a simple concrete structure spilling down into a river, a major tributary of the Black Volta, some 40 metres across, its brown surge flowing fast enough for there to be little eddies flecked with flashes of white. We were only an hour's drive from Sunyani, but I was told that the drive to the next bridge was some four hours on a very rough road. The alternative was to cross by canoe.

I walked down to where a jumble of four or five canoes was pulled onto the steeply sloping bank. The rare sight of a white man wanting to cross caused huge amusement and there followed some excited competition as to which canoe I should take. I eyed them dubiously – they were all of local dugout construction, hewed from a single trunk with rough pieces of wood nailed across as seats. Each already contained a fair amount of water slopping about in the bottom. I chose the largest looking one and we set off. One paddler in front and one at back. They were incredibly muscled; their torsos would have been the delight and envy of any Californian gym, and they were soon sheathed in gold as the sun reflected off a mixture of sweat and river water. I was continually wiping my glasses clear.

We set off more or less straight upstream, the men paddling like crazy with huge muscular strokes but still making very little headway, the force of their efforts rocking the canoe from side to side so that water poured in and I had to lift my feet clear of the floor while gripping the slimy canoe

---

49I think it was Tainano but my notes are not quite clear which of a number of towns I visited that day it was. I intend to explore this region again.

sides to try and retain my balance. That didn't feel safe, so I reluctantly planted my feet again, the water in the well of the canoe now over my ankles. We had started straight upstream in order to come back to a point opposite our starting one in a graceful arc. As we were broadside to the current in the middle of this manoeuvre, the water flowed over the side and along my seat, thoroughly wetting my arse.

I was in danger of wetting myself anyway. I have a terrible and irrational fear of water – I can bath but get scared in a shower for example, and even get scared in very heavy rainfall. Unsurprisingly, I have never learnt to swim. There was one other passenger, an old lady who had hoisted up her brightly flowered dress and knotted it beneath her loins, while balancing an improbably large cloth bundle of goods on her knees. I told myself that if she could do it, I should not be pathetic, but she didn't improve my mood by screwing up her eyes and yelling out "Lord have mercy" throughout the entire passage. This rather cancelled out my efforts to tell myself that the boatman must make this crossing scores of times a day and it must have been completely routine for the local villagers.

After turning at the top of the arc, we were racing down with the current on the other side of the stream at a quite alarming rate. As we sped past the road, the rear boatman threw a rope to someone on the bank who whipped it round a tree trunk, pulling the canoe up with a jolt that nearly pitched me into the water. I disembarked on shaky legs, deeply conscious of my wet trousers.

I had been vaguely aware of flashes of fluorescent orange in a large tree that was growing to the right of the collapsed bridge on the bank on which we had now arrived. After wiping my glasses again I could now see about a dozen life jackets, hung high in the tree. The effect was rather macabre.

I turned to the boatman and asked why they didn't use the life-jackets. He flashed me a wide grin.

"Oh," he said, "We don't use them since people drown in them."

The poverty and squalor of the town were as bad as I had seen in Ghana. Unlike most rural towns, which smell earthy but clean, this one had a palpable smell of sewage and the buildings were visibly decaying.

The brown spots on the corrugated iron roofs had swollen and merged, and in places the ensuing holes had gone rampant, reducing the covering to a fragile latticework of fern-like iron oxide tendrils.

As usual, I chatted with the local schoolmaster, and he firmly alleged that the government's failure to replace the bridge was because it was an opposition town which the government was happy to see dwindle. In his school I was impressed to find the electoral commission personnel with their cameras set up, quietly and methodically issuing photo ID cards to a queue of several hundred people. They had lost some film stock on the crossing but still had plenty.

I took a trip around the surrounding countryside in an old plum and orange coloured taxi, which had lost a door and whose bodywork was battered beyond recognition, but had a Peugeot badge on the steering wheel. The chrome front bumper was rather bafflingly tied across the roof, secured to the window struts either side with ties made from strips of old fertiliser sacks. The driver, Aaron, was a bright man who was going to vote NDC on the grounds that Rawlings willingness to hold a free election meant that he deserved support.

But my trip showed the surrounding farmers to be as impoverished as the town, and I determined on return to try to persuade DFID to rebuild the bridge. It seemed to me that the resulting benefit to an area which had been effectively cut off from economic interaction with the rest of the country, would justify the expenditure.

In fact I was to get nowhere with this. DFID were in the throes of changing from project work to a doctrine which is now the basis of their philosophy, that of budget support. The idea is that no longer will the UK do something for the aid recipient, like building a bridge, a hospital or some schools, or providing inputs and training to farmers. Instead we help the government, together with its civil society, to plan its budget and its programmes to maximise poverty alleviation. We then pump money into its budget to help it to achieve these agreed aims.

This has several advantages. It is more democratic, with the African country pursuing its own objectives. The consultation structures included boost the role of civil society. It also builds up the capacity of the

159

African administration and African professionals to deliver goods to the people.

Unfortunately, these happy ideas are hopelessly unrealistic. With the greatest will in the world, the capacity of African ministries to deliver anything to the people is in practice highly constrained – even in Ghana, which probably has the best civil service in Africa. There are numerous factors behind this. There is a lack of middle management capability, and a lack of incentive for ordinary civil servants to deliver. African bureaucracies almost entirely lack any link between performance in the job and reward or discipline, with family and tribal linkages almost always being much more crucial to your career than ability or performance.

There is also the sadly unavoidable fact that African governments are corrupt – all of them, to a greater or lesser degree. Now that is not to say that Western governments are not corrupt – of course they are, all of them, to a greater or lesser degree. But African governments are more corrupt. Why they are more corrupt, and whose fault that is, opens up another range of very interesting questions touched on from time to time in this book. But the sad truth is that African governments are rather intensely corrupt, and so simply to hand them over in effect large wodges - amounting to billions of pounds - of the British public's cash as "Budget support" is not a policy that is going to strike the man in the street as glaringly sensible.

DFID would argue, with some justice, that they then carefully monitor the spending of the African government and the achievement of the objectives of the programmes, to make sure the money is being well used. There are two problems with this. The first is a wonderful DFID word, *fungibility*. It means the ability to switch around funds and I think the meaning is clear if you think of it as *fudge-ability*. Put simply, it means that you put the £100 million DFID gave you for education, into education. Meanwhile you put the £40 million of your own taxpayers' money, that you had for education, into your own pocket. Nobody will notice amid the flood of resources coming from donors. *Fungibility* – where would the Swiss banks and London property market be without it?

The second problem is that in its decade of re-orienting to budget support, DFID has vastly reduced the percentage of funds it devotes to monitoring and evaluation – so it doesn't really know how much fungible leakage is occurring.

Anyway, Ian Stuart, the head of DFID's Ghanaian operations, advised me that there was no way DFID would do something as old-fashioned as building a bridge, and though I continued to try for another year, he was right.

Despite what I have written, there is a role for budget support in aid policy – an element of it is essential to have a real effect on primary education, for example. And other approaches can also be fraught. In 1999 the British Council organised for DFID the delivery of basic textbooks to every single primary school in Ghana – a programme of which I was proud. Again I made a point of journeying to the most remote locations to make sure they had got through, and in almost every case they had. But in a significant number of cases they were not being put to use. One headmaster proudly showed me that they were "safe" in a locked steel container in a locked cupboard in his locked office. The packets had not been opened. Another teacher told me they read to the children from the books but did not let them see them as "They would get them dirty."

But in deep rural districts the biggest problem in education I had found was teacher absenteeism. Talking to those teachers present, to local priests and others, I reckoned teacher absenteeism in rural areas ran at over 60%. Often schools would have no teacher present at all, or a single teacher holding the fort for all the others – I suspect they took turns. The simple truth was that educated teachers were not prepared to live in villages with no running water, little electricity and none of the delights of urban society.

I found DFID remarkably ignorant of the true state of affairs. The problem was that neither permanent nor visiting DFID staff or consultants would dream of calling in to a village school ten hours drive from Accra, certainly not without first giving warning and almost certainly arranging the visit through, and being accompanied by, officials from the local regional office. Whereas I would be driving through the bush and simply see a school and call in. DFID also credited official figures which, while acknowledging the problem, hid its true extent.

To return to the Ghanaian election in 2000, it would be foolish to deny that there is a tribal element in voting in Ghana. The Ewe vote over-whelmingly NDC, the Ashanti overwhelmingly NPP. The significant swing is among other smaller tribes. But then, it is foolish to pretend this is uniquely African. Look at an electoral map of the United Kingdom. The Scots and Welsh vote overwhelmingly Labour, the South East of England votes Conservative. Celts have a higher than average propensity to elect Liberal Democrats. Is all that tribal? Yes, up to a point. Ghanaian voting is tribal up to a greater point. But there are other social and economic factors at play, too.

In Ghana as in the UK, it is a matter of the community that you feel embodies and protects your individual interests, and a collective view or consensus within that community, on how best to take forward the interests of that community.

Nor was electoral fraud limited to the NDC. It was simply that, as the party in power, they had more opportunity. In fact there were different methods of fraud prevalent, with the Ewe areas going for multiple voting, while the Ashanti rather favoured under-age voting. The Electoral Commission had to guard against both.

One key weapon was indelible ink. When somebody voted, their thumb was painted. It is difficult to find an ink that is truly permanent, and DFID, who were paying for it, found India to be the only source of an ink that truly could not be washed or rubbed off. (Hence the term Indian Ink, which is what permanent markers were called when I was a child).

This special ink was applied with a little plastic tube that was rubbed inside the nail, where it joins the skin, to make it hard even to sandpaper the ink away.

Election monitoring abroad by EU member states normally comes under the purview of the European Union, but the EU reached the rather extraordinary conclusion that Ghana was a mature democracy and monitoring was not necessary. Ghanaian civil society had mobilised to provide a number of formidable monitoring organisations, as Ghana's middle class asserted itself. I managed to persuade the FCO to provide three experts from the Electoral Reform Society for several weeks in the run-up to the election, with a further team of volunteers for the voting itself. I was delighted that these included my old friend, Andy Myles, Chief Executive of the Scottish Liberal Democrats and a veteran of these monitoring missions worldwide.

There were a scattering of other European observers. For the poll itself we effectively closed the High Commission and sent almost all our staff, local and diplomatic, around the country to observe the poll. A few staff were also lent by other EU missions, who consented to put the ERS team in charge of the organisation of the whole effort. The ERS team carried out training and allocated the staff, in teams of two, to different regions around Ghana, with instructions to tour the polling stations ensuring all was in order, ballot boxes were sealed, ballots checked, ID shown etc.

A further valuable addition were two British MPs, Roger Gale and Nigel Jones, who came out under the auspices of the Inter Parliamentary Union. Their prestige with Ghanaian parliamentarians was a great help to our effort.

The United States did their own thing. This included, in what seemed to me an absurd example of political correctness, sending a delegation of blind election observers. In any event, as the Ghanaian elections followed immediately upon President Bush's fraudulent election, the US had no credibility on the issue.

Votes were counted in individual polling stations, and then the results sheet, signed by the polling station officers and local party representatives, would be sent to a constituency centre for collation, together with the sealed ballot papers themselves. In the constituency centres, constituency results would be tallied, declared by the returning officer, signed off and sent to the regional centre. In the regional centre they would be verified, and then faxed to the Electoral Commission HQ in Accra. We had supplied the fax machines, and back-up satellite telephone systems.

Once polls had closed, our monitors would follow the ballot boxes through the stages, until they all reached the regional centres. They would then telephone the results through to me at the Electoral Commission HQ, so I could check the fax eventually produced at HQ against the result declared in the region. It was at this stage that most of the fraud was to occur in the 2007 Kenyan and Zimbabwean elections, where vigilant local observers ensured accurate local results, but they were altered at the centre. We had independent international verification of every regional result before it arrived at the centre, where it was I who was actually taking it off the fax and moving it to the collation, so there was no opportunity for fraud.

The issue of photo ID cards brought perhaps the most startling example of people power in recent African history, exercised above all by the women of Ghana. Alarmed that they were going to lose a fair election, the NDC government brought a case against its own Electoral Commission to seek to have the photo ID card system declared illegal, on the grounds that it disenfranchised legitimate voters. I knew this to be nonsense, but ever since a sitting Court had been murdered, High Court judges were reluctant to oppose Rawlings, and they ruled against the electoral commission and the ID card system, despite the mass demonstrations around Accra chanting "No ID No Vote".

It appeared I had wasted £10 million of DFID money on the photo ID scheme. But I had seen two things from the court case. One was the courage of the Electoral Commissioner, Kwadwo Afari-Gyan, in being prepared to stand up to the bullying government. The second was the popular demand for the photo ID cards.

The people now took over. The polling station officers, all over the country, who had supervised the issuing of the photo ID cards, decided they were going to use them, whether the High Court wanted or not. These were local school teachers and bank or post office managers, and it was a quiet, middle class revolution. While the voters themselves, as people queued to vote, were checking the others in the queue and kicking out anyone without a photo ID. This movement was led, everywhere, by Ghana's formidable female market traders. This popular adoption of the Photo ID system was common throughout the entire country, even in government areas: and in most of the country spontaneously supported by the local police.

After myself inspecting polling stations all day, I entered the Electoral Commission on the night of 7 December, and carefully monitored the collation of the first round results. A more or less uniform swing to the opposition across the whole country was soon obvious, and my phone ran hot as results were telephoned in to me from the regions. There were just a very few suspect constituency results, in Brong Ahafo and Northern regions, sharply in conflict with the national trend, but 98% of the constituency results rang true. It became obvious that the opposition was heading for a small parliamentary majority, while no candidate would exceed 50% in the Presidential election, leading to a run-off. When the votes were finally tallied, John Kufuor had 48.4% against John Atta Mills 44.8%.

The NDC had woken up too late to the fact that they could not win a legitimate election. They had then made clumsy and unpopular steps to try and prevent a legitimate election. The failed attempt to thwart the voter ID scheme was one example. They also tried to move against FM radio when it was far too late.

On the evening before the poll, I was taking Roger Gale and Nigel Jones to visit Joy FM, possibly Ghana's most influential radio station, run by my good friend Sam Attah Mensah. We were sitting in the back office of the station when an armed posse of Rawlings' security men from the castle came in the front door and announced that they had come to close down the radio station on the President's instructions.

I appeared from the office and said:

"Good evening. I am Craig Murray, Deputy British High Commissioner, and these gentlemen are Mr Roger Gale MP and Mr Nigel Williams MP, members of the British Parliament who are here on behalf of the Inter Parliamentary Union."

Roger Gale then added: "Obviously there has been some mistake. I thought I heard you say that you were closing down the station, but we are here to visit our fellow democracy, Ghana, and democracies don't close down radio stations."

Nigel Williams then chipped in: "It must be a misunderstanding. Perhaps you can go back and ask for more instructions?"

The goons, thwarted by this unexpected manifestation of the British parliament, left in some confusion. Joy FM never was closed down. We returned to our tea, and Sam opened something a bit stronger to celebrate.

I had been able to predict the result of the first round with some accuracy, having spent the past year travelling all around Ghana and speaking to Ghanaians of all ranks in both cities and villages. I had also formed a view of how many people had changed their vote since the election. It was very obvious to me that the substantial change in Kufuor's vote – up from 39.6% in 1996 to 48.4% in 2000 – was more due to our reducing fraud than to a change in real votes cast. Put another way, I estimate the NDC cheated in 1996 by around 7% of the vote net (i.e. they cheated more than that, but some was cancelled out by cheating the other way). I am satisfied we reduced cheating in 2000 to under 2% net. A fair election is one where the margin of victory is greater than the margin of cheating – you can hope for no more than that.

Electoral fraud is everywhere. The glaring Bush 2000 election, with myriad black voters turned away from the polls and some very dodgy electronic voting machines, was no example. I was myself to encounter more electoral fraud in Blackburn than I ever did in Ghana.

With the second round looming, the NDC started to think that I was a part of their problem. They assigned a secret service team to follow me everywhere, which must have been very boring for them. Sam Jonah came round for a drink one day and remarked that the agents who used to shadow him had disappeared around a week earlier. Now he knew why – he had just spotted them all lurking around my gate. With my driver Peter I used to go for long pointless drives, because the security services had never been given enough money for petrol. We also used deliberately to go places our 4WD Mitsubishi Montero could go, but their saloon cars couldn't.

Rod Pullen, the High Commissioner and my boss, was also getting a bit alarmed that we were in too deep. He saw dangers that we could be accused of rigging the election if Kufuor won, or that if Mills won, the NDC might be vindictive against us for our strictness over the elections. But Rod was still new in Accra, and I still had influence with Africa Command of the FCO, and strong support from Clare Short. Anyway, the die was now cast.

DFID had to find more money to help fund the second round of voting, on 28 December. 16 million ballot papers had to be printed and distributed. Word was reaching me from many sources that the NDC was planning to increase its vote in Volta Region – which it called its "World Bank" as it was so safe – by a big effort on multiple voting. Minibuses and pick-ups were being assembled to bus voters around from booth to booth.

Our chief weapon against multiple voting was the Indian ink, but there was not enough of this for a second round. DFID had therefore bought more, but it had to be specially made, and the batch would not be ready until 24 December. With the election on 28 December this was cutting it very tight, and we found that we would have to charter a private plane to get it to Ghana. Chartering an inter-continental private plane to set off on the evening of Christmas Eve was more easily said than done. I also had no budget and no way of getting one, Whitehall having gone into festive mode, so I took a chance on using the Embassy's own local budget pending a resolution. Yes, that ultimately got me into yet more trouble.

The government plainly from various actions did not really want the Electoral Commission to get the India ink, and I was most concerned that it would get delayed by Customs. That is why, on Christmas Day 2000, instead of eating my Turkey I was baking on the heat of the tarmac at Ko-toko airport. When our plane taxied in, we quickly unloaded the boxes of little ink bottles straight onto two trucks. I escorted these straight out of the VIP lounge gateway, helped by a substantial Christmas tip to the guards. The truck drivers then set off around Ghana, taking the ink to the regional centres for onward distribution to the constituencies. I spent Christmas evening briefing election observers; that sounds crazy, and it says something extraordinary for the spirit of those times that we had 100% attendance of observers on a purely voluntary basis. I remember Fiona, herself an observer, striding though the volunteers distributing Mince pies, and Andy Myles making a number of serious and valuable points while wearing a silly paper hat.

As for Roger Gale and Nigel Jones, I cannot speak too highly of them. We British have a pretty scathing view of our MPs, and often it is justified. But while it was one thing for these MPs to come out in early December, it was quite another for them to give up their holiday and come out again between Christmas and New Year. Frankly, I had not expected it. Nobody could say that this trip was a jolly, or even comfortable, and they certainly both dived into the field and worked hard. Their presence undoubtedly was one of the small factors that combined to tip the scales in favour of a successful democratic transition.

It had been a major pre-occupation for some time to find a retirement role for Jerry Rawlings that he would feel commensurate with his dignity, and which would thus encourage him to give up power and move on. The UK had been making discreet soundings in the United Nations and other international bodies to try to initiate a tempting proposal that could be put to him. Our efforts were hampered by the widespread international perception that Jerry Rawlings was off his rocker, while the fact that he had been a military dictator who had executed (among others) his predecessor meant that we could not automatically count on support even from EU partners. "He hasn't murdered anyone for a while" is not the most compelling of arguments. In the end we decided that it looked like the best that might be done was some sort of roving UN Ambassador status on HIV awareness and malaria prevention, which might utilise his undoubted charisma and ability to communicate with Africans.

One of the problems of history is that there is a tendency to see whatever occurred as inevitable, whereas there may have been in truth a whole range of possible outcomes, with tiny factors tipping the scales. Nowadays people tend to take the view that Ghana's transition to real democracy was natural and easy. Some even measure Ghana's democratic era from Rawlings' 1992 plebiscite.

But in fact in 2000 nobody could be sure how Rawlings would react to losing power. The NDC had no shortage of hotheads like Tony Aidoo and indeed Mrs Rawlings – normally so influential over her husband – who wanted to react to a NPP victory with a military takeover and claim of electoral fraud. Rawlings held a meeting in a hangar at the military base of Burma Camp to judge the reaction of the army to a possible takeover. He spoke of the dark forces threatening to usurp the country. My sources in the meeting told me that the soldiers became restless, and some even started to drift away as Rawlings was speaking. But he had the security services and some military units still undeniably loyal to him, particularly his notorious "Commandos". Certainly at Christmas 2000 nobody was ruling out a military coup.

There was even a very real danger of civil war. The Ashanti, who had been the dominant political force for centuries, were furious at what they saw as the stolen elections of 1992 and 1996. If they were excluded from power again, there was a real danger that Kumasi, Ghana's most teeming and vibrant city, would explode into violence. In 2000, Ghana by no means felt safe from the spectre of violent conflict. Every Embassy was dusting down and updating its emergency consular evacuation plan. Once again I found myself slap in the middle of a game being played for the highest possible stakes.

Our election monitors dispersed again around the country. I saw the head of our commercial section, Malcolm Ives, depart for the North with his wife Sue, looking like they were off for a picnic, with straw hats, hampers, and even that most English of facilities, a windbreak.[50] The result of the second round of voting was a foregone conclusion. Kufuor's first round lead had destroyed Rawlings' aura of invincibility. I spent election day in Volta region, looking for evidence of multiple voting. I found a couple of minibuses full of young men who were plainly engaged in multiple voting. They all had traces of India ink on their thumbs which had plainly been sanded off. A couple were actually bleeding. I told them they were under arrest and to go and report to the local police station. Rather amazingly, in both cases they actually did this, although I was only bluffing, having no authority at all.

That evening with Peter at the wheel we raced back through the darkness to Accra, for me to take my place at the Electoral Commission. It is on a small back street near Ridge. I found both entrances to the street blocked off by soldiers. They said they were there to guard the Commission, but this seemed to me ominous. There was a definite tension in the Electoral Commission that night which had not been so obvious in the first round.

Slowly, from around 1am, constituency results started to come in. There wasn't much movement from the first round, but there was a slight additional and more or less consistent swing to Kufuor. You could have

---

50Malcolm and Sue were a really nice couple. Malcolm was always friendly and helpful, and I was extremely sad at his quite sudden and early death not long after leaving Accra

cut the tension with a knife. Party representatives came in and out, checking on what was happening. The Electoral Commissioner, Kwadwo Afari-Gyan, was the coolest man in Ghana that night. He and I sat in his office, collating the master register of the faxes from the constituencies and personally checking the addition of the votes. When there was a pause, we would stop for a beer and discuss how the election was going.

Kwadwo's phone kept going, and after a while it became clear that he was getting a whole string of threatening phone calls from the Castle, instructing him to fix the result. He replied very calmly: "The result will be what the result will be. I am just making sure it is fairly counted. I have no influence on the result." It became his mantra.

Then, suddenly, taking his umpteenth phone call, he stiffened. He summoned me to his side to listen. It was his wife. Soldiers had come to their bungalow, taking Kwadwo Afari Gyan's wife and children hostage. They were threatening to kill them if he did not deliver the "Right" result. As the pressure on him had mounted through the night, the only sign of stress that Kwadwo had given was to smoke faster and faster. Now he barked down the phone:

"Put their leader on."

A soldier quickly took the phone, and started repeating the demand to Kwadwo. Kwadwo interrupted him. It is very taboo for Ghanaians to swear, so I have edited what Kwadwo said:

"Listen you little *****. Do you think you soldier boys can still tell us all what to so? How dare you come to my house and threaten my wife and children. I am sitting here with the British Deputy High Commissioner, and he knows what is happening. Now get the **** out of my home before we have you thrown into jail!"

There was a short silence, and then the soldier said "Yes sir, sorry sir." Kwadwo then told his crying wife not to worry, and turned calmly back to his work as though nothing much had happened.[51]

---

[51] Remarkably, this story of the Electoral Commissioner's family being held hostage by the military has never become public. Kwadwo is not the kind of man to tell it, and I was the only other one there. Ghana has never given Kwadwo all the honour he deserves. I called on Kwadwo in February 2008 to confirm that my memory of this is correct. He confirmed that it is.

Two other unwelcome developments had started to happen. The first was armed soldiers appearing inside the Electoral Commission, not actually doing anything wrong, but just intimidating by their presence. I kept throwing them out. The second was that for the first time we started to get some apparently altered duplicate constituency results turn up. I had our observers phoning in the results, and these always tallied with those arriving on the main fax. But one or two different results from the same constituencies then started to follow, brought in by Afari-Gyan's deputy, Mr Kanga. It was not necessarily Kanga's fault, but it was he who happened to bring them in. I started to keep a jealous physical guard of the authentic results to avoid substitutions, and as the second night of the count moved into its early hours, I had been awake solidly for over three days, so I stole a couple of hours sleep with my head on the faxed originals of the election results for safekeeping. It is that image of me that has found its way into Ghanaian popular mythology.

I awoke again in the early hours, because we were now moving to the white heat of the crisis, and my mobile phone was constantly ringing. By 3am on the second night there remained only two remote constituencies still to declare. Afari-Gyan and I calculated that, even if every eligible voter in those two constituencies voted for Professor Atta Mills, John Kufuor could still not be beaten. Kufuor had been elected President. But Kwadwo Afari-Gyan was not legally entitled to make the declaration until all results were in.

This was now or never for the NDC; if they were to launch military action against the result, it had to be now. And my contacts were calling from all over Accra, giving me details of the movements and the sayings of key NDC figures and senior army personnel. There was undoubtedly a faction in the NDC that was looking to what could be done to cancel the result by military action.

At the same time, Kufuor and his people had become highly nervous. Why was the result not being announced? Were fraudulent results being prepared? Was it going to be stolen again? Was there a delay to enable the military to prepare? The NPP General Secretary, Dan Botwe, was pressing hard for a declaration. Then, around 3am, I received two pieces of news about the same time. Kufuor, on the advice of his key advisers including Hackman Owusu Agyemang, was going to declare himself President. Almost simultaneously the NDC had decided that, in the event that Kufuor declared himself the victor, they would denounce it as an unconstitutional coup and move in the military. Just at this time I also received a firm order from Rod Pullen; he had heard that things may be going pear shaped, and ordered me to leave the Electoral Commission building.

I phoned Hackman:

"Hackman, I hear you are going to declare victory."

"Well, it looks like we've won, and..."

"Hackman, please, listen to me. Do not declare."

"But it's been..."

"Please, Hackman, I beg you. Tell John. Tell him from me, personally, that Craig says he has to trust him. Do not declare. Then come to the Labadi Beach Hotel. I will see you there in half an hour."

"OK, Craig, I'll try."

Devonshire House was being watched, and I didn't want Hackman being seen scuttling around there in the early hours. With some of Rawlings' crew's anti-British views, that might itself have been enough to spark a coup. I shook hands with Afari-Gyan, and as I left the Electoral Commission, a squad of soldiers were coming up the stairs, guns carried rather than shouldered. I yelled at them that soldiers were not allowed inside the building, they could guard it from around the perimeter, Then I drove them before me down the stairs, and ordered the old man at the entrance to padlock the gate. So at 4am the bar of the Labadi Beach Hotel became my HQ, with George Opata joining me, Peter shuttling messages all over Accra, and Roger Gale and Nigel Jones adding weight when I needed (they were living in the hotel and extremely sporting about being dragged out of bed).

Hackman arrived and I explained to him urgently that Kufuor had, undoubtedly won. I told him that I absolutely guaranteed that Afari-Gyan would announce the true result when all constituencies were in. But I also knew that forces in the NDC were poised for a military takeover if Kufuor made an "Unconstitutional" early declaration.

The big problem is that, although I am a big fan of Afari-Gyan, the NPP were not, viewing him as the man who delivered the fixed 1992 and 1996 results. But I had seen that he could be both brave and honourable, given the resources and support. Finally I persuaded Hackman to trust Afari-Gyan, and the NPP did not make a premature declaration. The most dangerous moment had passed.

I then concentrated on encouraging a wide variety of respected and senior elderly Ghanaians to send messages to John Atta Mills conceding defeat. Atta Mills is an honourable man, and he did concede, to the absolute fury of Mrs Rawlings. Mills thus killed off the chances of a coup.

This all cleared the way for the formal declaration, made about 3pm, with Roger Gale and Nigel Jones supporting Afari-Gyan. I sat in the next room, enjoying a quiet beer. Then I went home and slept, completely exhausted.

On the Sunday afternoon, I drove round to the home of President-Elect Kufuor. We were both in shorts and T-shirts, and we sat in his garden with our sandalled feet up, drinking Chivas Regal and discussing plans for Ghana in the coming year.

After a whole generation of rule by Rawlings, Ghana had come through to genuine freedom and democracy. An African country had shown that real democracy was possible in Africa, with a change of power to the opposition after a good debate and a peaceful election. This was really the kind of progress I so desperately wanted for Africa. And I had helped to do it.

10
Local Hero

My main task was accomplished in Ghana, and I could spend my last year there undertaking important but not stressful tasks and basking in the friendship I had earned from Ghanaians. It should be stressed that I still had many friends in the NDC, who acknowledged that Ghana had benefited from a genuine election, and were even prepared to say that a short period out of power would do them good, enabling them to become a real party and not just a Jerry Rawlings fan club.

Fiona spent much of that last year in the UK, to get Emily started at a British primary school, leaving me alone in Devonshire House. We had been through the difficult need to sack the long-serving steward, old Nasser. Drink had been disappearing from our store at an alarming rate. Fiona had instituted a stock check system, and this had stopped the losses between functions, but Nasser was still reporting the use of improbably large amounts of spirit at functions.

I had initiated a monthly meeting of the British business community, and one evening, after one of these gatherings of about thirty people, Nasser reported that we had used thirteen one litre bottles of Gordon's gin. I thought that highly unlikely. We used small individual bottles of Schweppes tonic, and I asked how many of these had been used.

"Seven", he replied.

Nasser had to go, having been warned several times. He had been at Devonshire House many years, and lived in the servants' quarters at the back of the grounds, so it was a horrible thing to do. Once we actually fired him, the other staff quite cheerfully told us that he had regularly been passing crates of mixed spirits to an accomplice over the wall. It had been going on for years. It is very typical of Ghana that all my domestic staff knew, but nobody had told me, until after he was actually gone, when there was no harm in telling me. Then they were completely mystified as to why I might be angry with them.

174

My good friend Hackman was newly installed as Foreign Minister. His determination to protect Ghana's interests led him, very early in his tenure, to indulge in a rather feeble bit of populism that brought us into unexpected conflict.

Visa applications for Ghanaians to visit the UK continued to rise. We were processing about 300 new applications every day. Rather surprisingly, about two thirds of all applications were successful. When the application was refused, a small stamp would be applied to a page stating "Visa applied for", and this little statement would be underlined in ink, as a warning for future applications that an application had been refused. This would not lead to automatic refusal of new applications, but it would certainly cause the entry clearance officer to look hard.

As we had by far the largest and best staffed visa operation in Accra, our decisions were taken as a benchmark for other Embassies, In practice once you had a British "visa applied for" stamp underlined in your passport, you would be unlikely to be able to get a visa to anywhere.

This annoyed those refused, but we were surprised when Rod received an official letter from Hackman asking us to stop putting "Visa applied for" stamps in Ghanaian passports, as this amounted to a defacement of Ghanaian passports, which were the property of the Ghanaian government.

Having made this peculiar request to us, Hackman leaked his letter to the Ghanaian media. It made front page news and was indeed popular, with the media angle being that Hackman had requested the British to stop refusing visas.

As it happened, I was due that day to give a radio broadcast on Joy FM with a phone in on the subject of Gordon Brown's debt relief initiative. Needless to say, the first caller asked me about Hackman's request that we didn't put "Visa applied for" stamps in passports. The presenter added that surely the Ghanaian government indeed had the right to ask us not to put stamps in Ghanaian passports?

I replied that the argument about defacement of passports seemed to me nonsensical. Passports had pages specifically for the insertion of various stamps; that was what passports in practice were for. Furthermore, when we actually issued a visa, we put a much bigger visa stamp in the passport. That was a bigger defacement, if you wished to describe it in those terms. If the government of Ghana really wanted us not to put any stamps in their passports, then we couldn't issue visas. That seemed to me not a good road to go down.

Two days later, Rod called me in to his room. He had his gravedigger face on. He said that Hackman had issued a formal complaint about my interview. Hackman had said I was trying to make a fool of him on the radio, and that if we stopped issuing visas to Ghanaians, it would be a major diplomatic rupture. Looking fixedly at the floor, Rod went on to say that I had no right to threaten to withhold visas from Ghanaians. It was an extraordinary thing to do. Looking ever more mournful, Rod said he had been obliged to report this incident to the FCO, including to Personnel Department.

I replied that I had not threatened to suspend the issuing of visas to Ghanaians – I had merely pointed out the logical consequences of saying we were not permitted to stamp Ghanaian passports. I had specifically said we didn't want to go down that road. I pointed out that no other media outlet had picked up on my interview, so it couldn't have been that shocking; and I suggested that Hackman was being ridiculously thin-skinned. Besides which, Hackman's letter had been out of order and a bit of low populism at our expense. We should be robust. Rod pointed out that we had not had a reply from London yet on how to respond to Hackman's letter. He said he was banning me from further media appearances without consulting him first.

I returned to fume in my office. I phoned Hackman on his private mobile; Hackman denied point blank having complained in anything like the terms Rod had described.[52]

I especially enjoyed working with the various British charities and NGOs operating in Ghana, many doing great work. I have particular admiration for Sight Savers. I visited several of their mobile clinics around Ghana, and it was truly heart-warming to see their surgeons restore the

---

52At the time I believed Hackman over Rod, though with hindsight perhaps I was wrong. A few years later I sent Hackman a copy of *Murder in Samarkand* via a friend. According to that friend, Hackman tossed it aside saying: "Craig Murray! He's nobody now. Jack Straw was right to sack him."

sight of scores of people every day by simple cataract operations. In the UK, we think of this as an affliction of old age, but in Ghana Sight Savers were also helping many younger people. There is no better feeling than seeing somebody have sight restored to them – it is like a continuous generation of miracles. My favourite was a boy called Ben, who I spoke to in Hohoe the day before his operation, and again the day after. The second time I saw him he said:

"Oh, you're Craig Murray. Nobody told me you were ugly."

Raleigh International are a good cause in a slightly different way. Providing adventurous projects for young British people, who pay a lot to participate, their benefit probably lies mostly in the development of the young British people rather than of the host nation. But there was also a benefit to Ghana in having the Raleigh expeditions there. They worked on clinics together with Sight Savers, built schools, and undertook a number of projects with the Ghana Wildlife Department.

One of these was the forest reserve at Ankassa, near the Ivory Coast border. This is one of the few surviving stretches of primary rain forest for thousands of miles, and home to a good concentration of rare species including pygmy elephant and bongo. The idea of the project was to improve local livelihoods from the forest by means other than poaching, through developing controlled tourist facilities. Raleigh were building a visitor reception centre and educational walkway, a campsite, and an observation post. These were not small tasks. The walkway involved a bridge over a river, and construction included use of great timber uprights some eighteen inches square and twelve feet long.

The Raleigh volunteers were living for months in hammocks simply slung between trees in the middle of the rain forest. I went to visit them on what was billed as a "Morale-raising visit". It raised my morale, anyhow – I don't know if it worked for them.

It was the Easter holiday, so I took Peter and my private car, and we battled our way down to Ankassa though torrential rain. When it rains in Ghana, it feels like someone just lifted a bit of the sea and dumped it straight on your head. The rain is so dense you fear you might drown in it. You very quickly find yourself knee deep. It is an exciting and exhilarating experience.

The rain turned a five hour drive to eight hours, and it was dark as we threaded our way along a narrow, partly submerged track in the rain forest. The World was limited by the beam of our headlights, and that was hemmed in and foreshortened by the sheets of rain. Rounding a corner, suddenly our headlights hit a wet wall a few yards ahead. It was a dead end. Then, slowly, the wall moved away, and I realised to my amazement that it was an elephant. Peter pressed on. Eventually we were signalled to a halt by torches flashing from the track side, and met by half a dozen enthusiastic young volunteers from Raleigh. They led us by torchlight along a track, half a mile into the forest. There, in a dell – not a clearing, it was full of trees - was their camp, visible only as the odd flicker in the dark of torch or storm lantern.

I am not sure I had ever seen blackness as dark as the darkness of that night. A mature rainforest canopy is itself pretty impenetrable, even in daytime only letting through a dank green gloom. But any chance of star-light or moonlight was removed by the vast banks of storm cloud, many miles high and covering the entire sky, that invisibly separated us from view of the rest of the universe. Absolute, perfect darkness is something we rarely experience, and on which a torch beam has very little effect. Once I was in my hammock and the lights were off, the total absence of light was oppressive.

I had not anticipated that we would be straight to bed (it was only about 8pm), but the volunteers started backbreaking physical labour at first light, worked all day, then got into their hammocks before total dark fell. I hadn't eaten since breakfast, but it was straight out of my now sodden clothing and into my hammock. This consisted of a tarpaulin spread with sticks at both ends and suspended by ropes between two great forest trees, with a second larger tarpaulin bent over a single rope above it, tied to the ground both sides to form a roof.

The problem was, the torrential rain wasn't falling on to the roof, it was being driven in sideways under the roof and a substantial amount of it was collecting in the hammock. I emptied it out before getting in, but my sleeping bag was soon sodden, and within a quarter of an hour I was sleeping in a positive puddle. I considered cutting a hole in the bottom of the hammock with a penknife, but it wasn't my hammock. I could not empty it out every fifteen minutes all night, so I decided just to try to sleep in the puddle, which was surprisingly successful.

It says something for the ferocity of a Ghanaian storm that it could drive sideways a continual stream of great gouts of water, underneath the rain forest canopy and through the massed undergrowth, without any apparent diminution in the amount of the rain or speed of the wind. As the bottom of the large hammock filled with heavy water, it sunk down more steeply and I, sleeping, curled more and more into the bottom. I woke up choking. My head had fallen below the water level in my hammock! I cursed, wondering if anyone had ever drowned in a hammock. I got out, emptied it again, and got back in (getting yourself into a sleeping bag on a hammock in total darkness is not easy at all). As I lay there in the absolute dark, I heard from somewhere in the camp the distinctive noises of a couple having sex. I could only admire the fortitude of youth.

I awoke at 6.45 to a bright sunny morning with the camp bathed in green light, with my nostrils filled with the delicious mixed smells of wood smoke and bacon. Opening my eyes I looked down from my hammock, to where a heart-stoppingly beautiful young girl was frying bacon and eggs over a wood fire. She looked up at me and smiled, with her wide mouth and sparkling teeth and with her clear blue eyes. She had long light hair and a delicate, freckled complexion.

"Boz thought you'd be wanting your breakfast" she explained.

She was one of those light, Scottish girls so fey as to be almost invisible. She told me her name was Rose and she was on a gap year before starting at Edinburgh University.

She handed me breakfast on a metal plate and a cup of tea in a china mug with a picture of Lincoln Cathedral on it. The campsite looked like the Battle of the Somme. Now there was some light I could see that everything and everybody was covered in thick black mud, including all my clothes. In fact it took me quite a while to identify one heap of dirt as my trousers.

"They don't call it rain forest for nothing" Rose said, "you'll want those washing". She collected all my things and went walking down the path towards the river, looking like a mystical creature in the forest half light.

Boz appeared, staring at Rose's lithesome retreating back.

"Yes, mate. I know how you feel. Gorgeous, isn't she?" he grinned.

Boz was a large, heavy man, in his late twenties, fond of a beer and with a ready laugh. A self-employed builder from Birmingham, he was very different from the normal Raleigh participant. He had come for one expedition and stayed on for another. He wasn't paying Raleigh and they weren't paying him, but he was happy, and his skills were essential to directing his enthusiastic young volunteers.

We went to inspect the very impressive building projects Raleigh were undertaking. I was startled by their ambition. Peter, who used to be a carpenter in the gold mines, started helping out enthusiastically, while I posed for photos with a hammer and a gaggle of beautiful girls in boots and hard hats. The volunteers enjoyed showing off what they had done, and showing me around the reserve. It is a beautiful place. The "Bamboo cathedral", a vast natural space enclosed by hundred foot arches of bamboo, is amazing, with a truly numinous atmosphere. As I stood looking up, a green mamba emerged from the litter of bamboo leaves at my feet, whipped through my legs, and vanished into a great clump of bamboo.

Too soon I had to leave, as I was visiting another Raleigh project with Sight Savers in the afternoon. I was giving Boz a lift back to Accra.

"I know a good place for lunch; we are going past it anyway," he said. He directed us to the Ankobra Beach Resort. I felt in something of a daze as we walked in. I could not explain why. As we sat in the restaurant, I realised that it was again Easter Sunday, and one year later I was in exactly the same restaurant, at the same table, as I had been on Easter Sunday the last year when Buckman came in to me with the message of my father's death. I had not been back to Ankobra since, and would not have done so now if Boz had not suggested it. It was not too wild a coincidence, but it still made me feel closer to my father.

That put me in to a rather reflective mood, and Boz looked at me questioningly.

"Still thinking about Rose?" he asked. I said I was, and to lighten things up, I said that I bet him three beers I could get Rose's name at least five times into my two minute speech at the Sight Savers clinic. Boz readily agreed, adding:

"But "A rose by any other name" is not allowed, OK?"

I readily agreed. Arriving at the village housing the clinic, we found scores of local dignitaries seated under canopies, and then a large crowd of grateful patients. It was all very celebratory. The Sight Savers doctors and Raleigh volunteers, who were doing the organisation and nursing, stopped work for twenty minutes to watch. Winking at Boz, I strode to the microphone, acknowledged the local chief and other dignitaries, and then gave a brief speech:

"This morning, when I aRose, I was concerned how many people would bother to come out on Easter Sunday to this ceremony. Nonetheless I Rose to the occasion, and when I arrived I was delighted to see so many Rose upon Rose of beautiful people seated here. That is of course, not a tribute to me but to the excellent work being done by Sight Savers and by Raleigh, helping those who once having suffered the slings and aRose of outrageous fortune, their sight is now thankfully restored..."

Champs Bar in Accra remains my favourite bar in the whole world. The original Irish Rover in Warsaw was perhaps just better, but has long gone. Champs still goes strong, and the atmosphere has not really changed in ten years. Patrick, the Canadian owner, is a great host.

Those young NGO volunteers, mostly from the US and UK, form the backbone of the clientèle, and when they hit town they are really out to party. Add to that meandering backpackers, including a fair smattering of ageing hippies and rastafarians, a whole gaggle of young Ghanaian professionals, a few expatriates and prostitutes from West Africa, Eastern Europe and Morocco, and you have the most vibrant mixture I know. Somehow at least a score of extra totally random ethnicities get added into that mix on any given Friday night, and you have the most multi-cultural crowd imaginable. I used to be the oldest person there in 1999, and I am still going.

My favourite drinking companions were the girls who worked in our visa section. It was sadly not possible to give jobs on visa issuing and visa processing to Ghanaians – the social pressures on Ghanaians from family and friends to steal or defraud visas would be absolutely irresistible. You would be putting Ghanaians in an impossible position, and even possibly at risk, if it were known they had physical access to visas. I had a constant fight with London over this, because of the most senseless piece of New Labour political correctness combined with Treasury meanness – bluntly, it's cheaper to employ Ghanaians. I fought off the demands to "indigenise" visa issuing and processing, at one stage facing an accusation of racism for my insistence that it would be wrong to give the job to Ghanaians. The strange thing was, every one of my many Ghanaian friends agreed with me entirely that it would be crazy to employ Ghanaians in this role. It was people in Whitehall who had never seen West Africa who were pressing for it.

The upshot was, that I was able to reserve the jobs for non-Ghanaians, but at salaries too low to attract British people, even partners of those settled in Ghana or in the High Commission. So we ended up recruiting a number of young people who enjoyed being in Ghana and were not too bothered about money, and a number of Eastern Europeans. I made great friends with these girls. There was Michaela from Germany, a real party animal with a motherly soul; the very conscientious Luda from Belarus; pert little Nathalie who was half Russian and half Togolese; the beautiful ethnic Korean, Irina from Tashkent, who had a husband in the US Embassy, and the imposing Ukrainian Zhanna Horn, who with her Scots husband Keith formed a permanent party. These were the people I spent my weekend nights with. After Champs we would often go on to The Office, a great cocktail lounge owned by a friendly Sierra Leonean named Abdul. This venue was always very crushed and much given to spontaneous dancing. As I often had my arm in a sling or strapped, Abdul installed me on a cocktail stool on the barmen's side of the counter to save me from the crush. Just as had happened in Poland, I soon reached the stage where in my favourite bars they never charged me.

I came downstairs in Devonshire House one Sunday morning with a frightful hangover, one of those really piercing headaches you get when you have been mixing your drinks too foolishly. I staggered into the kitchen and filled the kettle from the big stainless steel water filter in the corner. Then I pushed the plug into the socket. Surreally, I met with no resistance and my hand just kept moving forward until my arm was fully extended. For a split second my rather blurry brain was trying to make out how this could be, then my eyes focussed on the kitchen wall, which seemed to be falling away from me in slow motion. Bloody hell, what had I drunk last night? Then there was a huge "Crash!" The wall hit the ground, and I was staring out at the garden through a cloud of dust

That would be pretty disorienting even if you didn't have a hangover. I had simply pushed the wall out trying to insert a plug. I had not discovered superpowers. It turned out that the kitchen, which was a single storey addition on the back of the house, had been built of a single file of bricks and without any foundation at all.

I didn't realise it, but I was in great danger as I stood there, bewildered. A single concrete slab had been cast on top of the wall for a roof. The concrete was over a foot thick, and the slab must have weighed many tons. The back wall having fallen out, it was held up only by the two equally flimsy side walls, which had of course just lost most of the little structural integrity they had. I stepped over the rubble into the back garden and sat down on the grass, still clutching my kettle. I had to go and live in the Labadi Beach Hotel for a couple of months while Devonshire House was partially rebuilt.

A very bright young Second Secretary, Greg Quinn, had replaced Mike Nithavrianakis on the political side, and Greg had organised an intern from the FCO to spend the summer with us. Her name was Adrienne Ramainian, an English girl from a French Iranian family, and she came with a very impressive CV. As Greg brought her in to my office on her first morning, I was even more impressed by her darks wells of eyes and by her dazzling smile. She was a witty, charming companion. I took her to Champs, and took her marlin fishing with my great friend Bryan Harris at his superb beach house at Ada, where we spent many lazy afternoons. I introduced Adrienne to President Kufuor. We spent her first week in Accra constantly together, and the hour got later every day in which I dropped her back at her flat, with a chaste peck on her forehead.

London had called for a report on child labour in the cocoa industry. Cocoa remains fundamental to the Ghanaian economy, but the major farming areas had retreated westwards before the spread of blackpod disease from the East. I asked Adrienne if she would care to join me, and we travelled by Landrover deep into the major cocoa producing regions. After a long, eventful journey, much of it on unmade road through forest, we arrived at the district capital of Enchi, and stayed there in a government guest house. We had a chicken supper, washed down with the champagne I always took with me when I travelled. After supper we called on the village chief, which involved a lot of Schnapps, and then visited a very pleasant Scottish volunteer named Donald, who came from Crieff and was teaching maths at the local teachers training college.

By the time we returned to the government guest house, it was late and we were not entirely sober. The staff had automatically taken my things into the master bedroom, which was large, clean and air-conditioned, with a double bed. The other available bedrooms were old and very dirty with no air-conditioning. Adrienne's stuff had been taken to one of these.

I gave Adrienne her customary peck on the forehead to say goodnight. "I was wondering," I asked, "would you like to sleep in the double bed?"

Crack. Her open palm slapped hard into my cheek, sending my spectacles flying across the room.

"I thought as much," she yelled, "you just brought me out here so you can try and screw me."

"No," I said, "I didn't mean that. I just meant would you like the single bed, and I'll take the crummy room."

I was telling the truth, and the misunderstanding was so funny that we both dissolved in giggles. They were a bit hysterical, partly because we were drunk, and partly because her remark had stripped away the cover on a whole mess of sexual tension between us. She declined the better bedroom, and we each went to our own beds.

The next day we started a slow sweep Eastwards through the cocoa belt. We stopped in many towns and villages, and then I would ask the farmers about their practices regarding child labour. I would also ask the chief and the local priest, if I could find one, and ask the schoolteacher if children were missing school through work on cocoa.

The results were consistent. Cocoa in Ghana is a smallholding crop, with individual farmers having a hectare or two of mixed crops, including cocoa. It is not a plantation crop as it is in Brazil or Ivory Coast. That is why Ghanaian cocoa is of higher quality, and commands a premium on commodity markets. Cadbury's chocolate in the UK uses 95% Ghanaian cocoa.

There is an old sailor's rhyme that goes:

"Beware, my boy, o'the Bight o' Benin,

There's one that comes back for twenty goes in."

That wasn't too much of an exaggeration. White people just could not survive the climate and disease of West Africa, before the advent of modern medicine. There are numerous sad little colonial graveyards all over Ghana, not just in Accra and Kumasi, but all along the coast in places like Keta, Ada, Elmina and Axim. The surviving gravestones show most of the occupants to be in their early twenties. Nor could their cattle survive the climate and pests.

A country where white men could not settle, and the cattle could not live, had the advantage of being subject only to the lightest form of colonialism. Locals were not forced from their land as they were in Kenya or Zimbabwe, and traditional land structures remained in Ghana, as did the chieftaincy institutions which control them. That is a major contributor to Ghana's social stability.

I used to be a devotee of the theory made popular by De Soto, that security of land tenure, giving a farmer mortgageable capital to raise cash for improvement, was a necessary step to development. Now I have my doubts. The violence in Kenya, Zimbabwe and Ivory Coast can all be traced directly to the uprooting of peoples entailing disruption of traditional land patterns.

We are also terribly arrogant about African farming, convinced that our science and techniques are better than the knowledge of those whose methods have accumulated from the experience of thousands of years winning a living from the soil in local conditions. In Ghana as elsewhere in Africa, farming has to cope with extremely friable soil, baking heat, and rain that comes in heavy torrents. No matter how careful the design of bunds and ditches, every attempt I have seen to introduce Western systems has resulted in massive soil erosion.

We also patronisingly underrate the productivity of African farms. A typical mixed and intercropped Ghanaian smallholding is actually highly productive from the available resource. Often to the untrained eye the spindly cassava and tufts of yam, mixed in with plantain, tomato, cocoa and even citrus, just looks like a bit of bush. I enjoyed walking Adrienne around and explaining all of this, and she had the politeness to look interested.

My conclusion was that there is no real problem with child labour in the Ghanaian cocoa industry. It is almost unheard of for children to work on any smallholding except their own family's. There they are simply helping their dad or uncle. They are not working long hours, and for someone to miss a couple of weeks school in the harvest season would be extremely unusual, and would be about as bad as it gets. In short, I concluded that the problem which existed on the plantations of Ivory Coast, does not extend into the smallholdings of Ghana.

After we finished our cocoa investigations, we went to visit Ashanti Gold's mine at Obuasi. Following my role in resolving their financial crisis, I was extremely welcome there. To enter Obuasi leaves you in no doubt that you are approaching an environmental disaster. A pall of choking red dust hangs over the town, and absolutely everything – buildings, trees, vehicles, clothing, people – is stained by it. The town is as sorry and dilapidated a shanty town as you can imagine, with cascades of rubbish on the hilly terrain. It is a disgrace that the town that produces the greatest concentration of wealth in Ghana should be one of the least prosperous. Ashanti was doing a certain amount in community programmes, but plainly not nearly enough.

By strange contrast, once you pass through the vast security fence into the mine area itself, the environment greatly improves. The offices and management housing have the air of a colonial hill station and are located upwind from the mine. We were very warmly received and taken on a tour. The sheer size of the opencast pit is breathtaking, with great vehicles roaring past and down the vast helter-skelter sides, until very quickly they look like small insects scuttling around below.

Best of all is to see a gold pour. In the gold house, a strapping bearded Ghanaian, in huge padded leather boots, a great leather apron and a welder's helmet, raked the slag off the liquid fire of the furnace. Then he tilted the crucible until a great stream of white hot gold gushed forth, falling down one, two, three, four, five steps and forming ingots in the hollowed out mould in each. This was the moment, the culmination, the apotheosis of thousands of tonnes of dirt milled, sieved, washed, sorted, reduced and fired. No matter how good the assay, you never really knew how much gold you had in your ore until this moment, when you saw how many ingot moulds the pour filled. Afterwards, Adrienne got to hold a whole ingot; I have never seen eyes burn with lust the way Adrienne's did as she saw the ingot and bent her knees to heft it. I only wish her eyes had looked like that when she saw me!

We stayed the night in the mine's guest house. Built in 1950's colonial style, with Crittall aluminium windows, it was built on a steep hill so that the ground floor entrance on one side led to the first floor balcony on the next. We had eaten a roast chicken dinner and the cook had just gone home. The living room led on to the balcony and we decided to go and sit outside. I had to put my shoulder to the metal door to get it open, with great difficulty and a nasty scraping noise. The hinges appeared to have dropped and there was a gouged arc in the concrete floor of the balcony. I pushed the door back closed again to keep out the mosquitoes. We sat on the balcony to enjoy our wine in the night. Being so isolated, a dense canopy of stars spread above us with astonishing clarity. I have never known the sky look so full.

As we sat, rather awed, suddenly there was a hideous shriek from the garden. It sounded almost, but not quite, human. It sounded like somebody in extreme pain. It seemed to come from very close, from the garden just below the balcony. We both got up to look; there was a Stygian darkness down there, and no sign of movement. Then more shrieks, unnervingly close and very human. I looked at Adrienne:

"Baboons?"

"No, thank you" she replied.

Suddenly, the whole garden seemed filled with wailing, so loud we had to shout above it.

"It really does sound like a lot of... things"– I didn't like to say people. "And it sounds exactly as if it is coming from just down there."

"Weird, isn't it?" said Adrienne, "must be a trick of the hills."

The suddenly, the noise stopped, with no prior abatement, just as if someone flicked a switch. The silence was extraordinary, and it was a good thirty seconds before the cicadas whirred into life again and the normal thrum of an African evening reached our ears.

We both agreed that evidently there had been some noisy birds in the garden which had been suddenly frightened off by something. I refilled our wine glasses and we tried to get back to normal conversation, when suddenly there came an angry scream, undoubtedly a human yelling at the top of his lungs, and it came from right beside us on the balcony – but there was no-one there.

"OK, now I am scared" I said.

Adrienne just nodded, wide-eyed. Then suddenly the balcony door slammed open with a great crash.

I tried to appear calm: "That's strange, I didn't feel any wind."

"That was really difficult to open earlier" said Adrienne.

"Yes, it was. Perhaps something fell back into place."

"Can we go inside now?"

"Good idea."

Sticking together, we walked to the door. It had opened with force and really wedged itself against the concrete at the end of its gouged arc, so as we entered the house it took both of us to wrench it back closed again. I then opened it once more to see if it could now swing freely outwards. No, it still took a great deal of effort to get it open.

"Look, don't worry. In this climate you easily get freak gusts of wind" I said, unconvincingly.

Adrienne curled up in an armchair with a book, while I closed the balcony door again. It had a hinged metal bar as a locking device. When you swung it into position two closed metal loops, one attached to the balcony door and one to the frame, passed through a slit in the metal bar. You then passed the hasp of the padlock through both metal loops and locked it, securing the bar in position. It felt very comfortable to have that door firmly locked against whatever was outside, even if it only was unnervingly noisy birds.

I got out a book myself and took another armchair. After a few minutes Adrienne said:

"Did you do that?"

"Do what?"

"Did you organise that performance to try to scare me into your bed?"

"Certainly bloody not! I'm sorry, of course I mean I'd love to have you in my bed, but I didn't organise – whatever it was that happened. How could I? I don't really know what happened myself."

"Well, it nearly worked."

Suddenly there was a metallic clang, then the balcony door flew open again with an almighty crash.

Adrienne looked at me accusingly.

"I thought you locked that."

"I did. I mean I was sure that I did."

Now I really was feeling scared; that cold, clammy feeling when all your skin starts to sweat and the hairs stand up all over your body, and you feel uncertain if you want to go to the loo or to run.

With a huge effort I stood up and walked calmly to the balcony. I looked out; there was no sign of anything or anybody. I must just have not closed the padlock properly. It was lying on the floor – I bent down and picked it up. It was firmly locked! This was impossible. The locked hasp had somehow passed through the two closed metal loops of the door and frame. I checked these and found them undamaged. What on Earth had just happened?[53]

I was shaken and confused. Again it took a great deal of effort to scrape the door back over the floor and close it. I fetched the key of the padlock, opened it, and went through the locking process again. I could figure out nothing which I might have done the first time which could have that result. Adrienne and I, by some unspoken agreement, did not talk about it further. We both resumed reading our books, and after a little desultory conversation, went to our respective bedrooms. I lay awake for quite some time, alert to every sound and moving shadow, but eventually tiredness overtook me. The rest of the night was uneventful for both of us.

The next day, before returning to Accra, I took Adrienne down to Cape Coast. We visited Elmina Castle and Cape Coast Castle. The castles of Ghana are an absolute wonder, and it is astonishing that they should be

---

53 Kind friends have urged me not to publish this story. I offer no explanation, I saw the impossible. If we shy away from recording events we cannot explain for fear of ridicule, we will not help to advance the cause of human understanding.

so little known in the UK. The rival European empires established forti-
fied trading posts along the coast, and these developed into fully fledged
castles. Elmina, built in 1480 by the Portuguese, was the first, and it is so
old and so thoroughly European that it is really hard to believe it is in
Africa. The Dutch, Danes and British all followed and all built massive
castles.

At first the traders sought gold and ivory, then the castles became the
great depots of the transatlantic slave trade, then in the nineteenth century they were headquarters to the British Navy West Africa patrol as
they fought to put down the slave trade. Cape Coast castle remained the
seat of the British colonial administration, and Ghana is still in 2008 ad-
ministered by its Presidency from the 450 year old Danish castle of Kristi-
anborg in Osu. My good friend Thomas Svanikier grew up in Osu, a des-
cendant of an 18th century Danish governor of the same name. Ghana is
full of living reminders of its long and mixed relationship with Europe.

Some of the castles are exploited as a tourist attraction, with a strong
eye on the interests of African American tourists. But they concentrate ex-
clusively on the slaving period of the castles. Slavery was a terrible thing,
and should be remembered. But there is a dishonesty in the ideological
presentation, which refuses to acknowledge the key role played in the
slave trade by Africans. Over 90 per cent of the slaves exported from
Africa were sold by Africans. Forget Alex Haley, white men did not go
out catching slaves. White men were of course far and away the chief be-
neficiaries of the trade. Slavery is a terrible blot on the history of Britain,
most European countries and the United States. But many African chiefs
did rather well out of it too. Later, there were thousands of Royal Naval
personnel based in and around Ghana's castles who died in West Africa,
mostly of disease, over almost a century of concerted effort to stamp out
the trade. They also deserve a mention. While we should always remember, we should remember the whole truth, not just the simplified black su-
premacist version which Ghana is now teaching.

After the castles, I took Adrienne to the canopy walkway. This is truly
spectacular, as you walk across rope bridges suspended in the rain forest
canopy, some 50 metres off the ground. It was built by a Canadian NGO,
and the fun is that, while it is perfectly safe and impossible to fall off acci-

dentally, it feels dangerous. It doesn't really have the claimed educational or ecological value, any wildlife having been scared away from the area years ago by all the people on the walkway. But it is certainly fun. I was later to take a party of British MPs along it. Diane Abbott had no problems, but one strapping male Tory MP could not cope with the heights.

Adrienne was now a little nervous, but managed OK. I had organised a private tour, so we were the only people up there. As we stood on a platform high above the ground, looking down at a sweep of rain forest through the valley, I decided that it was now or never, and leant forward to kiss her. I had only made the very first move of my head, when she screamed and leapt back. I thought that was a bit of an overreaction, then she pointed on to the walkway, just a few yards from us. It was yet another bloody green mamba! I know people who have been in Ghana sixty years and never seen one. They seemed to be chasing me everywhere.

The moment had passed. Back in Accra, Adrienne and I continued to spend almost all our waking moments together. She would invite me back for coffee in the evenings, and one night I sat up until about 3am, her head on my chest, stroking her hair, while she talked about her life and her hopes. Still I made no real move – I don't exactly know how it happened that way.

I was giving one of my spectacular parties for British volunteer workers in Ghana and their Ghanaian contacts. I was expecting about six hundred people. They came from Voluntary Service Overseas (VSO originated in Ghana), Raleigh International, Teaching and Projects Abroad and a host of smaller organisations.

These parties had a very special atmosphere. Most of the participants were in their gap year; they were embarked on what would remain in many cases the great adventure of their lives. They had mostly been working very hard, often living in what by British standards would be deprivation, eating local food with no drinkable tap water, no computer or satellite TV and sometimes even no electricity. Sometimes they came from very isolated locations. Certainly at least the Raleigh people had not been allowed to drink on expedition.

Now they were thrown into the grand surroundings of Devonshire House, with three hundred flickering paraffin lights lining the sweep of the drive between the large manicured lawns. A couple of football pitches worth of lawn was bathed for the occasion in bright halogen light, and the grass extended beyond into the darkness.

As I greeted young people as they started to pour out of buses, minibuses, taxis and battered Landrovers, I realised with surprise that I seemed a posh and important figure to these people, even remote. Then, as they wandered into and through the house, between verandahs and marquees, the guests were offered every possible drink by a score of white jacketed waiters, and ate fillet steak, cheese soufflé, or a vast variety of canapés.

Everyone had showered and the girls, their hair washed perhaps for the first time in weeks and glistening down long, tanned, bare backs, were each wearing their one party dress that had been retrieved from the bottom of the rucksack and lovingly ironed. The boys were fit and tanned, open neck shirts revealing strings of multicoloured beads, hair long and wild, bodies fit and bronzed. Eyes were bright and sparkling. There would be a huge amount of shagging after the party, and even some during, as couples discovered the guest wing or the distant swathes of unlit lawn and shrub. I signalled to my steward John to start the music, and the words and spirit of Supertramp seemed entirely apposite as it swept over the lawns and out over Accra:

When I was young
It seemed that life was so wonderful
A miracle, oh it was beautiful, magical
And all the birds in the trees
Well they'd be singing so happily
Joyfully, oh playfully watching me

And this was the night I was going to have Adrienne. Our flirting and our snogging had been building, and I had several times whispered into her ear during a clinch that we would do it after the party. She had shuddered, ground her hips against me and given me what she called a butterfly kiss, brushing my cheeks with her long fluttering eyelashes.

Tonight I would fuck Adrienne at last.

The excitement of the party was building; the excited buzz was near riotous, the dance floor was full, everywhere there was animated conversation, and my High Commission staff were doing their job in making sure that nobody was left out and lonely. Adrienne had arrived and was helping out everywhere. I was going from table to table and marquee to marquee chatting to guests. When Adrienne and I crossed paths, she would give me a sultry look. I snatched one moment alone with her, inside the house.

"I think you'll marry me now" I said.

"Yeah, right. You'll have to do a lot more than this" she replied. She kissed me and then quickly pulled away.

"Work to do!" she teased and vanished back towards the melee.

And it was a melee. The thirst of these young adults was quite astonishing. Even my battery of waiters were overwhelmed. They had taken to simply handing out bottles of wine and even spirits. Two of the five vast chest freezers used to chill beer were already empty. The drivers were shuttling around the city for ice. Table service had more or less been abandoned and the waiters had retreated behind the bar. Although the bar tables were heavy, they were not fixed to the ground, and the pressure of the crowd against them had moved the bar back about five yards until the space between it and the freezers was cramped. As people crushed towards the bar, it was like a scene from *Zulu!* only with the black people inside the barricade. Greg Quinn was helping out manfully. I went round the back, and started serving behind the bar.

"Bottle of white wine – certainly, here you are. Need any glasses? Three, OK. John how many people are on glass collection? Two? Detail two more, and one more on washing. And open some new boxes of glasses. Sorry sir, what was that? Guinness and two gins and tonic. OK, hang on. Greg, which freezer has the frozen lemon slices? Right. Hammer to that ice block John, quick! Here you are sir. What's that? Four Pimms. OK, take the bottle. Here's four glasses of ice. Fruit over there, here's a knife, cut it yourself. Yes? Three lagers. Coming up!"

I turned and lent over a chest freezer, plunging my left hand down and pulling up a crate of cold lager. Sudden, hideous pain.

"Aaagh!"

I fell down, the crate of lager landing on my chest. The world was full of nothing but pain. I had no idea where I was. I couldn't breathe. I had pulled my shoulder out of its socket again, hefting the lager.

I was carried inside the house. Despite the terrible pain, my brain cleared somewhat. George Opata and John were with me.

"Get my sling, John. It's in the bedside cabinet."

John and Opie fastened the sling, and I stood up. It was absolute agony. Every movement was so painful that I actually lost vision for an instant. I went down the stairs almost entirely blind, staggered outdoors to the very first table and sat down at it, to the astonishment of the young volunteers who sat there.

"Hope you're enjoying the party," I slurred, and grinned a rictus grin. My shirt was completely wet with sweat and beads of it were dripping off my brow. John had followed me.

"I'll have a Talisker, John."

The volunteers tried to make polite conversation, their party mood temporarily halted, but I couldn't really hear them and could hardly see them. I was making a monumental effort of will, and my brain was calculating my chances:

"I must shag Adrienne: must shag Adrienne. Christ I hope I can still get it up."

I stared at the breasts of the very pretty blonde girl next to me, to see if anything stirred. I could see her whole left breast through the armhole of her kaftan. Yes, things seemed to be working. My brain still worked too, but it was slowing:

"Must shag Adrienne. See doctor tomorrow. Arm a problem. Can't move much. I'll have to sit and she can climb on. Adrienne can climb on. Jiggle about a bit. Gently though. Hospital in morning. Where is Adrienne? Oh, here's Michaela."

And I passed out. The next thing I remember, I woke up again in the Trust Hospital around noon, with my shoulder reset and mercifully little pain. Apparently as I was loaded into an ambulance I had kept shouting urgently to Michaela and Greg: "Don't stop the party. Take over. Keep the party going." But they had closed it down as they were nervous about having hundreds of partying people in my home without me there.

This time they put my arm in a sling rather than tape it to my chest, and I had another week in Accra, continuing with Adrienne as before. This included a wonderful day as guests of Dick Barber at his little hut on the beach at PramPram. Dick was an old Scot who had been the representative for United Distillers, until it became plain that he might drink through the entire stock. He was a bright, wry man with a great knowledge of West Africa, and a genuinely kind soul. He was not a well man, but it didn't stop him enjoying life. I had organised British passports for his children by his long term Ghanaian partner. We now had lunch on the beach. It was an idyllic day, which I think Adrienne loved too.

The next night, I was returning to London for an operation on my shoulder. By the time I returned to Accra, Adrienne would have finished her internship with us, so this was the end of the great unconsummated love of my life. The FCO had told me that there was even a danger that, if Guy's Hospital were unable to stabilise my shoulder, I might not be allowed to return to Accra at all. So the gang were meeting up in Champs before I left on the midnight flight, just in case this turned out to be a farewell party.

We had been drinking and chatting for an hour or so, with me circulating round several groups of friends who had been summoned at short notice. Adrienne was looking at me strangely. Tears were forming in the corners of her eyes.

"Don't think I'll miss you. I won't" she said to me quite loudly. I was a little embarrassed by this, as there were quite a few people around.

"Do you want to talk outside?" I asked quietly.

"Not to you, I don't" she replied. I squeezed her arm, and she shook me off. Not wanting a scene, I moved on to talk to another group. After a while. Patrick the bar owner came and whispered in my ear "Craig, I think you'd better go and see Adrienne."

I walked across to where Adrienne was surrounded by a group of girls. She pulled me in and started insulting me, while I tried to calm her. Adrienne was by now in full spate, the tears flowing freely. She spoke with an unnerving sense of the iron control of extreme emotion. I was distressed that I couldn't understand her train of thought so was at a loss how to respond. I just stood there grinning weakly. She was laughing and crying simultaneously.

"You bastard," she said, "I hate you. I really do, I...firmly... hate you. That's forever. You thought you could make me fall in love with you, did you, and then coolly go back to your wife? Well it didn't work. I don't love you, you see. I don't love you, I hate you. You're stupid and arrogant. I hear you can't even get it up."

She turned to the bar in general and produced a large, firm booming voice that sounded suddenly and surprisingly sober and unslurred:

"Do you hear that? He can't get it up. The famous Craig Murray can't even get it up. He never fucked me. Do you hear that? He never fucked me. He wanted you all to think he did, but he didn't"

"What kind of man is this? Ask yourself, is this a man, standing here with that stupid grin on his face? Call that a man? What kind of man takes a young girl, here in Africa, she's young, she's scared she's thousands of miles from home, and this man, this man, her boss, he's supposed to take care of her. He's supposed to look after her. He's meant to be like ... like ...a parent. And then he abuses her. He abuses her emotions. What kind of man is that? He abuses her. He abuses a student in his care. Abuses without fucking. What does it mean, abusing without fucking? What can it mean?"

"I'll tell you what it means. I'll tell you what it bloody well means. Fucks with her head. He can't fuck my body. So he's fucking my head. He's scum. I hate him. You don't know how bad he is. He's scum. I hate him".

Adrienne then sat down again and started to sob. I went to move towards her but Michaela ushered me away. While Adrienne was addressing the bar, people had originally gone quiet and listened, but as the tirade developed they started talking again, and by the time she had finished the conversation level was back to normal. It was still early evening, there were only a dozen or so people in apart from our group, and almost everyone there was a friend of mine. A protective huddle of girls formed around Adrienne. Patrick discreetly came up to my shoulder and suggested it was time I left for the airport. He was right.

I had been trying to seem casual about my own feelings – indeed I had not really been quite sure what my own feelings were. But now the moment came to part from Adrienne, possibly forever, I felt suddenly overwhelmed by grief, like I was hollowed out inside. I believe I visibly swayed, as though recovering from a blow. Michaela later told me I had gone an awful blue grey colour.

I walked up to the girls.

"Anyone coming to the airport?"

Luda immediately bounced up and took my arm

"Of course, we all are" she said.

Adrienne looked at me with red-rimmed eyes, the lower lids still welling tears.

"I'm not coming with that bastard", she said. It was strange. She gave no impression at all of someone pretending hate to hide love, which I had rather hoped it was. It came over as deep hatred, plain and simple.

Michaela massaged her back.

"Come on Adrienne", she said, "you can't leave him like this. He did a lot for you."

So six of us left for the car, a strange group. I led and a knot of girls came behind, Adrienne almost being dragged along. She was still looking daggers at me. She sat in the back of the Land Rover with three other girls, while I squeezed into the front with Joe Domi the driver and little Nathalie. I felt a strong urge to stop the car, tell her I loved her, and not go to London. But with the agony from my left arm, held on by being taped to my chest, and a bed and operating theatre awaiting me in Guy's hospital, I could hardly just pull out now. I felt like a prisoner being led away.

Arriving at the airport, we all piled into the VVIP lounge. There I tried to raise the general spirits. I had to dictate my particulars to the immigration officer as I couldn't write without the use of my left hand; I got half way through spelling out my occupation as D R U N K A R D when he caught on and scrapped the first form.

"Mr Murray, you are our favourite but silliest customer" he said.

When it was finally time to go, British Airways insisted on pushing me across the tarmac in a wheelchair because of my arm, even though I pointed out I didn't walk on it. At the exit from the VVIP lounge, which has its own immigration and customs facilities, to the tarmac, Michaela pushed Adrienne forward:

"She's his wife. She must walk with him to see him on the plane."

So Adrienne accompanied me across the tarmac, now through streaming rain. She took my good hand when I held it out to her, and at last I started to cry. Now we were almost alone, apart from the man pushing the wheelchair, my soul yearned for some final words of comfort, endearment and hope for the future.

Suddenly, Adrienne produced a wild, primeval scream that echoed in the dark night along the miles of airport tarmac.

"You're fat. You're old, old and you're fat. You're a disgusting pervert, a disgusting, old old fattie. You're so old you'll die soon. Good. I hate you. I want you to die."

I was astonished. I still told myself that surely this was a reaction to her love for me, that in time she'd come round. But real doubt was undermining me.

The wheelchair reached the aircraft steps. I stood and turned, feeling foolish. The guy who pushed the wheelchair looked from one to the other of us in amazement, then discreetly walked away. I felt bewildered. Here, then was the end of a great love? As the rain streamed onto the tarmac, sparkling orange in the sodium light, this should have been our Bogart and Bergman moment. I would never get a chance like this again, so I tried.

"Well – here's looking at you, kid. We'll always have Obuasi".

"Just fucking leave" she said. She easily evaded my one-handed attempt at a hug, turned and stormed back to the VVIP lounge. The other girls were waving from the entrance.

A BA man came forward: "Please, sir. The aircraft is waiting for you."

"Oh, sorry. Thank you."

I walked up the forward steps, self consciously turning and posing halfway up to wave to the girls. I hope the rain disguised the tears now streaming down my own face. Of course I always had the excuse of a busted arm.

I was in first class so I could lay out flat. The seats were equipped with credit card phones that could call from the air, and I spent the first four hours of the flight calling Adrienne's Ghanaian mobile many hundreds of times. She never answered, and I was tormented with the thought that she had gone and screwed someone else because of her emotional state. I was utterly desolate.

Well, not quite utterly. Nathalie was a very pretty little thing indeed, with an extremely good figure. Adrienne would not still be in Ghana when I returned, but Nathalie would. As we were crammed together in the front of the Landrover, I had given her an exploratory lingering squeeze, right at the top of her left thigh, that could not have been construed as merely friendly. She had responded with a sparkling open-lipped smile.

One should never forget there is always a future.

I was in the UK for a few weeks, having a successful operation on my shoulder.

It won't surprise you that by now the diplomatic service really were scratching their heads as to what to do with me. Over-passionate, over-committed and given to complete no-nos like admitting that British firms were involved in corruption. Completely undiplomatic, and yet at the same time undeniably successful far beyond the limited goals of ordinary diplomats, and with a repeated history of earning respect and admiration for the UK wherever I served. In fact successive bosses had noted disapprovingly that they were unsure if I was gaining publicity for the UK or for myself: the point is the two went together without conflict, at least until I hit Uzbekistan where the last thing the government wanted was the high profile promotion of democracy. I had the definite respect of Robin Cook and Peter Hain and at least the goodwill of Sir John Kerr, who visited Accra while I was in Guy's Hospital and predicted to Rod Pullen that my career would end either in glory or in flames. He was to be proved right on both counts.

But I was delighted to find myself appointed as British Ambassador to Uzbekistan. I was judged to have done a very good job in Ghana, and particularly to be adept at pushing forward on democratisation. That was what was thought to be needed in Uzbekistan – until everything changed.

I was wandering around the FCO's Training Department with my arm in a sling. I had travelled in from Gravesend to discuss details of my future training needs for Tashkent. But there was a febrile atmosphere in the FCO, like nothing I had ever experienced before. Nobody was at their desk, and nobody had any time to answer my queries. People were gathered in little knots around the corridors, while one or two people were bustling around very fast, holding bits of paper and looking extremely self-important. I grabbed someone and asked:

"What's up with everybody today? What's happening?"

They looked at me pityingly: "Don't you know?", and steered me towards a television at the end of a long open plan office. It was showing, again and again, the planes crashing into the twin towers. It was September 11, and the first attack had happened just as I was catching the train at Gravesend station. As I watched the towers fall again and again, helpless and mesmerised, there was an overwhelming sadness at what must be the death of so many innocent people. But there was also an awareness that the world had just changed for me. The whole international climate would be thrown into confusion. Just how that was to affect me, I did not yet understand.

Returning to Ghana that September, I had just three more months to serve there. It was a pleasant time, more like a lap of honour. My name had firmly passed into Ghanaian popular culture as the midwife of the democratic transition – with which Ghanaians were still overjoyed. They became a bit disillusioned later, as is inevitable in politics.

I had one important task left, which was to persuade the Ghanaian government to accept debt relief under the HIPC scheme. I had been having lunch once a week in La Chaumiere, an excellent French restaurant, with the Governor of the Bank of Ghana, Kwabena Dufuor, who had brought respectability back to that institution. Kwabena told me that when he took over, he found that senior bank staff and political figures had been borrowing money from the central bank for personal use against handwritten IOUs.

The Ghanaian financial establishment were worried that accepting debt relief would damage the country's credit rating and remove access to capital for future development projects. I was arguing that freeing up over $1 billion per year of their own resources – then equivalent to their whole cocoa export – would outweigh this, and the end of so much debt would in the long term improve their credit rating. I had convinced Kwabena Dufuor, only to find on my return from London in the Autumn that he had been replaced. Paul Acquah was another excellent governor, but I had to start my convincing again.

Kufuor's first finance minister, Yaw Osafo Marfo, was a financial genius who prepared the ground for total GDP growth of over 70% between 2000 and 2008, meaning that the 2000s will be the first decade since independence that the Ghanaian economy hasn't gone backwards. He did it by reducing government interference in industry, but making government more effective in promoting services to support the nation and the economy. This does not mean only education and health, but projects which facilitate commerce such as rural feeder roads and credit and input schemes for farmers. Money from HIPC debt relief has been a major factor in this success. Yaw did not need persuading of the economic case for HIPC, but faced a huge political difficulty.

The problem was essentially one of pride. Yaw complained to me that the name summed up the problem – HIPC stood for Highly Indebted Poor Country. The NDC were already pillorying the government for considering the acceptance of this demeaning title, and were portraying HIPC as a major instrument of neo-colonialism. It probably does in fact say something about the attitudes of those who dreamt up the title for the scheme, that they did not consider African sensibilities on the subject.

I had several meetings with President Kufuor to discuss this, and a visit from Clare Short was the final catalyst in getting Ghana to sign up for HIPC. Rod Pullen held a dinner for Clare, attended by President Kufuor, Hackman, and four other Ghanaian cabinet ministers, plus John Mahama from the NDC. Most of the Ghanaian ministers present were also English barristers. Hackman had just made a polite after dinner speech about how much Ghana had learnt from the British Empire, when Clare Short stood up and expostulated:

"The British Empire! The British Empire! Don't tell me about the British Empire. I know about British colonialism. My father was Irish, and we know about British colonialism. I'll tell you what the British did to your country. They exploited it, that's what they did. They exploited it."

There was a few moments stunned silence at this unexpected line from a British cabinet minister. There is often a mismatch between the perceptions of the passionately pro-African Westerner, myself included, and the perceptions of African themselves. Also, as I have tried to explain, there were different kinds of British colonialism, and the Ghanaian experience was very different from, say, the Kenyan. There were Ghanaians who would have agreed with her - indeed I partly agreed with her – but the senior echelons of the NPP were staunchly pro-British.

President Kufuor rose to his feet and said "Well, the key point is, history is past and we are all friends now". He proposed a toast to our friendship, and the evening ended happily. I was happy. I loved my job, and felt I was working for my country, and that my country on the whole did good in the world.

Yet again, I was to find I was very wrong.

Epilogue – Seven Years Later

The concierge opened the door and the Nigerian detached himself from the rich leather upholstery of the sleek, silver, range-topping Mercedes. He stalked into the lounge of the Sheraton, as glossy as the sheen on his Italian silk suit and as smooth as the mirrored lenses of his designer spectacles.

My heart sank as he headed towards our little group. I had taken on the chairmanship of a Ghanaian energy company to help out some Ghanaian friends. Our little venture had prospered and we were looking to expand across West Africa. In doing so I was determined to steer well clear of capital tainted with corruption or drugs. My surest guide to doing that was to avoid people who looked and dressed like this man whom my colleagues had arranged to talk with us.

West Africa is now the third largest centre in the World for money laundering and narcotics capital formation. But in terms of the percentage of total capital formation which drugs money forms, it is far ahead. Money laundering is the raison d'etre of many West African financial institutions. In Accra in March 2008 a World Bank sponsored conference held in Accra on money laundering heard an estimate that over 60% of the capital of the mushrooming private banking sector in Nigeria could be drugs money. Recently Nigerian banks have started taking out huge poster adverts all over the UK's major airports. That is drugs money.

One consequence of this is that I have found it too easy to attract the wrong kind of capital to a legitimate business proposal in West Africa. These investors from West African banks and private equity firms are not even expecting the kind of high returns that a high risk market normally demands. With anti money-laundering regulations now so tight in the US and EU, their investors are looking to launder the money in the region before sending it to Europe. The proceeds of a legitimate energy company are accountable and clean; so we attract those wishing to put dirty money in to get clean money out. The actual bank executives and fund managers are of course not themselves necessarily involved in narcotics; they just fail to query adequately the source of their investor's cash.

So when the new arrival introduced himself as a manager of a Nigerian private equity firm, I mentally switched off. I giggled inwardly as he named his company as "Travant", because I thought he said "Trabant", which given the car out of which he had just stepped, would have been wildly inappropriate.

But I came to with a start when he said that his Nigerian private equity firm had access to DFID funds because Baroness Amos was a Director. To be clear, I asked whether Travant was an NGO or a governmental investment agency. He replied that it was not; it was a private, for-profit fund management company.

Baroness Amos was of course the Secretary of State for DFID until 2003 and until 2007 was Leader of the House of Lords. I though that it was impossible that DFID money would be given to a company of which she was Director. On the face of it, nobody could look further removed from the development aid ethos than the man in the designer suit. I went back to writing him off, deciding he was simply making it up about Baroness Amos and his access to DFID money. In West Africa among people who wear silk suits and are driven in Mercedes, the standards of truthfulness sadly leave in general a great deal to be desired.

I would have forgotten the incident, but in December 2008 I found myself sitting next to Baroness Amos on an airport bus heading for the plane to Accra. Once on board she moved to Business class while due to overbooking I was downgraded to Economy Plus. I shared this fate with John Paintsil, the Fulham and Ghana wing-back. We sat together and I must say he is delightful. He was flying back for two days mid-season to take his sick father to hospital. He was extremely polite and unassuming, helped other passengers with their luggage, put up with my conversation about football, and was evidently devoted to his wife and children. At the end of the flight I saw him search through the cabin to find one of the British Airways Unicef envelopes to make a donation, while not drawing anyone else's attention to his gift. We hear a great deal about the terrible behaviour of Premier League footballers. But I am sure there are other John Paintsils.

Baroness Amos was going out to Accra to head the Commonwealth monitoring team for the first round of the 2008 Ghanaian elections, as John Kufuor retired.

Sending Baroness Amos to monitor an election seemed to me another tremendous example of British arrogance. Valerie Amos is the very anti-thesis of a democratic politician. One of the Blair inner circle, she rose to Cabinet rank despite never having faced the electorate. Never, ever, at any level of politics. Her entire career was based upon New Labour internal patronage after making a very good living out of complaining about discrimination against minorities in the UK. She opened up a substantial income gap between herself and those on whose behalf she was claiming to work from a very early stage, and that gap has widened ever since.

All this came back to me as I looked at Baroness Amos quaffing champagne on that plane. So I did a bit of digging. Valerie Amos is indeed listed on their website as a non-executive director of Travant Private Equity, one of only five directors[54]. There is nothing about developmental goals, ethics, or the environment on the website. There is a lot about real estate opportunities in West Africa (by which they do not mean housing for the urban poor), and a boast that they have "the largest fundraising from domestic investors in sub-Saharan Africa"[55]. Remember what I said about the sources of local capital formation? Now Travant may have the most rigorous procedures for scrutinising the origin of the domestic money deposited with them. But if they do, they do not mention it on their website. Rather they emphasise that "we are deeply immersed in the business communities in which we invest".

Mmmm.

But have Travant received DFID money? On the face of it, Travant shouldn't even want public money – they are aggressive proponents of the capitalist ethos: "We believe that the private sector, with appropriate oversight and governance, is the best shepherd of Africa's resources. We

54 http://www.travantcapital.com/travant/view/travant/en/page48
55 http://www.travantcapital.com/travant/view/travant/en/page54

seek to empower entrepreneurs to pursue opportunities that they have identified, creating returns for investors, jobs and economic growth."[56]

Yet in 2007 the British Government financed Travant with £15 million of funds, provided through CDC, the investment arm of DFID[57]. CDC is owned 100% by DFID. At launch over one third of Travant's first equity fund came from DFID. A few months afterwards Baroness Amos, ex minister in charge of DFID, joined the board of this profit-making firm.

It says everything about New Labour that CDC, which as the Commonwealth Development Corporation used to run agricultural projects to benefit the rural poor, was rebranded as CDC with a new remit to provide most of its funds to the financial services industry. It says even more about New Labour's lack of the understanding of fundamental personal ethics, of their embrace of greed, that they see no reason why one of their former senior ministers should not move to benefit personally from the DFID money - even if through a 100% owned satellite - thus invested.

To turn this story full circle, let us turn back to Sierra Leone. 65% of the measured exports of this country come from its rutile mines. These were under guard by Sandline at the start of this memoir. Following the British invasion of Sierra Leone, it returned to its normal state of extreme corruption. Life is hard for most of its inhabitants, and UN donated food and pharmaceuticals, clearly marked "not for sale", are only available to the local population for cash they do not have, as the result of collusion between corrupt UN officials, government officials, and mostly Lebanese traders.

But the rutile mines are working full out, and extremely profitable, with armed white men again in charge of security. A major rutile miner, Titanium Resources Group of Sierra Leone says in its 2008 interim report: "the long term future of our markets is sound and the quality and scale of our mineral reserves underline our future prospects."

The Chairman of Titanium Resources Group is Walter Kansteiner III, George Bush's former Assistant Secretary of Sate for Africa and a founding partner of the Scowcroft Group, led by Brent Scowcroft, George

56 http://www.travantcapital.com/travant/view/travant/en/page53
57 http://www.cdcgroup.com/pdfs/cdc_annual_review.pdf

Bush's National Security Adviser and architect of the CIA's re-introduction of torture. The Scowcroft Group advisory consultancy did huge harm in Africa in the 1990s with their advocacy of privatisation and deregulation, particularly in the forestry sector, and with some influence advocated policies worldwide which contributed to the credit bubble and collapse of recent years.

But none of that prevented Kansteiner and Scowcroft from making money out of it, and Blair's invasion secured Sierra Leone's mineral resources to the neo-cons.

Not everyone benefits. Titanium Resources' Interim Report 2008 mentions the disruption in production as a result of the collapse of a dredger, without feeling the need even to mention the two Sierra Leoneans who died in the incident[58].

But New Labour believes in profit, especially for themselves, so it was no surprise to me when Titanium Resources announced in March 2008 the appointment of Baroness Amos as a non-executive director. For me that appointment[59] sums up the cosiness of the alliance between Bush, Blair and their acolytes. It was an alliance based on the acquisition of mineral resources by any means possible. The wars in Iraq and Afghanistan are the most infamous example. I saw it close up operating by war in Sierra Leone, and by the diplomacy of repression in Uzbekistan.

I served as a bit-player, but with a privileged view, in the Bush Blair years. I got to know many wonderful people of West Africa and of Uzbekistan, and formed strong views of how to assist them to make progress. But I was working for governments with quite a different agenda, that of international resource acquisition to benefit massive but specific commercial interests. I hope that my memoirs will, taken together, entertain with their tales of a very human and colourful life. But I trust that they will also throw some light on a most shameful period of British foreign policy, viewed from some unusual and fascinating points of vantage.

---

58 http://titaniumresources.com/media/78859/trg_interim_results_10september08.pdf
59 Though she later resigned

Select Bibliography

Achebe, Chinua; *Things Fall Apart*, Heinemann, London, 1962

Biddlecombe, Peter; *French Lessons in Africa*, Abacus, London, 1994

Drohan, Madelaine; *Making A Killing: How Corporations use Armed Force to do Business*, Random House, Ottawa, 2003

Durrell, Gerald; *The Bafut Beagles*, Penguin Books, London, 1965

Ferguson, Niall; *Empire – How Britain Made the Modern World*, Penguin Books, London, 2004

James, CLR; *A History of Pan African Revolt* , Charles H Kerr Publishing, Chicago, 1969

Keating, Frank: *Caught By Keating*, Andre Deutsch, London, 1979

Kampfner, John; *Robin Cook*, Phoenix, London, 1999

Kampfner, John; *Blair's Wars*, Free Press, London, 2004

Murray, Craig; *Murder in Samarkand*, Mainstream, Edinburgh, 2006

Pakenham, Thomas; *The Scramble for Africa*, Weidenfeld, London, 1991

Ross, Carne; *Independent Diplomat: Dispatches from an Unaccountable Elite;* C Hurst & Co, London, 2007

Saro-Wiwa, Ken: *A Month and a Day – A Detention Diary*, Penguin, London, 1995

Schama, Simon; *Rough Crossings*, BBC Books, London, 2006

Soyinka, Wole; *You Must Set Out at Dawn; A Memoir*, Methuen, London, 2007

Spicer, Tim; *An Unorthodox Soldier*, Mainstream, Edinburgh, 2000

Taylor, AA; *Sam Jonah and the Remaking of Ashanti*, Pan Macmillan, Johannesburg, 2006

Index

CM = Craig Murray
Footnotes are indexed as 120n